ARMED AND DANGEROUS

Savage, brutal, addicted to violence—they're hardened criminals without any respect for the law or the heroic men and women sworn to enforce it. They're cop killers, the most vicious breed of felon who strike down officers for a parking ticket, a pack of cigarettes or petty theft and never look back.

Now from the authentic files of TRUE DETECTIVE Magazine, here are twenty-five heart-stopping true crime accounts of cops killed in action and the dramatic police work that brought the murderers to justice!

PINNACLE BOOKS AND *TRUE DETECTIVE* MAGAZINE TEAM UP FOR THE GRIZZLIEST TRUE CRIME STORIES IN PRINT!

BIZARRE MURDERERS (486, $4.95)
Edited by Rose G. Mandelsberg

The crimes are too shocking to be believed, but they are true nonetheless:

* The "vampire" who drank his victim's blood
* The hooker who was cooked alive
* The killer who kept his victim's brain as a souvenier
* The murderer who fed his victim's to the pigs

BIZZARE MURDERERS recounts some of the most sensational slayings in the annals of crime. You won't believe what you read — but it's all true. And truly bizarre.

CELEBRITY MURDERS   435, $4.95)
Edited by Art Crockett

Some were in the wrong place at the wrong time, others were the victims of an obssessed fan. Bob Crane, Sharon Tate, Sal Mineo, Rebecca Schaeffer, George Rose, and tohers: stars of the screen and stage, darlings of the media. All had brilliant careers cut short by an act of bloody violence. Read the true accounts of the stars who last roles were played out on a cold, coroner's table.

SERIAL MURDERERS   (432, $4.95)
Edited by Art Crockett

Some of them, like Son of Sam, are known throughout the world. Others are not well known, like Henry lee Lucas, even though he killed 176 people. And there are those who are still unknown, their carnage gone unstopped, like the Green River Killer.

They are all serial killers, slaughtering their innocent victims for reasons known only to themselves. no one knows where they'll strike, or when. Or *why*. We know only one thing: Once they *do* start, they will write their stories in blood until someone stops them.

Available wherever paperbacks are sold, or order direct from the Publisher. Send cover price plus 50¢ per copy for mailing and handling to Pinnacle Books, Dept. 603, 475 Park Avenue South, New York, N.Y. 10016. Residents of New York and Tennessee must include sales tax. DO NOT SEND CASH. For a free Zebra/Pinnacle catalog please write to the above address.

COP KILLERS

Edited by ROSE G. MANDELSBERG

PINNACLE BOOKS
WINDSOR PUBLISHING CORP.

The editor wishes to thank the following individuals whose help was instrumental in making this book possible: Sara Heredia-Pearl; Inspector Alva Busch, Crime Scene Technician of the Illinois State Police; Detective Nelson Andreu, Miami Police Department; Lieutenant John Conklin and Detective K.C. Myers, West Palm Beach Police Department; Sergeant Leonard Muuss of the Bureau of Criminal Identification, Middlesex County Sheriff's Department; Sergeant Daniel Cosgrove, Public Information Unit, the New Jersey Division of State Police; and Commissioner Anthony M. Mosca, Westchester County Department of Public Safety.

A special note of thanks and sincere appreciation to Sergeant Lewis Beniamino, Westchester County Department of Public Safety, who went to great efforts to assist the editor.

PINNACLE BOOKS

are published by

Windsor Publishing Corp.
475 Park Avenue South
New York, NY 10016

First printing: May, 1992

Printed in the United States of America

TABLE OF CONTENTS

A PART OF AMERICA DIED

Somebody killed a policeman today and
A part of America died.
A piece of our country he swore to protect
Will be buried with him at his side.
The suspect who shot him will stand up in court,
With counsel demanding his rights,
While a young widowed mother must work for
    her kids
And spend many long, lonely nights.
The beat that he walked was a battlefield, too,
Just as if he'd gone off to war.
Though the flag of our nation won't fly at half mast,
To his name they will add a gold star.
Yes, somebody killed a policeman today,
It happened in our town or mine
While we slept in comfort behind our locked doors,
A cop put his life on the line.
Now his ghost walks a beat on a dark city street,
And he stands at each new rookie's side.
He answered the call, and gave us his all
And a part of America died.

—Angel Sparks

"TWO-NATION MANHUNT FOR A COP KILLER!"

by E.E. Gilpatrick

Some of it gets to be routine. In larger law enforcement agencies a pre-patrol briefing can be formalized into a classroom-like session with the shift sergeant reading off items on the hot sheet, issuing a departmental update, and melding the whole with a few sage words of advice. In smaller jurisdictions the briefing may take the form of asking the officer coming off his or her shift if anything's happening and sticking one's head in the chief's office on the way out to see if there are any special instructions.

Most departments fall somewhere in between. On Wednesday afternoon, April 12, 1984, Patrol Officer Martin S. Murrin, age 32, a 10-year veteran of the Joliet, Illinois Police Department was chatting with Officer Thomas Stein over coffee in the ready room. Murrin was getting an informal briefing prior to hitting the bricks. Joliet, often called the first, full-fledged, independent city south of Chicago, has the broad diversity of illegal activity any peace officer is likely to encounter in any city — from violent murders to irate neighbors. Among the items the two lawmen touched on was a warrant which had been issued for the pickup of Manuel Salazar Jr., age 18, for questioning with regard to a case of aggravated battery. Murrin knew of Salazar. Salazar was a member of the Latin Kings street gang and a resident hood, junior grade, of Joliet's east side. Murrin was intimately familiar with the area and some of its less desirable residents. Of late, Salazar, or "Junior" as he was generally known, had been hanging out with a fellow who was driving a green Buick Electra.

Murrin agreed he'd have no trouble spotting Junior if he saw him. Murrin was glad to get the tip on the green car. He'd keep an eye out for it. The two hit a few other high spots, then Officer Murrin and his rookie partner, Thomas Ponce, slid into the front seat of their cruiser to begin patrolling the streets of Joliet. They checked in with the dispatcher and headed east.

They drifted north on Draper Avenue toward east-west-running Woodruff Road in the northeast quadrant of Joliet. As the lawmen headed north on Draper Avenue a large, green car pulled out in front of them in the 1100 block. Murrin's head jerked forward to follow the car heading toward Woodruff Road. Murrin said to Ponce that Junior Salazar was in that auto. Ponce jammed the accelerator and the Joliet P.D. police cruiser sprang forward. The cruiser rapidly gained on the Buick. One can only guess that the occupants of the Buick spotted the marked cruiser as quickly as Murrin spotted Junior.

In only a few seconds the big, green machine began to accelerate visibly. Ponce hit the lights and the siren. The old green car was no match for the newer, well-maintained squad car. At the corner of Woodruff Road and Draper Avenue, Officer Ponce was able to force the fleeing vehicle to a stop at the side of the road.

There were four men in the green car. Two of the men jumped out and ran in opposite directions. Murrin, as he jumped out of the car, told rookie Tom Ponce to circle the block to try to cut off one of the fleeing men. Murrin took off on foot after the one who was running back down Draper Avenue tightly clutching what appeared to be a gym bag of some sort. Like a seasoned pro, Ponce was on the radio to call for help as he whipped around the block trying to find one of the men who had fled.

Ponce was not able to get a glimpse of him. As he'd expected when he'd completed his circuit of the block, Ponce could see that the green car was gone, probably fleeing on Woodruff Road. Ponce called it all in. Hoping his first pass might lure someone out of hiding, Ponce made another quick circuit of the block. No such luck. Making a quick decision, Ponce spun his wheels down Draper Avenue, sweeping both sides of the street. As he approached the 1100 block he heard a sharp report. He heard four more shots.

He spotted the location of the gunfire by the sound. They had come from behind a brown house with a chain-link fence around the front yard. Officer Ponce swerved off Draper onto the cement drive running along the brown house with white trim. Service revolver in hand and with little regard for his own safety, Ponce ran to the back of the house. His eyes swept a quick 270-degree arc of the back yard.

The yard sloped downward a few degrees. At the back end was a dip at the far edge of the mowed portion of the lawn. Off to the left was the corner of a chain-link fence about four feet high around a property on another street. The body of Murrin lay by the corner of the fence.

Stunned with disbelief, Ponce's own body refused to move for a moment. Ponce rushed to the side of his partner. The sirens of other cruisers were loud now. They pulled in behind the Murrin-Ponce cruiser. As a

11

newly arriving officer ran across the back yard, Officer Ponce rose, dumbfounded. He tried to grasp the logic of it, but there was none. He took a couple steps toward the approaching officer. His mind wouldn't work. All he could say was, "He's dead."

For several minutes the converging officers stood numbly looking at the body in the police officer's uniform. There would have to be a crime-scene investigation. Up until seven months ago one of the best crime-scene technicians the department had ever had was Martin Murrin. He had an uncanny grasp of criminalistics. To balance his high degree of technical skill he was put on the street to hone his practical application of law enforcement. He'd done such an outstanding job at it that he was chosen to give rookie Officer Ponce his field training.

It's in such situations that military-type training truly pays off. Devastated, unable to think or feel, the lawmen on all levels began the investigation immediately. The Will County Coroner quickly arrived on the scene. He pronounced Officer Murrin dead at 5:20 P.M. The coroner, Robert Tezak, noted the cause of death to be multiple gunshot wounds at close range in the head, neck, and chest. Only three wounds were apparent, but two which appeared to be ragged led Coroner Tezak to speculate the officer may have been hit more than three times. The autopsy would determine that.

About 20 feet from Murrin's body was a gym bag containing a 9-mm. semi-automatic pistol. In the yard encompassed by the chain-link fence, about 20 feet in the other direction from Murrin's body, was his service revolver. In the cylinder were five expended shells. No other hard evidence was found at the murder site. Men from all units swarmed into the area to check businesses, homes, and garages. Robbery, dope, traffic

12

all—sections were there. Even off-duty officers reported in at the scene to aid in the hunt.

The Joliet K-9 unit was on the job almost immediately, to be soon followed by another canine unit sent down by the Plainfield Police Department a few miles to the north. A command post was set up in a police staff car in front of the brown house with the white trim to coordinate the investigation, which would last through the night.

Early in the evening the green Electra was located. Its two juvenile occupants were taken into custody. The investigators soon had the names of the other two occupants who'd been in the car when it was first spotted by Murrin and Ponce. As the police had surmised, the previous occupant whom Officer Murrin took off chasing was Manuel "Junior" Salazar. The fourth rider in the car was taken at his home that evening. All three were questioned extensively, all three denied any knowledge of the killing. Their best corroboration was the fact that the driver of the Electra had pulled over as directed with no determined effort to avoid the stop. From the three the investigators learned that there had been another rider prior to the time they'd been spotted by Murrin and Ponce. This fifth possible suspect was contacted. He was living at the work-release house in Joliet. He said he and Junior had gone out into the country to do a little target-shooting about noon of that day, Wednesday. After they finished, they'd gotten high together till about 3:00 P.M. when he had to be back at the work-release home. He was driven there in the Buick. He said he'd already been dropped off at the work-release home before the car was spotted on Draper Avenue. The director verified the time factors, and the witness was released without being charged.

None of the witnesses had any idea where Junior Salazar was. The painful truth was that the investigation,

13

which had lasted into the bright light of Thursday's dawn, had, except for the two weapons, produced no specific testimony, no eyewitnesses, and no pertinent evidence. Several witnesses had seen the stop at Draper Avenue and Woodruff Road, but no one had seen the killing. Joliet Chief of Police Frederick Breen personally took charge of the investigation.

The nastiest job of all he saved for himself. He notified Officer Murrin's wife, the mother of his two children, that Officer Martin S. Murrin had been killed while fulfilling his duties as a law enforcement officer. It had been 14 years since an officer of the Joliet Police Department had given his life protecting the people of Joliet. Officer Murrin's father was a retired police captain of the Lansing, Illinois Police Department, and his brother was an officer on the Lansing force. Chief Breen said, Murrin was "an extremely fine officer who was well-adapted to working in all areas of the department."

The FBI immediately entered the case as witness testimony led the investigators to believe Salazar might well be beyond the borders of the state of Illinois. Joliet Police Lieutenant Arthur Schultz revealed, "He has relatives in Indiana, Texas, and Mexico. He might have fled the country." A multicounty alert was issued to cover the entire Chicago area. Salazar was described as being 18 years old, 5 feet 4 inches tall, 140 to 155 pounds, with brown eyes, and with combed-back black hair. One of Salazar's relatives admitted during an interview that the family car was missing. The auto was a black, 1975, Plymouth Valiant or Duster bearing Illinois license plate #XX7033. An all-points bulletin was issued for the vehicle on the possibility that the driver might well be Junior Salazar.

The autopsy on the body of Officer Murrin confirmed what Coroner Tezak had suspected. Murrin

14

had been shot five times with his own weapon.

The ballistics lab determined that the 9-mm. pistol had not been fired. The conundrum in the case was: what was the series of events in the killing? Murrin's service revolver with which he'd been shot lay some feet from his body across the fence in the next yard. The unfired, 9-mm. semi-automatic pistol was still enclosed in the gym bag which was presumably the one Salazar was carrying when Murrin took off running after him.

A reward of $4,000 became immediately available for any information leading to the arrest of the person who killed Officer Murrin. The reward money was contributed from a number of sources including the Will County Crime Stoppers, the Police Officer's Association, the Joliet Policeman's Union Local 807, and Lodge 58 of the Fraternal Order of Police.

Residents of the neighborhood were terrified to think that a policeman had been killed in their midst. Those who knew Officer Murrin were devastated by the news. One of the more incisive statements concerning the killing of this public servant came from Will County State's Attorney Edward Petka. Not many years before, Murrin had been a student of Petka's in a class on criminal law. State's Attorney Petka said, in part, "When a police officer is murdered, it represents a direct attack on each and every one of us, as a police officer is simply enforcing the laws that we have given him to uphold.

"We ask him to do things we would not do in protecting our freedoms. We pay him less than he deserves and ask him to make split-second legal decisions in which hindsight becomes the perfect judge.

"(The police) are criticized far too often and made to defend themselves against frivolous brutality charges. Yet, it is the rare individual who champions the cause of opposing civilian brutality against the police."

On Saturday, September 15, 1984 Badge number 215 was permanently retired as a troop of brother officers from Joliet, Chicago, and other cities and towns said a last farewell at St. Patrick's Catholic Church in Joliet to a colleague who'd given his life in the defense of his community.

By Monday, the reward fund had grown to $8,000. The FBI working with the Joliet P.D. contacted the U.S. Customs Service which alerted all of its stations at border crossings into Mexico. Investigators continued to evaluate notes, data, and diagrams but could come up with nothing concrete. Chief Breen said, "The shooting was at close range, and it appeared a scuffle could have ensued between Murrin and Salazar. Somehow, the suspect got possession of his (Murrin's) weapon. We don't know specifically how." Although there were no actual witnesses to the killing, a meticulous review of interview notes indicated Murrin may have yelled, "Freeze!" at the suspect.

The suspect's mother understandably expressed deep concern for her son. Such a situation too often moves fingers too quickly on the trigger. The mother said she recently was angry with her son and threw him out of the house briefly when he refused to answer charges of aggravated battery. It was on those charges that Officer Murrin was attempting to stop Salazar when the deadly pursuit occurred. The charge was so new it hadn't even been posted on Salazar's rap sheet. Although some of his relatives denied it, police knew Salazar to be a loyal member of a street gang. He was not in a leadership position of the gang, the Latin Kings, but he was acknowledged to be a dedicated follower. Much of Salazar's troubles with the law occurred while he was a juvenile. However, under Illinois law, at age 17 a person can be prosecuted as an adult.

16

Since his 17th birthday, the suspect had been arrested on three different occasions. On November 11, 1983, he was arrested for the unlawful use of a weapon. Eleven days later he was again arrested for illegal possession of an alcoholic beverage. On July 19, 1984, the charges in the second incident were dropped.

The weapons charge stated Salazar had been frisked after a complaint had been filed against him while he was at Woodland School in Joliet as a student. He was discovered to be carrying a concealed .357 Magnum on his person. The occasion for his second arrest was the stopping of a carload of seven youths. They'd been stopped for being disorderly and boisterous. Most of them were in various stages of inebriation. More serious was the discovery of three .22-caliber pistols under the seat of the auto. All three weapons were loaded and ready for use.

The current warrant which had been issued against Manuel Salazar Jr. described the shooting in the legs of a 15-year-old youth. He'd been shot with a sawed-off shotgun. The shooter had been, according to the warrant, Junior Salazar.

Detective David Saxon investigated the matter. The victim told the detective it was Salazar who'd shot him, but the victim declined to press charges. He said he intended to "handle the matter himself." That statement gave investigator Saxon an uneasy feeling. At the instigation of Detective Saxon a warrant was issued for the pickup of Salazar for questioning in connection with the shooting, but at the time Murrin began the fatal chase, Salazar didn't know such a warrant had been issued. A relative, however, had told Junior he was wanted by the police.

Testimony unearthed revealed that on another occasion Salazar had fired a 9-mm. pistol into the air on a Joliet Street in an act of bravado. Others were stand-

17

ing around him. One of the onlookers was a child who was frightened by the noise. The youngster began to cry. At the behest of an older brother of the child, Salazar put the gun away. The demonstration involved a close friend of Junior's. Junior and his friend had been talking of shooting a member of a rival gang who'd "messed with" the friend when he was a student at Joliet Township West High School. Junior's friend had already been convicted of one murder. The investigation continued, but none of the answers elicited seemed to point to the whereabouts of Manuel Salazar Jr.

On Thursday, October 11, 1984, Captain Albert Hentz of the Milwaukee Police Department flashed a wire to the Joliet Police Department that a Milwaukee patrol officer had spotted a black, 1975 Plymouth Valiant on a Milwaukee city street. The auto bore Illinois license plate number XX7033. Joliet investigators were alerted to prepare for a mad dash to Milwaukee. The Milwaukee police staked out the black Valiant. The Joliet lawmen waited. Several hours later Captain Hentz called Joliet to notify them a subject had been taken into custody. The subject was a suave-looking, mature man. Frankly, Captain Hentz guessed, the subject showed little resemblance to any of the photos of Junior Salazar which the Milwaukee police had received with various bulletins.

The subject identified himself and advised the Milwaukee police he was a relative of the owner of the Valiant, and if he had no absolute legal right to take the car, he had, at least, a sentimental, kinsman's right. That he'd not advised the owner of the car was simply an oversight. The subject was questioned at length but had no connection with or knowledge of the where-

18

abouts of Junior Salazar. The owner of the vehicle in Joliet was contacted and declined to press charges for the unauthorized use of the vehicle. Joliet advised Captain Hentz of the outcome of the matter and thanked the Milwaukee police for their splendid cooperation.

Salazar was known to have a relative in Indiana. Indiana State Police and local investigators conducted an exhaustive investigation in the area. They found nothing. Months passed.

The death of Officer Murrin was by no means forgotten, but all of the leads and all of the investigatory effort led nowhere. Bulletins had been sent out to every law enforcement agency the Joliet peace officers could think of. Those Joliet missed, the FBI didn't. Every lead that came in had been run down. Detectives stood ready to pounce on any new leads that might come in. None did. More than half a year passed since a law officer had been shot to death in the back yard of a home on Draper Avenue in the heartland of America.

If it's true that every dark cloud has a silver lining, it could also be said that one of the worst mistakes the kingpins of the Mexican drug traffic ever made was to kill U.S. Drug Enforcement Agency operative Enrique "Rickie" Camarena. A rapid series of lightning raids on facilities of the Mexican dope dealers came close to causing total chaos among the coke controllers. By dint of world opinion and diplomatic necessity, full and total cooperation on the part of Mexican authorities was the wisest course of action.

The lesson was not lost on the dope barons. Drug base after drug base was abandoned as raid after raid ensued. Some of the dope bases which only a short time ago had been armed fortresses where millions in dope had been stashed were now only way stations along the route of the snowy death with only a few flunkies to keep the trail open. One morning the sun had barely risen above the horizon in eastern Mexico to illuminate a Mexican rancho in Monterrey about 140 miles southwest of Laredo, Texas.

A convoy of cars and FWD's raised a cloud of dust as they sped toward the rancho. Veering into the yard in the middle of the ranch buildings the vehicles came to a sudden, dusty halt. Men with riot guns and other weapons piled out of the vehicles. Some of the cars were plainly marked cruisers of the Mexican federal police, the "Federales." Some were provincial police of Nuevo Leon in which Monterrey is located. One group, those in the unmarked jeeps and Broncos, wore no uniforms, only jeans and polo shirts. Some of those in jeans seemed to be Latinos who spoke Spanish with a Castilian ring instead of the typical Mexican accent. A few were obviously *gueros* (white). Their speech was more heavily accented.

Each player fanned out into various areas of the rancho, the barn, the house, the stables, other outbuildings, even a pile of straw. All of the individuals rounded up on the rancho were taken before one of the more mature-appearing men in work clothes. Among those rounded up was a young Mexican, he said, who'd been caught sleeping in a pile of straw with a rifle across his knees. When the young man, about 20 or a little less, awoke enough to realize what was going on, he was staring down the barrel of a 12-gauge riot gun.

The lawmen looked over their catch. Some were known dope dealers; all were frisked, identified, and questioned. As the searching went on and notes were taken, the older man in everyday clothes pulled a sheaf of papers out of the hip pocket of his jeans. Uncharacteristic for the scene, one of the sheets looked like an

APB (all points bulletin) one would expect to find on the clip board of any American patrol officer. With the sheet unfolded, the man in jeans with salt and pepper hair stepped up to the young man who'd been asleep in the pile of straw. The older asked the younger what his name was. The younger man said his name was Manuel Sierra. The other looked at the picture of a wanted suspect on the APB.

There was a small mole on the young man's upper lip just under his nose as specified on the APB. The mole was apparent on the photo. In the first English heard that morning, the older man said, "That's funny, you look just like Junior Salazar from Joliet, Illinois."

A Mexican officer put handcuffs on the younger man and put him in a Mexican patrolcar.

One source says that the raid had been called by the U.S. Drug Enforcement Agency, and a cache of dope was their objective. Another story is that they'd been tipped off by a covert source that a cop killer, Junior Salazar, was there on the rancho. Rumors and unsubstantiated reports from unknown sources are a part of any investigation.

Fingerprints confirmed that the young man in jail in Monterrey, Nuevo Leon, Mexico, was Manuel Salazar, Jr. of Joliet, Illinois, U.S.A. There was jubilation in police headquarters in Joliet when at about 8:30 Saturday morning on May 18, 1985, word was received that Manuel Salazar, Jr. had been taken into custody.

The previous November, Police Sergeant Fred Hafner had been assigned full-time to the Murrin case. Sergeant Hafner spoke for the entire department when he said, "We've been waiting a long time. We're ready to get the wheels of justice in motion. I can't wait until we bring the justice system down on this guy."

State's Attorney Ed Petka was ready to get right on

the problem in the best tradition of American justice. "Probably the first step would be that since he's an American citizen, the Mexican government would initiate deportation proceedings against him. Once he's deported, he would be returned at the nearest point of entry."

Americans of today seem to have a difficult time understanding that our concept of constitutional law is a freak in time and place. Most governments in the world today and at any time previously in history do what they want to do, when they want to do it, the way they want to do it, simply because they want to do it. Salazar was an American, he had no passport, he had no Mexican identity papers, and he could help remove some of the egg which had gotten on the face of Mexican officialdom from the killing of Rickie Camarena. A few days later at a border crossing, Junior Salazar was escorted out of Mexico and into the United States. There were men there to meet Junior Salazar, among them an agent of the U.S. Federal Bureau of Investigation, a special agent of the U.S. Border Patrol, and a Texas Ranger. Extradition from Texas to Illinois in a capital case is a relatively routine matter. When advised of this, Salazar waived extradition.

On his return to Joliet, Junior Salazar said that Officer Murrin chased him down the drive of the brown house with the white trim to the fence which cut off Salazar's escape. A struggle ensued in which the gun went off. Salazar said he had no intention of shooting the officer as indicated by the fact he threw away the gym bag which contained the 9-mm. pistol. That was proved by the fact the gym bag was found some feet from Murrin's body.

After the killing Junior Salazar said he ran to a friend's house. His friends had heard on the radio and TV what had happened. All feared that Salazar would be shot on sight. Within hours of the slaying, a man was found who drove Salazar to California. Junior had a relative in Monterrey and decided that would be the safest place for him to be. He crossed into Mexico at Tijuana. From there he took a bus to Monterrey in Nuevo Leon. He lived with his relative until a few days before his capture at the rancho.

On December 6, 1985, after having been found guilty of the murder of police officer Martin Murrin, Manuel Salazar, Jr., now age 19, was sentenced to die by lethal injection. Under Illinois law, all death sentences are automatically appealed to the Illinois Supreme Court.

"EXECUTION HIT OF
THE HERO COP"
by Bud Ampolsk

In the TV world of Kojak and Hill Street Blues, there is a certain neatness. Stakeouts last only a matter of minutes. At the end of an hour-long program issues are pretty well resolved. The cops have done their job. The bad guys are in the holding tank. It's time for male and female law enforcement officers to pick up the threads of their off-duty social lives (often with romantic overtones) over a pizza.

In the real world of flesh and blood anti-crime activity it's something else. Surveillance goes on for months or years. Cases often have no starting nor finishing point. Men and women detectives work side by side, depending on each other for their sense of security but limiting their relationship to being good friends and trusted partners. Rather than lingering over pizzas when a tour is done, they rush home to spouse and kids. The biggest problem they face revolves around making their pay check stretch just a little bit further.

In the real world of cops and robbers, there's discomfort and frustration. There are the endless hours of sitting cramped in an unmarked car. There is the stress of keeping the subject in sight without alerting him that you are on his tail. There is the need to defy your instincts. You know the guy is a bad one. But you don't move in to make the collar. You hope the mark will lead you to something or somebody more important.

You fight to maintain your concentration. Boredom is your worst enemy. You keep reminding yourself anything can happen.

If you're Detective Anthony Venditti, you may allow yourself a moment to reflect on how one of the six women in your life — this one your nursery school aged little charmer — just put the bite on you for a new dress to wear to class. You may think of how you had to bring her into the adult world of family finance a good deal sooner than you wanted to.

It's tough on "the old man" when he has to discuss budgetary limitations and promise that if he can earn enough overtime this week, he'll see what he can do about the request. It's very hard to tell her as she snuggles closer and regards you with those large eyes of hers that at this very moment there's no financial surplus for school dresses.

But if you're Detective Anthony Venditti, you may also feel a compensating glow of knowing how deeply you love, and in turn, are loved back by those six women — your mother, your wife, your four daughters — who range in age from one month to five years.

Perhaps you even reflect on the pride you take in your work. You're a good cop. If you weren't, you wouldn't be carrying a gold shield. You wouldn't be assigned to the FBI-NYPD Organized Crime Task Force. At age 34, you've already amassed 17 awards for bravery to show for your 13 years on the force.

If you're Detective Kathleen Burke, perhaps you take just a moment to think of your role as the wife of a highly respected inspector in the New York City Police Department. You might allow a very warm and human glow to run through you as you think about your own two daughters, one five years old, the other seven and growing up fast.

You might reflect on the fact that at age 41, with 17 years on the force, you've proved yourself. Although you stand a scant 5-feet-2, you have three departmental commendations, eight meritorious service awards and four excellent police duty honors in your record.

You're every inch a good cop. That's why you're at the wheel of an unmarked police vehicle assigned to the FBI-NYPD Joint Task Force Against Organized Crime . . .

At 8:25 P.M. on the evening of Tuesday, January 21, 1986, Detective Anthony Venditti and Kathleen Burke were working in Ridgewood, Queens. Their assignment was to keep a 1984 maroon BMW under surveillance. The driver of the BMW was considered by the Organized Crime Task Force to be involved in gambling operations. He was also reputed to be a soldier in the Genovese Crime Family.

Venditti and Burke had tailed the BMW to a spot at the junction of Myrtle Avenue, Woodbine Street and St. Nicholas Avenue.

It was at this point that the detective partners had lost sight of the expensive maroon car in the early evening traffic congestion.

Venditti, realizing that contact with the BMW had been broken at least temporarily, suggested that Kathleen Burke pull to the curb at a diner so that he might avail himself of the restaurant's rest room facilities. It was agreed that Detective Burke would remain at the wheel of the police vehicle and await the return of her partner.

A moment after Venditti had alighted from the police vehicle, Burke glanced up at her rear view mirror. She saw the maroon BMW now pulling in behind her.

Not knowing the purpose of the BMW driver's action, Burke relied on her street-wise surveillance instincts. She eased her own car from the curb and began circling the block. There were two reasons for the detective's action.

First, she did not want to tip her hand that her own reason for having parked near the diner was to keep the place or anybody entering or leaving it under surveillance.

Second, she wanted to determine whether the BMW occupant would follow her car — an action which would have indicated that he was aware that he'd been tailed.

The plucky detective tooled her way under an elevated section of subway track and past a series of low industrial buildings which are typical of these which dot the border between Brooklyn and Queens. A quick check behind her indicated that the driver of the BMW had not taken the bait. Burke was not being followed.

Some moments later, she arrived back at the diner, ready to pick up Venditti.

What she saw there galvanized her into instantaneous action. Service revolver drawn, Kathleen Burke bounded from the police car and moved toward the group of men who had congregated in front of the diner. The group consisted of four men. Detective Anthony Venditti was at its center.

Venditti had been pushed against a brick wall. It was obvious that he was being menaced by the three who now surrounded him.

Doing a quick make on the scene, Burke spotted the hand weapons toted by the assailants.

"Look out!" Detective Burke shouted. "They've got guns!"

Venditti never had a chance to reply. His voice and

his very life were cut off by the two slugs which tore into his face.

Even as Anthony Venditti was reeling to the pavement, a series of shots rang out. There was the staccato bark of Burke's service revolver as she emptied it at the killer trio. There was the sound of their answering fire.

Then there was a slight pause. It was followed by two more shots as one of the three men bent over the fallen Venditti and pumped two more bullets into the dying police officer's body.

The searing pain in her own left chest told Detective Burke that she, too, had been hit.

Mindless of her own condition and thinking only of her responsibilities as a cop, Kathleen Burke managed to stagger to a nearby pizzeria.

Later, describing the scene, the pizzeria's manager was to say, "She was a woman cop and she told us to call the cops." He also told how Detective Burke had been bleeding profusely from her chest wound.

The manager recalled running out into the street and having seen Venditti lying on the sidewalk, the male detective's body drenched in gore.

Said the witness, "He was facing up, and looked like he was shot in the face. He looked dead. They tried to revive him and couldn't do anything."

One woman had vivid recollections of the harrowing street scene in the moments following the shootout. She commented, "I was already walking up the street when I heard shots. I was carrying my three-year-old daughter, so I just started running to get away.

"There were police driving up everywhere," the young woman added.

The witness was not the only person scurrying to leave the immediate area. As the frenzied drama rolled on, a middle-aged man raced on foot away from the diner. He was Frederico Giavinello. Later he would be identified as the driver of the maroon BMW and the subject of the Venditti/Burke surveillance. At this moment, he appeared to be somebody with good reason to distance himself as far as possible from the spot where one New York City detective lay mortally wounded and another awaited the arrival of backup support.

As fast as Giavinello moved, he wasn't quite fast enough. He was only a block away from Woodbine Street when he ran into the arms of uniformed Sergeant Derrick Jones and Jones' partner, Police Officer Elaine Claiborne of the 104th Precinct. Jones and Claiborne had been answering the Signal 1013.

While the arrest was being made, paramedics from Brooklyn's Wyckoff Heights Hospital arrived. Recognizing the dire nature of Venditti's wounds, the paramedics fought valiantly to save his life as the Wyckoff ambulance, siren shrieking, sped to the hospital's emergency room. At one point the ambulance crew lost Venditti's heartbeat, but managed to shock the organ back into action.

The victory was a temporary one. The heroic officer's life ebbed away as he was being treated in the hospital's emergency room.

Serious as was Detective Burke's chest wound, she was not considered in a life-threatening situation. She was to spend the night at Wyckoff before being transferred to Bellevue Hospital where she could benefit from its more sophisticated medical facilities.

Police activity remained at a fevered pitch. Scores of uniformed and plainclothes officers converged on the Ridgewood section of Queens. They donned bullet proof vests and armed themselves with shotguns as they undertook an inch by inch search of the surroundings.

With Giavinello now in custody, the lawmen were going all-out to bring in the suspect's alleged two companions. At this point of the probe the police were not sure which of the three alleged assailants had fired the fatal shots.

One seemingly promising development was the recovery of a .25-caliber Beretta pistol from under the elevated tracks on Palmetto Street, five blocks away from where the shooting had taken place.

A profile of Frederico (Fritz) Giavinello was given out by police spokesperson Alice McGillion. She said that Giavinello was "a gambling person" in the Genovese family.

Intensive interrogation of Giavinello got underway at a command post set up at the 104th Precinct. Cops there worked through the night in an attempt to determine his role in the street crime. Sometime early the following morning, the suspect complained of "not feeling well." He was taken by ambulance to nearby City Hospital in Elmhurst.

A nursing administrator at that hospital reported that Giavinello had "been seen by a physician and released into the custody of the person (a police officer) who brought him here.

"I can't divulge his diagnosis but it apparently wasn't serious enough to keep him here," she added.

An entirely different act in the tragedy was now taking place at Wyckoff. There, New York City's top brass, led by Mayor Edward Koch and Police Commissioner Benjamin Ward, gathered at Kathleen Burke's bedside. They offered what comfort they could to Inspector Robert Burke, the commander of three mid-town Manhattan precincts and the wounded detective's husband.

It was revealed that the bullet which had entered Detective Burke's chest had collapsed her left lung. Although the Wyckoff corridors were jammed with police associates of Detective Burke who were standing by to give blood, it was determined that no transfusions would be necessary.

After spending some time with her, Inspector Burke reported, "She's tired and pale, but she's in good spirits."

Commenting on the rallying of friends and associates, Inspector Burke said, "It looks like a flower shop in there."

The outpouring of concern and admiration for Burke was represented in a statement by Mayor Koch who called her, "amazingly plucky." Koch had talked to her while she was still in the Wyckoff emergency room. The mayor said Detective Burke had expressed great concern over Venditti, fearing the worst for her partner. She had told Koch, "I don't think he (Venditti) made it."

Chief of New York City Detectives Richard Nicastro said, "What she did was praiseworthy. She emptied her gun. She saw her own partner being killed.

"I don't see anything done other than something very commendable and heroic."

Others who had worked with Detective Burke over a period of years noted that her actions in the shootout were entirely in keeping with the courage she'd shown throughout her career.

Stated former head of the Queens District Attorney's Narcotics Bureau Gabe Leone, "She is a natural for undercover. She acted any role she wanted to play and was not afraid."

As the details of what had happened were sorted

out, a more clear picture of the stakeout and the resulting shootout emerged.

According to Chief of Detectives Nicastro, Venditti and Burke had indeed been assigned to tail Giavinello on the night of the murder. The detective chief's account included the fact that the partners had lost sight of the Genovese soldier's car, that Venditti had decided to use the restaurant's rest room, that Burke had circled the block in the unmarked police car and had returned to find her partner surrounded by three men.

Nicastro alleged that one of the men fired at Venditti as Burke was approaching the group and warning her partner, "Look out! He has a gun!" He said that Venditti had been shot four times—twice in the head and twice in the back.

Expanding on this theme, Nicastro added, "We believe all three men shot at detectives and that Detective Burke was shot by the man we have in custody (Giavinello)."

Police sources also revealed that the bullets fired at the two detectives were copper-jacketed. The department does not use this type of ammunition, they contended.

Further details were given by Queens Assistant District Attorney Gregory Lasak. He said police had three witnesses—one of whom had identified Giavinello as the gunman.

Commenting on the .25-caliber Beretta, recovered on Palmetto Street, police believed that it might have been dropped by one of the three assailants. However, they did not think it had been used in this particular shooting.

A curtain of secrecy remained tightly drawn concerning the Giavinello surveillance. Thomas Sheer, deputy assistant director of the FBI's New York office, refused to explain why Giavinello was being tailed, other than to say it was part of a "larger surveillance of organized crime activities." Other sources noted that the probe had begun about six months before Venditti's murder.

A check of Giavinello's yellow sheet showed that the 53-year-old alleged killer had an arrest record dating back 34 years. These in the know referred to the suspect as "a low level mobster."

On Wednesday, January 22nd, Giavinello was taken before Queens Criminal Court Judge William Erlbaum on charges of second degree murder, aggravated assault on a police officer and criminal possession of a weapon.

Although a Murder One charge could apply in New York State in the slaying of a police officer, the lesser charge was determined in the Giavinello case because there appeared to be some question as to whether Detective Burke had identified herself as a police officer when she approached the scene, or whether the gunmen knew beforehand who the detectives were or that they had been following them.

Citing the suspect's extensive criminal record, which included past charges for assault, bookmaking, gambling and loan sharking, the Queens District Attorney's office asked that he be held in no bail. Judge Erlbaum granted the DA's request.

Arguing in behalf of Giavinello, defense lawyer George Meissner claimed that his client had been a victim, not a criminal. He said that the defendant had been carrying $4,700 in his pockets at the time of the assault. He alleged that "one or more people" tried to rob Giavinello and "then all hell broke loose."

For his part, Assistant District Attorney Lasak had an entirely different construction of the events. He alleged that Venditti had been felled by one of the first shots fired — and that Giavinello had then stood over the wounded detective and pumped two more bullets into his face.

Meanwhile, the police search went on for the other two as yet unnamed suspects in the case. No trace of them had been developed, since they'd vanished an instant after the shootout.

Veteran crime fighters expressed puzzlement over a crime—the killing of a police officer—which was considered atypical of organized mob activities.

Edward McDonald, chief of the Organized Crime Strike Force in Brooklyn, called the cop-slaying "unprecedented."

Another expert on mob thinking predicted, "The two who got away will be found, all right—dead."

Robert G. Blakey, a law professor at the University of Notre Dame and a former Federal prosecutor who specialized in organized crime cases, had this to say:

"There's an etiquette between law-enforcement officers and the mob.

"The mob knows in its heart that if they actually attacked law enforcement directly and law enforcement responded in kind, the mob would be wiped out. But it's not a code. It's better to describe it as a practice that is often breached."

Professor Blakey said it was his guess that the gunmen "did not know who the cops were." He added, "The fact that they went back and shot him again is an indication they wanted to kill him."

The Blakey theory received support from no less an authority on criminal behavior than Ronald Goldstock, head of the New York State Organized Crime Task Force.

Said Goldstock, "By and large, organized crime has restricted themselves from attacking law enforcement, and the reason has not been out of any great sense of love or respect."

The "enlightened self-interest" aspects of the uneasy truce on physical violence between cops and mobs had been cited by Professor Blakey in this case.

Blakey pointed out that in 1963, six men related to Carmine Lombardozzi, a reported leader of organized crime, were charged with having beaten FBI Agent John P. Foley, who was on assignment at a Lombardozzi family funeral in a Roman Catholic Church in Brooklyn. The agent was hospitalized with a concussion and a fractured skull.

According to Blakey, "Thereafter a series of guys from the Lombardozzi family ended up beaten up in ashcans."

Ultimately, Blakey noted, the head of the family assured authorities "it wouldn't happen again and everything got back to normal."

One theory attracting the attention of investigators in the Venditti slaying was that mob members had been jittery since the December 16th assassination of Gambino family boss Paul Castellano and his lieutenant, Thomas Bilotti. One source in the federal government noted that mobsters had been "incredibly jumpy" after the Castellano/Bilotti rubouts on Manhattan's West 46th Street.

However, if the killing of Venditti and the wounding of Burke had been inspired by an attack of "mob nerves" there had been nothing unusual in the surveillance techniques employed by the two heroic detectives.

The FBI-NYPD Joint Task Force On Organized Crime had been formed in 1982 to monitor illegal activities of the Genovese family.

According to FBI spokesman Joe Valiquette, the 36-member task force composed of 18 city detectives and

18 federal agents had originally been looking into gambling, loan sharking and labor racketeering Genovese enterprises.

Authorities stressed that Venditti and Burke had been tailing reputed mobster Frederico Giavinello as part of "routine surveillance procedures."

Explained police spokesman Lieutenant Tom Fahey, "It's a blanket term that covers many levels of police work, but it generally means that you watch and record someone's movements but you are not necessarily going to pick him up."

In recent years, the task force has been expanded to cover other known crime families and other forms of organized mob activities. It now numbers some 300 city detectives and FBI personnel as its operatives.

The influential *New York Daily News* wasn't buying the idea that mob blood-letting was confined only to crime family members. In its January 23rd edition, the newspaper published this editorial:

"THE MOB AT WORK: MURDER IN QUEENS . . .

"Detective Anthony Venditti, 34, father of four, 14 years on the force. Dead. Detective Kathy Burke, 42, mother of two, 18 years on the force. Severely wounded. The first New York City police officers to be shot in the line of duty in 1986.

"Veteran undercover cops, they were partners on the joint police-FBI Organized Crime Task Force. All indications are that they were shot by a Genovese 'family' hoodlum.

"That shoots hell out of the myth that the mob, La Cosa Nostra, the Mafia—whatever you want to call it—is some kind of benign sub-culture that kills only its own.

"The Mob and its operatives do kill their own. And kill, maim and ruin lots of others by pushing narcotics, by spreading terror, by corrupting public process, private businesses and labor unions. It's a genuine evil, every day. It must be brought to heel and stamped out.

"Anthony Venditti knew. Kathy Burke knows."

On Wednesday, January 23rd, there were two major developments in the case.

Police went to the office of a law firm which represented Steven Maltese, 52 years old, of Greene Avenue in the Ridgewood section of Queens. There Maltese awaited their arrival at 2:05 P.M., because according to Deputy Commissioner for Public Information Alice T. McGillion, "he knew we were looking for him."

Three hours later, word came that a man identified as Carmine Gualtieri, 55, had been arrested at his home in Flushing, Queens. In discussing the arrest, Lieutenant Edwin LeSchack, a Police Department spokesman, would only say, "The investigation led to this guy."

The two latest suspects in the Venditti murder and Burke shooting were charged with second-degree murder, attempted murder, aggravated assault and possession of a deadly weapon, LeSchack reported.

Police refused to speculate on whether the two men who had just been charged were linked to organized crime.

As the legal machinery concerning the three suspects in custody began to crank, relatives and friends of the fallen Detective Anthony Venditti now prepared for the sad task which lay ahead of them. His funeral had been scheduled for Friday, January 25th.

They also took time out to think about the enormity of their loss.

One close relative told of Venditti's four daughters and how they hadn't been told of their father's death.

She noted that the police had not as yet driven the slain detective's automobile back to his home, because the four little girls would expect their daddy to be stepping out of it.

She said of Venditti, "Aside from being a great son, he was a sensitive, loving man who loved his daughters so very, very much."

She called Anthony the core of his family, "the one that you could always rely on for anything.

"I'll tell you something," she said, "Anthony, aside from being a wonderful cop, took care of and loved his family.

"I don't know how these little girls are going to live without him, I'll tell you — it's going to be toughest on the kids."

The relative remembered her last moments together with Anthony. They occurred on the morning of the day in which he was destined to be killed.

"I hadn't seen Anthony in a week and I don't know why he stopped by that morning.

"He was in a great mood and he told me that he would be by on Saturday to help dad fix the car."

A brother recalled, "We always teased him about not having a son. But he said, 'I'd rather be surrounded by beautiful women.' "

Friends, one of whom had been his partner during Anthony Venditti's three year stint in a Bronx precinct, told of his courage and ambition.

Said the former partner, "From the moment he put on his uniform for the first time he had a goal; he wanted the gold shield. I never expected Tony to die like this, but in this line of work it can happen. It comes with the territory."

Former colleagues of Venditti's on the force found tangible ways to pay respect to his memory. They had raised $6,000 for his bereaved widow and children. In addition, they had accumulated a $20,000 reward for information leading to the conviction of the three suspects in the case.

Friday dawned cold and raw, a typical, penetrating winter day in Flushing, Queens. The 5,000 law enforcement officers from some 25 departments formed a guard of honor stretching six blocks in front of the Roman Catholic Church of St. Mel.

The big brass arrived. They included the mayor, the police commissioner, United States Attorney Rudolph W. Giuliani and New York Senator Alfonse M. D'Amato.

Four hundred people managed to crowd themselves into the church itself while hundreds of others occupied a downstairs room.

In his funeral oration, Monsignor John P. McCullagh issued a stern warning to the criminal element in the country. He said, "We issue a warning to people who enter into crime, organized or not. You face an eternity of God's wrath."

Praising "those who unselfishly lay down their lives for the good of others," the monsignor turned toward the slain detective's widow. He said, "You and your four children are members of a much larger family, his 27,000 fellow officers of the New York Police Department, and their friendship will last for the rest of your life."

He told of a visit he had made to Detective Burke in her room at Bellevue Hospital.

"In the room I saw retired Police Officer Salvatore (Richie) Pastorella standing there," McCullagh said. "He couldn't see me. (Pastorella had lost his sight in a terrorist bombing near police headquarters on New Year's Eve, 1982.) "He was there to offer any help he could."

39

After the homily, a tenor sang, "Be Not Afraid" and "Ave Maria."

The pall-bearers moved out into a swirling snow-storm, carrying the coffin of the slain officer to the cadence of the mournful wail of the massed pipers of the Police Department Emerald Society. As the casket reached the waiting gray hearse, a bugler sounded taps. The snareless drums began their steady roll. The tolling bells of St. Mel's added their note to the dirge.

Detective Robert Benedict, who had worked with Venditti when the latter had first joined the force, put his sorrow into these words: "It saddens you to lose somebody like that. It's like losing a brother, a member of the family."

Mayor Koch, who had led the official group of mourners, commented, "Nothing is more painful than attending the funeral of a cop or a fireman killed in the line of duty. It tears me up inside and I am almost unable to talk to the widow, particularly when they have little kids.

"Killing a police officer is the most outrageous criminal act one can do," he continued. "Those who kill, I believe, should be executed."

Police Commissioner Ward pledged that law enforcement officials would "fight not just against the criminal in this act but also those who are behind them."

Inspector Burke attended the Venditti funeral, although his heroine wife, Kathleen, still remained under medical treatment at Bellevue. The good word there was that she was making a satisfactory recovery from her chest wound. She was now able to talk to her two daughters on the telephone. The intrepid and diminutive officer who had once spent two years sleeping on boards in order to make the minimum height requirement to qualify as a cop, was now expected to regain her health completely.

How much had the public identified with the plight of the fatherless Venditti family? The answer came less than a week after the murder of the police officer. It was manifest in the action of an 83-year-old owner of a retail store chain. The executive, Milton Petrie, announced that he had set up a fund to pay Patricia Venditti $20,000 a year "for the rest of her life."

In addition, he said he was setting up a trust fund of $100,000 each for the four Venditti daughters to guarantee them a college education.

Said Petrie, "When I opened the newspaper and read about the poor detective's death and his poor family, I just felt terribly sorry for them. My heart went out to her and her children.

"I've got children of my own. My son, Bernard, is 60 and a lawyer in San Francisco, and I've got two daughters, Patricia, 51, and Marianne, 49, who are housewives."

The first $20,000 check was delivered to Mrs. Venditti through Mayor Koch. In an accompanying note, Petrie told the widow that she would receive a similar check each year "for the rest of your life, to help you bear the impact of the unfortunate death of your husband."

Koch relayed the check and the note through Edward Blasie, president of the Detectives Endowment Association.

Blasie said Mrs. Venditti "was very appreciative and told me she will send a thank you note to Mr. Petrie."

As Detective Burke continued to make progress and the Venditti family tried to pick up the pieces of their smashed lives, the investigations of the shootings went forward. Frederico Giavinello, Steven Maltese and Carmine Gualtieri remained in jail without bail.

At this writing, the three men have yet to be tried

41

before a jury of their peers. Unless and until such a jury finds them guilty of the charge of second-degree murder, attempted murder, aggravated assault or possession of a deadly weapon, they must be presumed innocent of these charges.

"CAN THE RAMBO DEFENSE FREE A COP KILLER?"

by Arne Arntzen

The call came through to the dispatcher's office at the Newton, Iowa, police station at 9:00 P.M., September 13, 1985. "There's a robbery going on here at the Westside food market," he said excitedly. "A black man with a gun. Hurry."

There were five police officers at the station who immediately sprang into action. Officer Daniel McPherren, 36, said, "I'll take a position behind the store." Minutes later, the officers arrived at the scene. They staked out the building and McPherren went around to the back. Officer Leland Groves spotted the robber leaving the front door and pursued him around to the front. He had not yet rounded the corner of the store when he heard two or three gunshots. When he came around the corner he saw McPherren standing in the middle of the driveway exchanging shots with two men.

One of the men was in front of McPherren, the other on his side. Officer Myrna McFarland, who was following Groves, saw McPherren being shot.

"I saw his knees buckle and he went down," she said. "At first I thought he was just taking a kneeling position, then when he went on his back, I knew he was down."

She said that after the men fled, one in a car and the other on foot into nearby woods, she hurried to McPherren. He told me he was hurt and couldn't move his legs. "Myrna," he said. "I think they got me."

"We have an officer down!" Lieutenant Harry Harger, who was in charge of the police force, shouted, "Get an ambulance out here!"

When it arrived, McPherren was rushed to Skiff Memorial Hospital; from there he was flown to the Iowa Methodist Medical Center at Des Moines on a Life Flight helicopter. He died in the emergency room at 11:09 P.M. from a single gunshot wound to his left chest.

At the time of the shootout, McPherren was wearing a bulletproof vest that protected him in the front and back. He was shot in his unprotected left side.

Questioning the people who were in the store at the time the robbery occurred, the police learned that the intruder was a black man. He had a gold tooth, wore a black mask and was armed with a handgun. He was of medium build and height. When he entered the store, he made the employees empty the money from the cash registers and the safe into a pillow case he had with him.

Another witness saw him get in a car and drive rapidly away. The other man, he said, fled to the nearby woods. Witnesses described the car as a brown, older model Chrysler. There were bullet holes in the left side fender and the rear window was shattered.

An alert was flashed over the police radio describing the car and its occupant, stating that he was armed and considered dangerous and probably heading for Des Moines.

Polk County Sheriff's Deputy Mark Brenen called in

to report that a civilian from the Polk County Crime Stoppers saw the suspect's car going west on Interstate Highway 80 near the Mitchellville exit.

"He saw the car flying on the Interstate and got the license plate number. Then he flagged down one of our cars," Brenen said.

Detective Charles Soderquist of the Des Moines Police Department said he was eating when he heard a broadcast that a Polk County sheriff's deputy had spotted a car matching the description of the vehicle involved in the robbery and shootout.

Soderquist, who was driving an unmarked police car, followed the suspect's car when it turned off Interstate 80 and continued south on Avenue Fredrick M. Hubbell.

When Soderquist radioed in for back-up, the suspect noticed he was being followed and began driving at a high rate of speed along a winding course through northeast Des Moines, while police and sheriff's deputies converged within the area.

At the 1400 block on Searle Street, the fugitive jumped out of his car and escaped the pursuing officers by running through the backyards of the neighborhood houses.

Some cash had dropped on the curbing on Searle Street, which was stained with blood. They followed a trail of blood from the back of a house and lost it.

No shots were fired during the chase, according to Sergeant David Noel, or when the suspect jumped out of the car and fled. The sergeant stated he didn't think the man was seriously injured because he ran at a quick pace.

"We didn't shoot because at the time we did not have positive identification and because of the danger to surrounding residents and civilian bystanders," Noel said.

Law enforcement officers sealed off the area and searched it on foot and in cars but were unable to find the suspect, who was described as a black man about five feet six inches tall and weighing about 175 pounds.

The two suspects were identified as Dennis Lamar, 38, and Lawrence T. Gladson, 41, both walkaways from the Riverview Release Center near Newton. Lamar was on a weekend furlough, while Gladson had left a hospital where he was to have had one of his hands treated.

Early Saturday morning, Des Moines police continued searching an eastside neighborhood for the suspect, identified as Dennis Lamar. They were also seeking warrants to search one or more residences in Des Moines.

In Newton, police were searching the wooded area back of the grocery store where McPherren had been shot. Bloodstains were visible on the ground, indicating that the suspect identified as Lawrence Gladson had also been wounded in the shootout. But despite an intensive search of the area, no trace of the fleeing gunman was found.

Later in the day, a report came through from the Des Moines Police Department saying that one of the suspects, Lawrence Gladson, had been apprehended and taken into custody. The law enforcement officers would not comment on the arrest, but sources close to the police said that the suspect had stolen a car from an inmate of the Release Center and was apprehended without incident at an undisclosed location.

On Tuesday, September 17th, at one o'clock, funeral services were conducted for Officer Daniel McPherren, 36, at the First Methodist Church. Over 500 officers from all over the state attended the funeral rites. After the services, the officers filed slowly out of the church and stood in rows. As the casket and McPherren's wife emerged, she was helped down the stairs by family members. The officers snapped to attention and saluted. The widow went to Governor Terry Branstad, who stood at the base of the stairs, and wept in his arms. Also surviving Officer McPherren were his three children.

Meanwhile, both Lawrence Gladson and Dennis Lamar were charged with first-degree murder and three counts of first-degree robbery. Because of the furor throughout the state at the escape of Gladson and Lamar from the Riverview Release Center near Newton, the state ombudsman began investigating the minimum security prison assignments given to the two convicts. The probe was conducted at the request of Gary Sherzan, Democratic Representative from Des Moines, considered a prison expert in the Iowa State Legislature.

"I know that Dennis Lamar received disciplinary reports at Newton. Why on earth was he given furloughs?" Sherzan asked.

"We are making an inquiry into Gladson and Lamar's progress through the prison system to determine if they moved in violation of any policy and if there were any warnings or indications that they would engage in violent behavior," State Ombudsman William Angrick said.

"The report could bring wide scrutiny of the state's policies on prison assignments," he added.

Meanwhile, the search for Dennis Lamar continued. Several sightings of him were reported to the police. One was by a man in Prague, in eastern Nebraska, who reported seeing him on a farm. A woman who lived there fired a shot at the man, who fled into a cornfield. According to Nebraska State Patrol Lieutenant Larry Korbelik, law enforcement officers launched a search for the fugitive but were unable to find any trace of him.

After obtaining information which they believed to be reliable, Des Moines police in their search for Lamar sealed off an area of six square blocks around the 1800 block of Eleventh Street.

The people living in a house on Eleventh Street were evacuated while police searched it.

Police also searched another house on the same street, but found no trace of the fugitive.

The last house to be searched was also located on Eleventh Street. In the 1984 directory it was listed as belonging to a relative of Lamar.

Before police entered, negotiators were unable to reach anyone in the house by telephone. An unidentified friend of Lamar's used a megaphone to issue a plea for Lamar to surrender.

"Walk out the door so nobody gets hurt," the man said. "Dennis, we have an attorney here. We have things arranged. We'll come up to the building and walk right out that door with you."

The officers waited. There was no response.

At 11:00 P.M., heavily armed police entered the building. They searched the house thoroughly. The man they wanted was not there.

Reporters questioning Donald Knox, chief of detectives for the Des Moines Police Department, were told only that they had information that Lamar could be in one of the houses. Knox said that the police were checking out other leads and had no further comments to make at that time regarding the investigation.

Because Jasper County has no county jail, Gladson was confined in the Story County Jail at a cost of $35 per day during the time of his incarceration, according to Jasper County Sheriff Alan Wheeler.

At the request of the Newton Police Department,

Canadian law enforcement authorities were tipped off on October 3rd that Dennis Lamar was heading for Canada from an undisclosed location in Wisconsin. The Royal Canadian Mounted Police alerted officers across Canada to watch for the fugitive. The Canadian alert is similar to an FBI all-points bulletin. It described Lamar as being armed and dangerous.

Toronto Police Sergeant Don Jackson said the alert indicated that Lamar had no known associates in Canada.

The Canadian authorities issued an arrest warrant for Lamar, according to Jasper County Attorney Charles Neighbor. The warrant gave the Canadians power to detain him if he were apprehended.

On October 10th, Newton Police Chief Mike Quinn revealed that another inmate from the Riverview Release Center, also on a weekend furlough, reported to police that the day after the shooting of McPherren, Lawrence Gladson appeared at his apartment and, at gunpoint, stole his black-and-blue Monte Carlo car and drove away. Gladson was arrested the same day at a friend's house in Des Moines. The inmate was serving a five-year burglary sentence. He was brought back to the Riverview Release Center after the incident and then sent to the Iowa Men's Reformatory at Anamosa. Ron Matthews, assistant superintendent of the Release Center, declined to say if the man was in any way linked to the grocery store robbery and slaying of Officer McPherren.

In another development, Jasper County Attorney Neighbor conceded that Gladson would not be able to get a fair trial in Jasper County and that he would not contest defense attorney Roger Owens' motion for a change of venue.

Jasper County District Judge Michael Streit agreed to the defense request and moved the trial to

Winterset in Madison County.

A reward fund amounting to $7,500 was contributed by several law enforcement agencies and the food market where Daniel McPherren was slain. The reward was not made public, but information that the money was available was passed to police informers "on the street" by word of mouth in Des Moines. The officers hoped that doing this, with the understanding that the identity of the informant would be kept in the strictest confidence, might bring results. Almost five weeks had passed since Dennis Lamar successfully eluded the police.

Their assumption proved to be correct. On Thursday, October 17th, Newton police received information revealing that Lamar was in Minneapolis, Minn. The address was spelled out and police were told that Lamar was still in hiding at that address.

At 11:00 P.M., Newton Police Sergeant Mark Diamond called the Minneapolis Police Department and told them that Lamar might be found at the address. A number of squad cars staked out the building and waited for the suspect to emerge.

According to Lieutenant Pat Hartigan, Lamar, wearing a beard and dark glasses, stepped out of a southside Minneapolis apartment accompanied by another man and a woman. They got into a rusty old car with a police car following them. A police car was directed to drive in front of the suspect's car and stop it. Minutes later, Lamar was arrested in the car after an officer approached him and inquired if he was Dennis Lamar.

The suspect said he was, and was taken to the Hennepin County Jail. In his wallet he had $50 and a Greyhound bus ticket from Chicago to Minneapolis.

After waiving extradition proceedings in Hennepin County, Lamar appeared in a Polk County courtroom on October 30th before District Judge Louis A. Laborato, who set his bond at $270,000. Lamar was charged with three counts of first-degree robbery, as a fugitive from justice, and the first-degree murder of Daniel McPherren.

In a soft voice, Lamar told the judge he had no money to engage an attorney and asked that Des Moines lawyer Robert Kromminga be appointed as his counsel at Jasper County expense. The judge approved the appointment and scheduled Lamar's formal arraignment for November 11th before Jasper County District Court Judge Streit at Newton.

Because Jasper County has no county jail, Lamar was lodged in the Polk County Jail to await his trial. Jasper County paid Polk County $45 per day during the time of his incarceration.

Lamar's formal arraignment was held in the Polk County courthouse in place of Newton as originally scheduled, with Judge Streit presiding. Lamar was charged with three counts of robbery and one count of first-degree murder. Judge Streit accepted his innocent plea.

Trial proceedings in the Gladson murder case began March 17, 1986, at Winterset in Madison County with the selection of a six-man, six-woman jury.

In his opening statement, James Ramey, assistant Iowa Attorney General, said the case was "about two different kinds of people, those who give to the community and those who take from the community."

"McPherren," Ramey said, "gave himself. Gladson took from the community."

The attorney said that while both Gladson and Lamar were believed to have taken .357-caliber handguns to the robbery, "the only one who could conceivably have fired the weapon that killed officer Daniel McPherren was Gladson."

But defense attorney Roger Owens said that Gladson was "not a taker, but gave his life for his country" while serving in Vietnam from December, 1969, to December, 1971. "He got a bronze star, and you don't get that for selling creampuffs on the corner.

"Gladson," Owens said, "suffered a mental disorder when he emerged from Vietnam and the army.

"It's not an excuse, but it mitigates what happened," Owens said.

Early in the court proceedings, Prosecutor Ramey had a tape recording of a police radio transmission played for the jury. It revealed hectic and somewhat dramatic chatter among the Newton officers who had answered the call of a robbery at a westside grocery store.

McPherren was heard saying he would take a position behind the store. Moments later, he had been shot down and was lying on his back in the store parking lot.

The prosecutor then called Curtis Brown, an inmate of the Riverview Release Center and close friend of Gladson, to the witness stand. He testified that before the shootout, Gladson and his friend Lamar, nick-named "Limo" of Des Moines, had come to his place to discuss plans to "case" the westside grocery store.

After the robbery, Brown said, Gladson staggered into his apartment. He was wounded and bleeding. He said, " 'Limo blew it,' or something like that."

Another witness, a relative of Brown's, testified that Gladson and a friend had come to see Brown before the robbery to ask him about the sale of some jewelry and guns. Lamar had arrived the evening of the robbery and cased the store. He said he needed money to repair his car, the witness said. Both men left armed.

When Gladson returned the following morning, wounded and bleeding, he said he had been shot by a woman cop.

Another witness, Frank Tarasi, a laboratory technician for the Iowa State Division of Criminal Investigation, stated that a handgun found near the food market had Gladson's thumbprint on it. A package of Pall Mall cigarettes found at the scene of the crime also had Gladson's prints on it, the lab technician testified.

However, another DCI lab technician told the court that the gun with Gladson's thumbprint on it was not the one that killed McPherren. He stated that a bullet lodged in McPherren's vest after it had killed him didn't match the gun.

The bullet, the technician said, had been damaged. He stated that a weapon taken from Gladson at the home of a friend in Des Moines had the same class characteristics of the bullet that killed the officer. There were no prints found on the second gun.

Harry Valdes, a friend of Gladson, told the court that he and Gladson held up a sporting goods store in Des Moines and came out with an armload of weapons they intended to sell for a trip out West. At the time, Valdes had criminal charges pending against him and is now in prison for a Tampa County burglary.

Two days after the holdup, two .357-caliber Magnum handguns taken from the store robbery were allegedly used in the shootout that resulted in McPherren's death.

"We wanted to get money to go on a trip to get out of the state," the witness testified.

"The day after the shooting," Valdes stated, "Gladson drove to my place in Brown's car. I knew more or less what had happened in Newton," he said. "They had a shootout, and he (Gladson) was getting out of a car when somebody shot him. He said he had shot someone and that Limo went down and he thought he was dead," the witness said.

Several other witnesses testified that they had been in the grocery store the night of the robbery and shootout, and had seen Lamar put a black mask over his face and draw a handgun from out of his pocket. Then they watched him rob the store. Following their testimony, the prosecution rested its case and attorney Owens began his case for the defense.

Owens pleaded what is called the "Rambo defense," contending that the stress of the Vietnam war, coupled with excessive drinking, destroyed Gladson's ability to cope with reality.

The only witness called by Owens was a psychiatrist who had taught psychiatry for 23 years at the University of Osteopathic Medicine and health Sciences in Des Moines.

Called to the witness stand, the psychiatrist stated, referring to the defendant, "When he drinks he goes nuts. When he's sober, and when you talk with him, he has reason, he has insight."

In his cross-examination, Prosecutor Ramey portrayed Gladson as a convicted felon before he went to Vietnam, a man who had fathered three illegitimate children and who was court-martialed for stealing while in army basic training.

Addressing the psychiatrist, Prosecutor Ramey said, "You sort of likened the war's effects to the destruction of Camelot. Could you call it waking up to reality?" Ramey asked, adding that many soldiers who returned from Vietnam did not resort to crime.

The witness said Gladson told him his mind was blank from the time shortly before the shootout until his arrest in Des Moines. Ramey then asked how Gladson could have told him he drank a lot of beer before the robbery.

The witness answered, "I was in error."

During earlier testimony, defense attorney Owens asked the doctor whether Gladson had the mental capacity to plan a crime.

"Whatever he did, his judgement went out of the window. There was no logic."

Speaking of his client, the doctor went on to say, "He has an unresolved conflict, a submerged reserve of fear, hurt, hostility and confusion. He has highly volatile emotions in a deep freeze with a lid on it. Pile booze on top of that, and the lid becomes fragile . . . Boom, it's a lousy combination," the psychiatrist said.

Gladson fits the criteria for the disorder, including a "recognizable stress-combat," "estrangement" from his surroundings, recurrent recollections of the war, a suppression of emotions, "a constant state of tension and anxiety" and has trouble concentrating, said the doctor.

The disorder "was not an excuse but a legitimate, bona fide disorder," he concluded.

The defense did not dispute the state's case—that Gladson was wounded in the shooting, that he had been at the scene of the robbery, that his print had been found on a weapon fired during the shooting, and that when he was arrested in Des Moines he was carrying a gun with similar characteristics to the gun that fired the bullet killing Officer McPherren.

The crowded courtroom filled with spectators had expected Lamar to take the stand in his own defense, but Owens decided it would be in the best interest of his client to rest his case after the conclusion of the psychiatrist's testimony.

Judge Streit then instructed the jurors, who retired to their chamber, to consider the testimony and evidence submitted to them during the trial.

After deliberating for nine hours, the jury returned

with a verdict of guilty of first-degree murder and three counts of robbery. Gladson displayed no emotion when the verdict was read, got up slowly from his chair, left the courtroom and went into a hall where he was handcuffed and led to the Madison County Jail about a block away.

Appearing before Judge Streit on April 25, 1986, with his attorney at the Jasper County Courthouse, Lawrence Gladson was sentenced to life in prison for the murder of Officer Daniel McPherren and an additional 25 years for three counts of robbing the Newton westside food market.

After sentencing, Gladson turned to his attorney, smiled and was led handcuffed out of the courtroom to begin his term in a state penitentiary.

Dennis Lamar's murder trial was moved from Jasper County to Polk County at the request of the defendant's attorney, Robert Kromminga, who felt Lamar could not get a fair trial in Jasper County. Jury selection began on Monday, April 14th, in the Polk County Courthouse in Des Moines, Iowa, with Judge Streit presiding. Lamar's trial began three weeks after his accomplice, Lawrence Gladson, was convicted of murdering Officer Daniel McPherren.

Prosecutor Ramey had contended in Gladson's trial that Gladson had fired the shot that killed McPherren. However, according to Iowa law, Lamar could have been convicted of first-degree murder even if he didn't pull the trigger in the fatal shooting of McPherren. The law specifies that all persons who participate in a robbery in which someone is killed are equally guilty.

Ramey said his case would not be substantially different from the evidence and testimony presented in Gladson's murder trial.

After opening statements from both attorneys, the prosecutor called several witnesses to the stand who had been in the store at the time of the robbery. They identified Dennis Lamar as being the man who robbed the food market.

One witness said he saw Lamar enter the building and identified him as a black man with a gold tooth. He said he wore a mask, carried a revolver and ordered the employees to empty the money from the cash registers and the safe into a pillow case he carried.

Several crime lab technicians from the Iowa Division of Criminal Investigation and other witnesses who had testified at Gladson's trial repeated their testimony when called to testify for the state, after which Prosecutor Ramey rested his case.

Lamar's lawyer, Robert Kromminga, called only one witness to the stand, the defendant, who testified for 40 minutes. He refused to answer some questions from Ramey, and Judge Streit threatened to cite him for contempt of court if he didn't answer.

Speaking of the robbery, Lamar said, "I looked over the market and said I'm going to get me some money there." He parked the car on the westside of the store and told Gladson, "You stay here. I'll be right back."

Lamar testified that after the robbery he ran out of the building to his car and threw the gun and the money bag into the car.

"Then this man, Mr. McPherren, said, 'Freeze! Hold it right there!' I put my arms up in the air and said, 'All right, all right, don't shoot.'" About that time, Lamar stated, he heard Gladson get out of the car and then heard two shots. He denied firing any shots at the police, saying that the shootout was between Gladson and the officers.

However, when police officers recovered the gun Lamar allegedly had used, they discovered the weapon had been fired three times. Two of the officers involved in the shootout testified that they saw shots fired from the spot where Lamar was standing.

At the end of Lamar's testimony, the defense rested its case.

In his closing arguments, Prosecutor Ramey told the jury that even though Gladson fired the fatal shot that killed the Newton police officer, Lamar was equally guilty of murder regardless of which one pulled the trigger.

But attorney Kromminga disagreed, saying the theory did not apply, because Lamar acted alone in robbing the store. This was a case, the defense attorney said, in which the prosecution said Lamar should be held equally responsible for McPherren's slaying even though Gladson had killed the officer. Kromminga accused the prosecution of stretching the felony murder rule.

But Ramey contended that while Lamar actually robbed the store, Gladson was acting as his "getaway man."

"When two people commit an armed robbery, they're taking responsibility . . . for a chain of events that can very easily lead to the death of a human being," the prosecutor told the jury.

Turning away from the jury, Ramey looked Lamar directly in the eye and said, "Because a police officer was shot and killed in the line of duty, you're responsible; you're responsible for his murder."

At the completion of the closing arguments, Judge Streit instructed the jurors, who retired to their chamber to review and consider the testimony and evidence submitted to them during the trial. They deliberated for only a short time before returning with a verdict of guilty of three counts of robbery and one count of first-degree murder.

Lamar sat with his hands crossed in front of him and his head bowed as the judge read the verdict of guilty, after which he was led handcuffed to the Polk County Jail to await sentencing.

Appearing before Judge Streit on Tuesday, June 24th, Dennis Lamar was sentenced to life in prison without the possibility of parole. He displayed no emotion when the sentence was pronounced.

EDITOR'S NOTE:
Curtis Brown and Harry Valdes are not the real names of the persons so named in the foregoing story. Fictitious names have been used because there is no reason for public interest in the identities of these persons.

"THE BIG APPLE'S MANHUNT FOR A COP KILLER!"

by Bud Ampolsk

In his short lifetime, Scott A. Gadell represented both a throwback to a golden era and a hope for a better future. At 22, the young police officer held staunchly to the type of personal values which had once made the Far Rockaway section of New York's borough of Queens a bastion of middle-class decency.

He was totally dedicated to his family, his girl and his friends. The simple joys of life were his happiness. He had direction, knowing where he was going and how to get there.

Looking at him, those whose lives he touched on would recall what Far Rockaway once had been. They'd remember Saturday evenings when dating couples would hold hands as they reveled in movie double features and how those couples would tarry over triple scoop ice cream sodas at Keeler's Drug Store. They remembered how housewives would move up and down Mott Street in complete security as they searched out the bargains at Brody's Furniture Store and the H.L. Green Co., and Woolworth's.

Scott Gadell reflected the values of that time and place.

And Scott Gadell also represented what those who now lived in Far Rockaway hoped their neighborhood might again become.

The proof of this could be seen in Scott Gadell's reasons for having become a cop. Although he was dedicated to law enforcement, his real inspiration for joining the New York Police Department had come from knowing that up to 90 percent of a patrolman's work is concerned with aided cases rather than arrests. Scott sincerely wanted to help people, and felt the best way to accomplish this purpose was to join the force.

When the women of Scott's family worried over the dangers of his job, he'd reassure them by repeating his plans for the future. In a couple of years, he would be working inside. Long range, he would be climbing the department ladder. There would be exams for sergeant, for lieutenant, even for captain. Scott would study hard and pass these tests. He would go all the way.

On the afternoon of Saturday, June 28, 1986 Scott Gadell was more concerned with the immediate future than he was about long range goals. As he and his partner, Officer James Connolly, tooled their sector car through the narrow and aged streets of Far Rockaway, Scott had his thoughts focused on the commencement exercises which were to take place that very evening at Wantagh High School, and the fact that a very close relative would be a member of the graduating class.

It was for this reason that Scott had transferred to day duty from his usual nighttime hours and was working with Connolly. Nothing was going to keep him away from the Wantagh ceremonies.

At 2:45 P.M., Gadell and Connolly were cruising near the intersection of Beach 31st Street and Seagirt Avenue, a rundown section where decrepit beach cottages and ancient houses, whose history went back to

61

before the turn of the century, commingled in a picture of sprawling blight.

As the car rolled slowly down the street, the two officers' attention was captured by a pedestrian who was frantically attempting to wave them down.

The two cops stopped and listened. The man's tale was a breathless one of a shooting incident on Seagirt and Beach 28th Street. According to the man, he and his sister had been the targets of a gun-toting assailant. The gunman had fired at both of them.

As he talked to the two officers, the pedestrian pointed at a figure darting between houses and identified him as the troublemaker.

Both Gadell and Connolly left their sector car. They pursued the suspect on foot for about two blocks, only to lose him in the maze of narrow driveways and backyard fences.

Following standard enforcement procedure in such cases, Scott and Connolly immediately returned to the police vehicle which they had left on Beach 28th Street. They invited the complainant to join them in the search, hoping they would be able to intercept the culprit at some other point.

Their strategy worked well. Within a block, they spotted the suspect running into an alley next to a rooming house situated within one street of the beachfront.

Once again, the two officers instinctively followed time-honored techniques for dealing with this type of situation.

Gadell fearlessly moved into the alley behind the man while Connolly remained in the patrol car just long enough to call in a 1013 (officer needs assistance). Then Connolly was out of the car and racing around the other side of the house. Should the man try to escape that way, he would be blocked off by Gadell's partner.

It was at this precise moment that the apprehension and questioning of the suspect, which should have been a routine matter, became something very different.

Suddenly, the gunman leaped from a side door of the rooming house. In his hand he gripped an ugly-looking 9-mm. semi-automatic weapon.

At that instant it became obvious that a bullet-riddled showdown between lawman and suspect would ensue.

The gun-wielding man now took cover behind a large wooden cabinet next to the door. For his part, Gadell leaped behind a concrete stoop. The two adversaries stared each other down from a vantage point of less than eight feet.

Gadell crouched, his .38 grasped in both hands, as the wanted man opened fire with the semi-automatic. There was the whine and splat of slugs as the gunman squeezed off nine rounds and Gadell answered with six of his own. So close were the two men that the fugitive's bullets formed a pattern hitting within one square foot of the far side of the stoop. At least one of Gadell's bullets nicked his assailant in the arm or head.

Despite his marksmanship and courage, the odds were against the valiant young officer. This because a semi-automatic weapon features 14 bullets in its magazine while a .38 can only fire six times before it must be reloaded.

Gadell knew this. He was desperately trying to get six more slugs into the chambers of his service revolver when it happened.

This is the way eyewitnesses described it:

A lodger in the rooming house: "All of a sudden, this guy comes running from the backyard and I see a cop chasing him.

"The cop said, 'Don't pull out that gun; don't pull out that gun!' He went and pulled out the gun anyway and that's when the shooting started."

A street-wise 11-year-old: "I saw the cops pull up in their radio car on Beach 31st, alongside the house. This cop, he ran up into the yard and when he got to the front I heard about ten shots.

"I threw my bike to the ground and I got behind the telephone pole behind the house."

The gunman hid behind a large wooden cabinet. The culprit and the cop were about eight feet apart, according to the boy. He recounted the details of the exchange of fire at point blank range. Then he added:

"I saw the cop's partner in a shooting crouch in the back side of the house, near the detached garage. I saw the cop get down and fire at the guy.

"I was scared. I just wanted to get out of there."

The boy also reported that the gunman had run out of the alley, gun still in hand, and had commandeered a car.

By now, scores of police units were flooding the area in answer to Officer Connolly's 1013 call. Connolly, knowing that Gadell had been gravely wounded in the head, was rushing his mortally injured partner to Peninsula General Hospital in his own squad car.

The wanton brutality of the shooting would be discovered by investigating officers at the crime site when they came upon two 9-mm. shell casings right where Gadell's head had been. The execution-style murder had occurred at the exact moment when Gadell had been attempting to reload.

One lawman would comment, "He (Gadell) knew he was going to die. He just buried his head in his chest and he got it in the back of the head."

While surgeons at Peninsula General fought frantically to save Gadell's life, his fellow cops moved through the Rockaways, asking questions, seeking clues, piecing together what they could about the events of early Saturday afternoon. They were under the personal supervision of New York City Police Commissioner Benjamin Ward. Veteran top department brass, such as Chief of Operations Robert Johnston and Chief of Detectives Richard Nicastro, were busy at the command post which had been set up at the Far Rockaway headquarters of the 101st Precinct.

From eyewitnesses, the probers learned that the wanted gunman had driven away from the shooting scene in a vintage 1970s model black Cadillac with a blue vinyl roof. Bloodstains discovered in alleys between the shooting site and the place where the fugitive had gotten into the car gave weight to the theory that at least one of Gadell's bullets had found its mark.

In the early going, there was some confusion as to whether the assailant had commandeered somebody else's car at gunpoint or whether the Cadillac had been his.

However, the accounts of the man racing through backyards and vaulting over wooden fences were vivid.

The wanted man was described as being black with short cropped hair, about 30 years old and about 5-feet-9. He was said to be dressed in a brown safari jacket and brown slacks.

Meanwhile, stunned relatives and city dignitaries were gathering at Peninsula General as the futile all-afternoon battle to save the promising young officer's life was running to its tragic conclusion. At 6:17 P.M., exhausted doctors gave the word. Scott A. Gadell had succumbed. He had never regained consciousness.

Commissioner Ward said Gadell had suffered "massive brain mass loss from the bullet."

He commended Gadell and Connolly, who had been partners for only three days. Ward said they had taken appropriate action in confronting the gunman. "They split up and surrounded the house and called for assistance," he noted.

As night-time darkness swept in from the sea to claim the beachfront area, hundreds of uniformed and plainclothes personnel spread out. Knowing they were in a hotbed of drug-dealing and street crime, the police believed they were seeking someone who might be notorious enough to have killed a cop rather than risk the consequences of a routine trip to the precinct house.

Investigators alerted hospitals to be on the lookout for anyone seeking treatment of gunshot wounds to the head or upper torso. Stakeouts of all major airports and railroad stations were set. Homes in the neighborhood as well as in outlying districts were canvassed. A number of drug sweeps were undertaken in the belief that known dealers might have something of interest to say once they were brought in.

The intensity of effort brought quick results. From a number of sources, the detectives learned that the alleged gunman was 32-year-old Robert Roulston, a Jamaican. Roulston was said to be using a number of aliases.

The suspect, known by the street name of "Darvy," was said to have had a criminal record which had been amassed in his native Caribbean island as well as in New York.

His last known address had been in New York City. His yellow sheet showed that he had last been arrested in the city on December 14, 1984 on charges of robbery, burglary, possession of a gun and unlawful imprisonment. Outcome of the 1984 case against Roulston was not immediately known.

Deputy Chief Joseph Borrelli, commander of Queens detectives, circulated photographs of the suspect while enlisting the public's aid in locating Roulston. A special hot line was set up to receive confidential information on the alleged killer.

Now that the detectives had a prime suspect in mind, they noted that Roulston had been a low-level dealer in narcotics, including the powerful cocaine derivative, crack. There had been some reports that crack had played a role in the original confrontation between Roulston and the man he had allegedly fired at in some type of dispute on Saturday. However, the police were playing this aspect of the case down.

A female relative of the original complainant now came forward to give further details of the altercation which led to Officers Gadell and Connolly having been flagged down.

The woman said that Roulston had been her friend for several months. She had learned that he had recently been released from jail. The girl had sent out word that she would like to see Roulston.

The invitation to Roulston had caused the woman's relative to try to break off her relationship with Roulston.

Said the woman, "This is not the first time he (the relative) got into my life. He's got no business trying to get into my life."

At about 2 P.M., on the day of Gadell's murder, she alleged, Roulston had been lying shoeless on the double bed in her apartment. The relative called and there was an argument between the two men on the telephone. The relative warned that he was "coming over to fight my friend," the woman said.

"When he got here, my friend was sitting on the bed and said, 'It's cool. It ain't no problem.' And he (her relative) still wanted to fight him."

The men scuffled with each other, according to the woman. The verbal argument continued on the street.

"He (Roulston) ran outside without his shoes. I passed him his shoes, and he left," she said.

The complainant told police that while the men had been on the street, Roulston had fired two 9-mm. shots at the complainant and a second man.

Working around the clock, probers searched for solid clues which would give them hope they were zeroing in on Roulston. Their first break in this direction came on Sunday, June 30th, when the blue 1976 Cadillac Seville showed up on a street in Queens. Police held a tight cloak of secrecy around the recovered vehicle. They even refused to reveal the site on which it had been recovered.

Deputy Chief Borrelli would only report that the Cadillac was registered to a woman who was a friend of the missing man. But he would not divulge her name. He said investigators had been unable to question her because she was out of the country.

The gut feeling of the cops was that Roulston was still holed up somewhere in the city. Steady pressure was being maintained on his usual haunts. It was also said that Jamaican police, who had been seeking Roulston in the Caribbean on charges unrelated to the murder of Gadell, were cooperating by conducting sweeps on the tropical island.

The theory that Roulston was still in the Big Apple was given weight by the type of wound the suspect might have suffered in the fire fight with Gadell. Such injuries would have made it difficult for the wanted man to travel any great distance, it was felt.

Despite periodic forays into neighborhoods populated by Jamaican immigrants — both legal and illegal — Borrelli could offer no quick solution to the baffling case.

"If you want me to tell you we're hot on his trail, I can't tell you that," he said. "We're just sniffing around the edges."

The sense of mourning for the fallen hero cop hung over the city as preparations went forward for his funeral. A $20,000 reward for information leading to the arrest and conviction of his killer was announced.

But nowhere was the loss more deeply felt than in the neatly kept Wantagh home where the 22-year-old policeman had lived so happily with members of his immediate family.

Relatives came and went. Midst their tears were moments of consolation given to them through the recall of happy memories of a young man who had been universally loved and admired.

They remembered the basic decency of Gadell, who had been so opposed to violence in any form that he had refused to wear his service pistol while off duty.

They talked of how much he'd cared for senior citizens and the way he was always available to help — whether among his own relatives or for others.

Said one elderly relative, "He came to stay with me earlier this year. I told him, it's too dangerous to be a police officer and he said, 'Don't worry. I'll only be on the streets for a year.'

"He was going to be a sergeant, and then a lieutenant, and then make captain, he told me."

One cousin noted that Scott had first thought about becoming a police officer when he was only four years old.

His best friend, who had trained with Scott Gadell at the Police Academy and had served with him while both had been members of the New York City Housing Authority Police (Gadell had served there until his appointment to the NYPD) told of a pact the two young lawmen had made.

"We promised each other if something were to happen to him, I would take care of his family — and he did the same for me.

"I thought the world of him," stated the friend. "Even before he became a cop, he was a great guy."

The two men had shared a number of off-duty interests and had frequently spent their vacations together.

According to the friend, Scott Gadell had felt that when he'd been transferred from his Bronx beat to the one at the 101st Precinct he'd drawn a safer assignment.

"He would tell me to be careful. He left the Bronx for Queens, a nicer neighborhood — so much for a nicer neighborhood."

The close friend told of how the two had matured since having become police officers.

"Becoming cops made us both grow up," the grieving man commented. "You change your priorities. When you go into the city, you really find out what life is all about."

Others talked about how closely knit the family had been and Scott Gadell's deep and abiding love for his relatives.

On Tuesday, July 1st, a soft summer sun looked down on the spit and polish blue uniformed and white gloved officers who stood in rigid ranks as mourners gathered at the I.J. Morris Funeral Home in Hempstead, Long Island. The columns of officers stretched for four blocks. In all, there were 5,000 lawmen on the street. As one, their gloved hands touched visored caps in a final salute to their fallen comrade.

Inside the jammed chapel, mourners heard Rabbi Alvin Kass, a police chaplain, say of Gadell, "He began many labors, the end of which he will not see.

"But if the day comes when we can walk the streets in safety, it will be because of the dreams of men like

Scott Gadell . . . Scott made God's work his own."

As the flag-draped casket was carried by pallbearers from the chapel, a bugler sounded the mournful notes of "taps."

An escort of 100 police motorcycles formed a phalanx around the hearse. The cortege of limousines moved slowly to the gates of New Montefiore Cemetery, Pine Lawn, Long Island, where Scott Gadell was laid to rest.

Even at the moment of burial, New York City detectives were still going through the exhaustive and exhausting tasks of searching for Robert Roulston. In one sense, they felt left out because they had been unable to attend the funeral. But in another, they recognized that they were doing what was expected of them.

Said one, as he went through the business of knocking on doors and asking the same questions over and over again about Roulston, "You know where you are needed. You know where you belong. When the death of a member of your family occurs, emotions are high."

By now it had been firmly established that the prime suspect was allegedly a low-level crack user and dealer. Officers assigned to the murder investigation said they felt they were making "progress every day."

The sweeps of known drug users and dealers went on in the Rockaways. It was hoped that the street people who were brought in might have some useful knowledge.

Deputy Chief Borrelli left little doubt that he considered Roulston a hardened criminal when the top detective revealed that records showed the wanted man had been sentenced to 15 years in a Jamaican prison in 1974, having been convicted of committing a series of armed robberies on the island. He had been paroled in 1982.

Said Borrelli, "When he got out, he committed additional robberies, and they were looking for him there.

"Roulston had fled to New York and had been living in the city illegally since 1983," Borrelli said.

Once again, Borrelli described Roulston as being 5-feet-11, weighing 160 pounds and having a close-cropped mustache and beard. He was also known to use the name "Errol Campbell."

The weeks began to drag by as the frustrating hunt went on. Seven were to pass as detectives followed every lead, hoping one of them would point to the wanted man.

The task force headquarters was maintained at the 101st Precinct. A great deal of effort was concentrated in Brooklyn, the last place where Roulston (or Campbell) had resided before the Gadell murder.

Chief of Detectives Nicastro said there had been several confirmed sightings of Roulston by "reliable sources." Detectives were almost positive they had missed their quarry by only two hours when they had arrived at a hot location only to discover that Roulston had fled.

One problem plaguing the lawmen was the fact that Roulston did not appear to have strong roots in the community. However, detectives were reasonably sure that the wanted man did have some contacts who were willing and able to hide him out.

Just as the search appeared to have grown cold, three separate calls were received. The callers suggested to the police that the wanted person was holed up in a building on Marcy Avenue in the Bedford-Stuyvesant section of Brooklyn.

Although there had been many disappointments before, weary detectives found cause for optimism in the latest tips because they had come from three separate sources.

During the middle of August, the Marcy Avenue building was placed under surveillance, a certain third floor apartment in particular. Once again, there were disappointments. To all appearances, the flat seemed unoccupied. There were no sightings of lights going on or off. There were no human figures moving across the windows.

Despite all this, the assigned officers refused to let their concentration waver. They kept telling themselves that something positive might happen and they must remain on the alert for it.

Then, out of a clear blue sky, the long awaited big break came. It was Detective Sergeant Robert Plansker who first spotted it. The time was shortly before 3 P.M. on Monday, August 18th.

It was such a subtle change that it could have just as well been missed had it not been for Plansker's diligence and sure instincts. Staring up at the tenement, Plansker realized that one of the window sashes in the third floor flat was in a slightly different position than it had been for better than a week. Somebody had to be inside the apartment to have raised the sash that way.

There was a hurried conference among the officers. For long moments, they studied the change in the window. Then somebody said, "Let's go!"

With Plansker in the lead, four detectives entered the tenement. Stealthily, they moved up two flights of stairs and waited before the apartment in question. Plansker and his detail wanted to make sure that enough time had elapsed for their comrades to have taken up positions on the building's exterior fire escape. Once all members of the detail had moved into place it would be time for the climactic showdown.

If indeed one of the people in the apartment was Roulston, his only two avenues of possible exit would be past the five detectives in the corridor, or out the window and onto the fire escape. Should he choose the latter, he would find himself in a dead-end situation. The fire escape reached only to the tenement's top floor and offered no access to the building roof.

Once assured his people had been deployed to his satisfaction, Plansker knocked on the apartment door.

A voice from inside asked, "Who's there?"

Plansker offered a one word reply — "Detectives."

A long moment of silence followed.

Then there was the sound of a doorknob turning. Slowly the door swung inward. An unidentified woman stood before the five officers.

By this time, Roulston was already out the window and climbing the fire escape. The fourth floor was to be the end of the line for him.

From the street below and from the roof above the muzzles of police guns were unwaveringly trained on the suspect. Gruff voices ordered him to "Freeze!"

Then, two detectives leaped out onto the fire escape from inside the apartment and wrestled Roulston down.

This is the way one of the arresting officers, Detective Mike Falciano, would describe the action later.

"He looked down at us with our guns pointed up at him and attempted to climb the fire escape, but it only went to the fourth floor.

"He thought about pulling his handgun for a second, but the other officers jumped him. There was a brief scuffle and he was arrested."

The woman who had been with him in the apartment became hysterical. Detectives took her into temporary custody, but they released her when she convinced them she had not been an accessory.

Police, with Roulston now under arrest, searched for a second woman whom they believed had rented the apartment for the wanted man.

A check of Robert Roulston showed that he was indeed the same man as Errol Campbell. It was further learned that Campbell had been indicted by a Queens grand jury just a week before his arrest in the Gadell murder for a totally unrelated homicide which occurred in the Edgemere section of the Rockaways in the early morning of July 13, 1985.

In that case, it was charged that Campbell and an accomplice had shot to death one Albert Small, a 23-year-old Brooklyn man. It was said that the Small killing had been drug-related.

According to law-enforcement authorities, the charges in Small's murder had been developed during the course of investigation of Officer Gadell's killing.

Roulston (Campbell) was taken immediately to the 101st Precinct for questioning. When he was led out of the station house for booking later on the evening of August 18th, he was greeted by a cheering mob of street people.

Said one of the officers assigned to the convoy, "It wasn't exactly clear if they were cheering for him or just out of relief after waiting to see him for several hours."

Strong praise was accorded the Queens task force which had captured Roulston.

For Gadell's family, there was some sense of comfort that at last a prime suspect was in custody.

Said one relative, "The only thing I can say is I give the men in blue credit."

Added another, "He (Roulston) did a horrible thing to take our boy away. He (Gadell) was one beautiful human being, and I feel the loss terribly. I knew the police would never give up."

On August 19th, Queens Assistant District Attorney Jeffrey Levitt appeared before Judge Allen Beldock in Queens Criminal Court. The A.D.A. said at arraignment proceedings that Roulston (Campbell) had confessed to the murder of Scott Gadell. According to Levitt, Roulston had made a complete videotaped statement.

The A.D.A. alleged that in addition to having shot Gadell to death, Roulston had admitted to having fired on a second officer and two civilians. (The three other persons had escaped injury.) Following the shootings, Roulston had discarded the 9-mm. weapon he'd used.

Alfred Pillero, a Legal Aid lawyer assigned to defend Roulston, argued that his client had told him the confession had been beaten out of him by police. Roulston had said he had been "struck by fists and clubs in the face, eyes, stomach and legs while being taken to the 101st Precinct headquarters by car and then at the station house itself.

"His face was swollen," the lawyer said. "He has a black eye. He was hit in the face, in the eyes, in the stomach and legs.

"A cop indicated the beating would stop if he made some kind of statement."

Later, giving the police position on the allegations of a Roulston beating, Captain Michael Julian said that Roulston had not been beaten, and that any marks he might have, including the black mark under his eye, could have been the results of the brief fire escape struggle which preceded his capture.

As this is being written, Robert Roulston, alias Errol Campbell, is being held without bail on second-degree murder charges in the unrelated slayings of Police Officer Scott A. Gadell and street person Albert Small. He is also wanted in his native Jamaica on robbery charges.

It is his constitutional right to be considered innocent of all of these charges unless and until proved otherwise before a jury of his peers.

"A HERO COP WAS AMBUSHED!"

by Barbara Jahns

Sometimes, a call to settle a domestic disturbance may be humorous in rehashing the story for comrades at the stationhouse. Take the cop who drove to a rural home and found a woman lying prone on the ground, apparently banged up badly. The officer arrested her husband, and as he was placing handcuffs on the culprit's wrists, the battered wife leaped up and began beating the policeman with her purse, yelling, "Leave my husband alone!" Sometimes a case doesn't end this way at all.

There is always the isolated case where a dispatcher's report of a domestic disturbance can be deadly.

On the night of March 9, 1985, Officer Greg Williams received a dispatcher's call to investigate a domestic disturbance taking place in his jurisdiction of Huntsville, Texas. It was 1:20 in the morning of a Saturday night, when families seem to fight the most. A lot of times they are lovers again by the time the weekend is over.

Greg Williams was 27 years old and had been a police officer for three years. Congenial and easygoing, he knew it was never wise to assume a call like this would have a peaceful ending. Greg was always ready to give a guy a break if he could, and make an arrest only if necessary.

He arrived at the apartment complex in the Huntsville city limits in Walker County, parking his cruiser on the side of the building. He was met by two apartment security guards, who drove into the area about the same time. Before he could take note of anything else, two women dashed toward him. One of them was more undressed than dressed and hysterical. The weeping women had run from different directions and it was evident there was a lot of confusion. The parking area was well-lighted and the buildings large and fairly spacious.

He could see that the women were scared of something, fleeing from someone unseen. He stepped in front of them, using his body as a shield of protection.

One of the women pointed with trembling finger to the rear of the apartment building. Williams had time to ask "Where is he?" Following the line of direction, the uniformed officer turned and could see a lone gunman pointing a long firearm in his direction. It was clear that there was a scope attached to the barrel of the gun. Williams reacted quickly as he always did when confronted by an armed assailant. He stepped in front of the ladies and yelled "Freeze!" to the unknown gun wielder.

In the same instant, his hand reached to his side where his service revolver nestled in its holster. He had just managed to loosen it before the gun held by the suspect began to spew flame. Greg Williams was shot twice. The first bullet pierced the cartilage and flesh of his right shoulder. The second plowed into his head, right between the eyes, and he toppled to the ground. His skull was punctured, and the vital elements of his brain were destroyed.

The rifle kept firing. One of the security guards fell as a bullet ripped into his left arm and a graze wound on his side could have been caused by another bullet. One slug ripped into an automobile parked on the lot. In all, seven shots were fired. Williams had ceased to move after he fell, and the guard was helpless, but he tried to shield Williams from further injury by rising to one knee.

Lieutenant Mike Horner of the Huntsville Police Department drove into the area. The first thing he saw was Williams lying prone. He knelt beside his fallen comrade to render first aid and CPR, but the officer's pulse was very weak and he was apparently breathing with much difficulty. One of the security guards had regained his feet and, despite the pain and bloody trauma of his own wounds, shielded the policeman as he tried to revive his friend. Residents were peering through their windows and entering the parking lot by now.

The other security guard drew his weapon and raced after the gunman. One man had placed a call to headquarters, stating that a policeman was shot and down. Later it was learned that this man had been looking at the security guard when he was shot, and was unaware that two men had been hit by the flying bullets.

"An officer is down" are among the most ominous words known to law enforcement. As the dispatcher radioed the words they were picked up immediately and response was rapid. Officer Frank Hidalgo was off duty that night, just kind of walking around his own apartment, but the message sent a chill of fear down his spine. He broke into a dead run, calling into his car radio, "I'm on my way!" All over the city, other officers were answering the summons in a similar manner, concern for a comrade spurring them to the scene of the crime. As Hidalgo arrived, he saw policemen and two security guards loading a suspect into a patrolcar.

Later, Hidalgo would learn that the man with the gun had been trying to get to his car, which was parked on the street. As he started to enter the vehicle, the other security guard caught up with him. Lieutenant Horner was right behind. The gunman saw the grim looks on the faces of the men confronting him, saw the drawn service revolvers, and he wasn't so brave anymore. He dropped his rifle and raised his hands in the air. He was taken into custody without further incident.

His rifle, recovered at the scene, was a .22 Marlin semi-automatic, Model 60. Mounted on the barrel was a 48-power scope. Magnified by the scope, if the suspect had been looking through it when he opened fire, Williams must have made an outstanding target. The man had stood on a slight rise when he fired, and the ambushed policeman had not had a chance.

Ambulance attendants were doing their best to revive the fallen policeman, though it was clear to see he was critically injured. As gently as possible, they loaded him onto a stretcher and transported him to the local hospital. Williams gave no sign of life other than a very faint, fluttering pulse.

The suspect was identified as Patrick Curtis Havard, 24. As Williams went to the hospital, the other man was transported to the Walker County Jail.

Havard was worried that night. Though he had shot two men, he was more concerned about being at work on time by Monday morning than he was about his victim's welfare. He talked to the chief of police from his cell in the Walker County Jail, and this seemed to be the main theme he could find to speak about.

He confessed to the shooting. He had been caught

dead-to-rights and couldn't very well deny it, anyway. But he felt his actions had been justified, and he had a tale to recite of having been involved in a conversation with officer Williams and firing in self defense. He was to worry all weekend about getting out of jail in order to be at work on time Monday morning.

Jay Hubert, the wounded security guard, was treated for his injuries and released. But he, like other decent people, was worried about Greg Williams' condition. The fallen officer's family kept vigil at the hospital, but he had lapsed into a deep coma, holding onto life only through medical skill.

It was hard to associate the energetic Williams with the laboring figure on the hospital bed, lingering in a state more dead than alive.

Hidalgo was worried, too, and other officers canvassing the area shared his concern, but there are duties to perform in any crisis which a good lawman never omits. Walt Pinegar, criminal investigator for Walker County, joined Hidalgo and they began to reconstruct the events leading up to the shooting.

Patrick Curtis Havard had gone to the apartment complex, parked on the street, and walked to the first-floor apartment where his estranged wife and a roommate had been living. Once he was admitted to the apartment, it is said that he became involved in a violent argument with his wife, even to the point that she was shoved across the coffee table.

He had left the weeping women, frightened and vulnerable, while he ran to the bedroom to grab the gun — which belonged to his wife's roommate. Investigator Pinegar, in examining the apartment, entered the bedroom where Havard had gone to secure the weapon. Scratches on the wall showed where and in what haste Havard had grabbed the gun.

He did not know it, but the roommate had called

the police. She had been run out of the apartment by Havard and had stood outside waiting for the police, though she knew that her friend was being threatened and pushed around inside. Apartment security men had been summoned, too, and one of them arrived on a motorcycle, the other in a car, just as Officer Williams drove up in the cruiser.

Havard's wife had run from the building and raced around the side of the building, believing that she would be shot at any second by her angry spouse. She had no time to gather her clothing and was almost nude. With her life in jeopardy, the girl could not be concerned with modesty. Seeing the uniform and the safety it symbolized, she ran to Williams.

The officer had taken in the situation at a glance and he had moved in front of the women. "Where is he?" he asked.

The scared, trembling girl raised a shaky finger to point at the other end of the building. The policeman had time only to see that a gunman stood alone there on a slight rise, pointing a long rifle at him and the people around him. Maybe in that second Greg Williams thought of his own family, his own three children safe at home. He may only have thought of his duty, though, for he moved with speed and agility in an attempt to carry out his duty, as he called out "Freeze!" and tried to protect the others. He reached for his own gun in its side holster.

After this, it was easy to tell what had transpired next. Williams' holster was opened but he had not had time to draw his weapon before he was fired upon. Witnesses to the violent scene were easy to locate, but here Pinegar knew he had to work to sift the wheat from the chaff, so to speak. Sometimes a person comes forward who really hasn't seen anything at all, but who wants the attention of saying he saw something, anyway.

Tall, curly-haired Walt Pinegar was well experienced in sifting through statements from witnesses. He had been working in criminal investigations for the district attorney's office in Walker County since 1977. He reflected that although he had worked on many important cases, he had to spend a great deal of time away from home because so many of them were tried by change of venue—in a different place from where the event had happened. He hoped that would not be the case here.

Officer Hidalgo had not worked closely with Pinegar before, but during this investigation, he was to become more involved with the district attorney's office than he anticipated. He and Pinegar worked hard, and they made a good team. When finally they were through interviewing witnesses and isolating the crime scene, it was 10:00 A.M.

In the early hours of the afternoon, Officer Greg Williams was pronounced dead. To those who had waited at the hospital the news came as no surprise, for, to all intents and purposes, he had died in the parking lot the night before when he was gunned down.

Patrick Havard, it seemed, would not make it to work on Monday morning despite his worrying. He expressed no concern for his victims, though one had died. He did not express any remorse for the shooting.

But, in looking at Havard's background, one found this was typical of the man. He didn't have a lengthy police record. Though numerous charges had been filed against him in the past, most of them had been dropped before they ever went to court. But a profile of a bullying, threatening, violence-prone man was to emerge during the course of the investigation.

Greg Williams left behind a devoted wife and three

young children, besides a host of friends and relatives. He had worked for the Texas Department of Corrections at the state prison before he became a cop. His background was exemplary, and his death caused much grief on the force. He had been well-liked by his co-workers.

In his initial statement to the police, Havard had stated that he had seen a flash of gunfire and had only retaliated when he opened fire. The police did not feel this was true, but in order to safeguard their case, each officer in the vicinity had to undertake a gunpowder particle test to determine if indeed anyone had fired a gun. The test had to be administered within the first few hours after the shooting.

If any man had fired a weapon, the evidence would be on his palm. One by one, all participants in the night's tragic occurrence were tested. The security guards had not fired. Neither had the downed police officer. Though Lieutenant Horner had handled a gun, he had not fired one.

The results of the test proved that no one except Havard had fired a weapon on the night of March 9th. Witnesses further bore out these findings. From all evidence collected, it appeared that Havard had fired without justification or provocation.

If the city of Huntsville was shocked by the slaying of a gentle cop like Williams, no one in his acquaintance was really shocked by the arrest of his killer. Pat Havard did not have a lengthy police record; he did have a long series of complaints against him by people who would have ordinarily filed charges. But a look at his background showed that Havard had such an intimidating manner that his threats were often worse than the violence he had exhibited. Some people said they were afraid to go to the police because he might have hurt them even worse than he already had.

Some did file charges against him, but these were usually dropped before they came to court. The reason, it was to be learned, was that they were simply afraid of Havard, who was known as a bully and a merciless thug.

One man said Havard had put a rifle barrel in his mouth and torn away precious flesh when he yanked it away. He would be physically scarred by the experience. Then there was the other man who said Havard had broken a gun barrel over his head. Both men were afraid to press the issue in court and the charges were dismissed against Havard.

His wife told again of how Havard had entered her apartment and threatened her roommate and herself, causing her to fall over the coffee table. At the time he ran for his gun, she thought he meant to kill them both. This story would later be repeated on the witness stand in court.

It became a joint effort of the city and Walker County to gather as much pertinent information as it took to gain a finding of guilty when Havard came to trial. They ran into no snags in reaching an indictment for capital murder in the case. Meanwhile, Havard remained incarcerated at the Walker County Jail, where he did not want to be, even though the building was new. The jail had not been built to escape-proof specifications, either. The top of the cell bars were located too far from the ceiling to be secure, due to lax work by the builders.

Pat Havard was aware that he might face the death penalty when he was brought to trial, so he began to plan his escape.

He figured it would be easy to remove a portion of the wall and escape through vent pipes. Once free of the bars, he could find outside aid which would help him to flee the country. One night he began to put his plan into action, carefully and quietly removing a portion of wall. He worked industriously at this. Other prisoners had talked of how easy it was to escape from the new cells. He plotted to put into action a plan which would prove this was true.

However, he didn't go anywhere, because a tipster told the guards what was happening. They caught him red-handed, and he was moved to a safer place of confinement. He had gained nothing for his efforts.

During pre-trial hearings, Havard's defense attorneys asked for a change of venue for his forthcoming trial. They cited widespread publicity as the reason.

But the case had been kept low key, with few releases to the press and other media in anticipation of just such a motion. Thus, this motion was denied and Havard was slated to stand trial for capital murder in Walker County.

District Attorney Frank Blazek was to prosecute the case. Tall, studious, and completely engrossed in his work, Blazek felt the man deserved the death penalty for his unwarranted killing of a police officer whose only wrong doing—and this was from the killer's viewpoint—had been to respond to a domestic disturbance call in the line of duty.

Blazek had delved into the victim's background and found that the policeman had been gentle and easygoing. For years he had worked for the Texas Department of Corrections in Huntsville State Prison, and it is to Williams' credit that even the prisoners in that facility did not have anything derogatory to say about the dead officer.

Blazek had also studied the confessed killer's background, and found a sharp contrast to that of Williams. Pat Havard had been known as a man not to be trifled with. He had an uncontrollable temper and it was common for him to explode, with those around him bearing the brunt of his anger. He had been terrorizing his wife and her roommate on the night he shot and killed Williams, but he had spent most of his adult years terrorizing other people.

The jury selection began in September, 1985, but it was to be October 13th before the actual trial began. During that time, Investigator Pinegar and Officer Frank Hidalgo had worked unceasingly to help build the case and have ready the evidence which would lead the jury to a finding of guilty. One rather unique part of the trial was the filming of a videotape of the dispatcher's clock. Every word on the transmitter that night had been taped. The jury could gain visual impact by watching the seconds tick away as the voices told graphically of the events which had taken place.

First there was the distress call. The dispatcher advised Officer Williams to respond to a report of domestic disturbance.

Then there was silence for a moment, and then the terrible words, "officer is down," followed by a jumble of responsive voices. Frank Hidalgo's hurried message, "I'm on my way," were played on that tape, as well as other statements. And then the clock stopped ticking. Time had run out for Officer Greg Williams.

Since that day, Hidalgo has resigned from the department and gone to work for the Walker County Sheriff's Department, where he has responded to many types of criminal activities. But it is doubtful that he has been called to answer any summons which affected him so deeply as the death of his friend, Greg Williams.

He was acutely aware of the widow and orphaned children who had been left behind. He was aware of the loss of his buddy, the feeling of something being missing whenever he walked into the police department. Though he had helped plan the videotape, he was visibly touched by the clock's ticking and its sudden silence.

· The jurors were affected, too, as they saw the pugnosed defendant before them and could only imagine the reality of Greg Williams' figure moving spectrally through the courtroom.

For the prosecution, this phase of the trial was a great success. However, Pat Havard had his own line of defense strategy in store. Defense claimed he wasn't guilty because of his state of mind. They never pleaded insanity, but if they had, Blazek would have been prepared with his own rebuttals.

Havard admitted having problems with his wife and her roommate on the fatal night, but claimed he had gone to the bedroom and grabbed the gun merely to scare her. He never meant to harm anyone, he claimed. But the women had run outside, and he followed them, still holding the gun. He saw his wife standing beside a man—in the dim lighting he didn't know he was looking at a cop. Suddenly, the other man stepped in front of his wife. Havard, amazed, had called to him to "Get away from my wife!" The other man yelled back an insult. Then he saw the security guards.

He felt really outmanned then, he said. All three of them were armed to the teeth and coming at him with drawn guns pointing. He then raised the weapon he held and stood in the marksman's stance, but they kept coming. He saw a flash of light which he thought was flame from a firing pistol, and he shot in retaliation. He saw the two men fall, but he did not know he had fired at a police officer and he only fired in self-defense. He fired at random only in an effort to save his own life. It was really all an unfortunate accident and he felt he should be freed, since he had not planned to kill anyone, he repeated.

Testimony proved that only Havard had held a gun in his hand. Williams had reached for his revolver but had not cleared leather before he was gunned down. Havard had been angry and hurt and distraught at the time, and his uncontrollable temper had caused the whole thing. It was implied that he had become jealous when the stranger stepped in front of his wife.

But Pinegar and Hidalgo had brought pictures to the courtroom which proved to the jury that the area was well-lighted and Havard had to have known he was looking at a policeman when he opened fire.

Frank Blazek had been district attorney since January of 1983, and he was prepared for any eventuality which might surface during the course of this trial. Having worked in private practice before, then as an assistant to the former D.A., he was experienced in legal work and was constantly striving to perfect the functions of his office.

His assistant at this trial was Bob Choate, who has been a member of the staff for almost as long as Blazek. The younger man was quiet, attentive, and knowledgeable. The two worked well together, and they both shared a common goal. They wanted Pat Havard with his lies and his uncontrollable temper to be locked away where he would terrorize nobody else, where he would shoot no more unsuspecting cops.

Testimony revealed that all witnesses to the shooting could agree on one point. There had been no conversation of any type between Havard and the man he had gunned down. Greg Williams had only shouted "Freeze!" and then he was killed, though he had reached for his gun but had not cleared leather.

Pinegar and Hidalgo had done their homework well, too. By careful searches at the scene, by tedious re-tracks and series of photographs, they could help Blazek and Choate prove that Havard could not have seen a random streak of light which he took to be gunfire.

The trial began on October 1, 1985, and lasted a week and a half. It took the jury about an hour to find the defendant guilty as charged for capital murder.

The penalty phase of the trial lasted two days, but it only took the jury 55 minutes to agree on a sentence of death for the defendant.

Currently, Patrick Curtis Havard is on death row at the Ellis Unit of Huntsville State Prison in Texas, awaiting his execution date and applying for all appeals at his disposal.

"DID BONNIE SUE ACTUALLY SNUFF A COP?"

by Krist Boardman

The last time anyone in civilized society heard from Richard Bowser was 11 o'clock at night on October 22, 1987. For the 47-year-old police officer and security guard, this was highly unusual. With a full-time job as a policeman for the Lower Paxton Township Police Department in suburban Harrisburg, Pennsylvania, and another full-time job as a security guard for a local supermarket, Bowser's life was well-structured.

When he did not report for his security guard job, his supervisor became concerned. Bowser didn't answer his phone, either. The police department in Lower Paxton Township was eventually called, and Patrolman Norm Kegerreis showed up to look in on his brother-in-blue.

Outside the ground-floor apartment where Bowser lived, Patrolman Kegerreis discovered that an outer screen had been forcibly removed from the window on the northwest corner of Bowser's dwelling.

Inside the apartment, entered through an unlocked door, Patrolman Kegerreis noticed something unusual: the telephone in the bedroom had been pulled from the wall. On the dresser in the bedroom was Bowser's wallet, but there was no cash in it. In addition, his .38-caliber service revolver was missing. But Bowser's false teeth, eyeglasses, jewelry, driver's license and watch were still there.

A relative told the police that she thought some of the furniture in the living room was disarranged, but there had not been any of the usual signs of struggle, such as smashed glass and overturned lamps.

The evidence did indicate something, however. If Bowser's teeth were out and his watch was off, he was most likely in bed sleeping. Maybe he had interrupted a burglary in progress? How else to account for the missing cash, which Bowser normally had plenty of, and the missing gun?

Investigators later learned that Bowser had another gun that was missing. This was a 9-mm. pistol in a holster that he normally kept in the trunk of his car. When he completed one shift as a police officer, he always took off his gun belt with the .38 and switched it for the belt with the 9-mm. that he wore as a security guard.

And then there was Bowser's car, a black 1984 Chevrolet Monte Carlo. Where was it? Did that also explain his missing car keys? A description of the car and its registration and VIN numbers were registered with the NCIC network, and the information was distributed to police agencies throughout the U.S.

The law enforcement task force searched for any kind of clues. Could the perpetrator be someone Bowser had arrested as a police officer? What about a shoplifter nabbed by Bowser the security guard? All the names of the possibles were sifted through, but nothing promising came up. Then what about Bowser's other contacts?

One thing learned about the burly 5-foot-8, 280-pound lawman was that he liked to frequent Harrisburg's massage parlors in off hours. The massage parlor connection was probed carefully by sleuths trying to find out what if any link there was between this custom and Bowser's disappearance. But none of the leads led anywhere.

Fingerprint technicians didn't come away as empty-handed, however. They lifted some usable latent prints from the outside window where the intruder seemed to have gained entry, and also some from the phone that had been torn from the wall in the bedroom and from the wall itself. These were forwarded to the FBI fingerprint repository and lab in Washington, D.C. for comparison with prints on file. Unless something else came up, this was the best hope there was.

A week later, Bowser's black Monte Carlo showed up in Richmond, Virginia, minus its license plate.

The car was originally found abandoned on the night of October 23rd in the parking lot on West Broad Street in Richmond. The following morning it was towed to an impoundment lot by an unsuspecting tow-truck operator. Some days later its VIN was entered into the NCIC network. There was a hit.

The car was pored over by FBI investigators. One first impression they had was the car's putrid odor. There was a tremendous amount of blood in the trunk and also feces. The trunk also contained evidence of human hair and flesh.

What seemed to be more useful were the Newport cigarette butts and the bloody prints. There was a large, smeared, bloody handprint on the inside of the rear window. Technicians also dusted for other prints in the front seat.

The car's rear stereo speaker was torn out, apparently by the passenger in the trunk — presumably Bowser. Insulation was also removed from inside the trunk, and the taillights seemed to have been tampered with—all signs of a man desperately trying to figure out how to save his own life.

If anything, the discovery of Bowser's car seemed to eliminate the possibility that Bowser himself escaped a violent and bloody end.

In Leon County, Florida, something else was happening. There, at a rest area off Interstate 10, near Tallahassee, Leon County Deputy Sheriff Stephen P. Shaw saw a 1978 Chevrolet van with a North Carolina registration number. Although there is no record of why Deputy Shaw decided to check on its registration, he did. And he discovered that the van was stolen from Hills Borough, North Carolina.

One person in the van was a woman who identified herself as Tina Marie Brown. She said she was from Lebanon, Pennsylvania. The other was Samuel Lee Green, 29, from Harrisburg.

After a day, Tina Marie Brown was released. But there was a detainer out for Green, and he was held at the Leon County Prison.

FBI print examiners were notified and they processed the van for latents. These were collected and returned for comparison with other samples.

Green was detained for allegedly stealing a television set from a relative's home. Pennsylvania authorities initiated extradition proceedings to remove him from Florida.

A month after the crime, Green was back in Pennsylvania. Pennsylvania State Police investigators scheduled some interviews with him. He waived his right to remain silent and, in the presence of Corporal Thomas P. Brennan and Troopers John J. Holtz and Gregg Benedek, as well as a detective from the Dauphin County D.A.'s office, he made the following statement . . .

"On the night of October 22, 1987, or early morn-

95

ing of October 23rd, I saw a window cracked open on the ground floor of Bowser's apartment," Green said. "I took the screen off the window and placed it by the bushes. I then pushed the window open and crawled inside. It was very dark inside and I crawled on the floor, being very quiet. I remember seeing a door and an opening. I crawled into the bedroom and saw people sleeping. They did not move.

"I checked the dresser and found car keys. I had my hand inside my shirt and patted my hand on the dresser until I found the keys.

"I then left the apartment using the door, and went into the parking lot. I checked the cars in the parking lot until I found the car that the keys fit. I remember it was a black car.

"I then drove to Allentown to Bonnie Sue Pflugler's residence. I found her sleeping on the sofa. Bonnie asked if I got any cash from the apartment. I told Bonnie no. Bonnie then said let's go back and check it out.

"Bonnie and I then drove back to the apartment. When I got there I went through the window again, closed it and opened the door for her.

"I then got a knife from the kitchen counter or drawer. I was going to use the knife to cut the phone cord. I remember finding the phone and pulling the cord from the wall. I found a wallet on the dresser and took cash from it. I remember we lit matches to get our bearings.

"In the bedroom Bonnie handed me a gun in a holster. It was a small gun, a .32- or .38-caliber gun. I eased the gun back onto the dresser. I was wearing a tan jacket and I put the money in the pocket of the jacket.

"I left Bonnie in the bedroom and I left the apartment. I went outside and started exploring. When I returned to the car I saw Bonnie standing outside the car.

"I then drove us back to Bonnie's house and parked the car. After a while we left the house and we got into the car and I started to drive. Bonnie gave me directions. Bonnie said we are going to a secluded area. I remember smelling an odd odor in the back seat of the car and there was a blood smear on the back window.

"When we got to the secluded spot I opened the trunk and saw a fat, white, naked guy laying on his left side, balled up like a baby. He wasn't breathing or making any sound.

"I said to myself, I don't need this, and started to walk away. I heard Bonnie say, 'Get out.' I then heard a sound, like scratching in the leaves. Then I heard a pop, maybe two shots.

"I turned around and saw the naked guy laying face down. Bonnie had a gun and I was sitting in the car. I grabbed the guy by his arms and pulled him a couple feet off the side of the road. I then covered him with branches and a cut tree.

"Bonnie then took the registration plate that was on the car and some papers from the car and threw them near the body. I recall that I threw an umbrella near the body. We drove away.

"Bonnie and I then drove to Richmond. When we got to Richmond I had it with the car. I got out and bought some beer while Bonnie parked the car. We then walked to the bus stop, and Bonnie bought some bus tickets to Raleigh, North Carolina.

"When we arrived in Raleigh we got off the bus and started walking to Hills Borough, North Carolina. In Hills Borough we saw this place across the street so we went over to it. I was cold so I started walking to get warm.

"Bonnie then drove up in the van. We took off for Florida. Bonnie had two guys' credit cards which I got in the van. Bonnie put them on the dash and we used them to buy gas. On the trip to Miami, we used the cards at least eight times. We both signed the cards.

"We stayed in Miami overnight. We headed for Interstate ten and Bonnie was driving. Bonnie parked in a rest area near Tallahassee and this is where I got arrested."

The investigators asked Green to show them where the body was. Soon after, Green, dressed in an orange jump suit and with cuffs on his hands, led the investigators to the sleepy borough of Northampton.

The picturesque town, with aging frame homes and a smattering of small factories, could have been the subject of Simon and Garfunkel's popular song, "My Little Town." There, on the outskirts of town, off a long, winding country lane, lay the body of Richard Bowser.

The investigators stopped at a small pull-off from the road. Beneath branches and leaves lay the badly decomposing and nude body of the police officer. After the site was identified, Green was taken away and the proper technical personnel arrived to process the scene and remove the body.

Later that same day, the forensic pathologist, Dr. Isidore Mihalakis, determined that Bowser had died from two gunshot wounds to the back of his head. Because of the actions of rodents, he was unable to determine whether Bowser had been beaten on the head and face, however.

Dauphin County District Attorney Richard Lewis said at a news conference at the Bethlehem, Pennsylvania State Police Barracks: "We believe he (Bowser) was forcibly abducted, brought here and dumped."

But that version of the crime soon changed. As Dauphin and Northampton County police and prosecutors huddled to go over the existing evidence, it seemed apparent that although Bowser was abducted in and kidnapped from Dauphin County (Harrisburg area), he was likely murdered in Northampton County. Prosecutors and investigators there began to assume control.

Mark Refowich, First Assistant District Attorney from Northampton County, announced to the press that "we will seek the death penalty" for the person or persons responsible for Bowser's death.

At about the same time, Bowser's body was returned to his hometown of Huntingdon, Pennsylvania, for funeral and burial with full police honors. And on November 25, 1987, flags at all city buildings in Harrisburg were flown at half-mast.

But there was still plenty of work to be done on the investigation, before Richard Bowser could rest in peace.

The focus turned to Bonnie Sue Pflugler, also known as Tina Marie Brown.

At 29, the divorced mother of three pre-school children was charged with murder. When she showed up for arraignment, wearing cuffs, leg-irons and a pink jogging suit, she had little to say to members of the press.

But they had plenty to say about her, a fact that later caused her to complain in a petition to the court that she was the subject of an "open hunting season" by the press.

She was no stranger to law enforcement.

Just two days before she was charged with murder she was arrested in Lehigh County with a male suspect on charges related to a September 1987 burglary at the Shimerville Inn in Upper Milford Township. In addition, she had a long record of brushes with the authorities.

While Bonnie Sue Pflugler was in jail, she told

another female inmate of her involvement with Green in the Bowser murder.

On December 2, 1987, Troopers John J. Holtz and Cynthia Transue both interviewed the inmate at the women's detention center in Dorneyville. The inmate said that the following information was given to her by Pflugler on or around Thanksgiving. The police report of the interview, as obtained from court records, stated that the inmate "said that Bonnie told her that Bonnie and an unnamed co-conspirator and Bowser had a fight. Bonnie helped the unnamed co-conspirator get Bowser in the car. The only thing they took from the apartment was cash and guns. Bonnie said she knew Bowser was a cop because she looked at his I.D. The I.D. was laying on the top of the dresser in the bedroom.

"Bonnie said she knew a spot to take Bowser. Together they drove Bowser to Easton. The unnamed co-conspirator shot Bowser once and then Bonnie shot Bowser once. They then covered Bowser's body and left. They then came back to Allentown and then traveled to Virginia.

"Bonnie told (the inmate) that law enforcement officers talked to her (Bonnie) about Bowser's murder. Kennedy said she asked Bonnie if she did it and Bonnie said, 'Yeah, girl, me and (unnamed co-conspirator) killed that mother f----r.' "

Pflugler's attitude remained mean and feisty. She battled with her own court-appointed defense attorneys and tried to have them dismissed for incompetence and partiality. She claimed that the appointment of Defenders Steven Shields and William Zaun did not compare with the appointments that Green received.

"In general this invidious discrimination violates her civil rights to equality under the law," her petition read. Pflugler "feels victimized because her co-defendant is black and has received *experienced* and *seasoned* trial attorneys and to date the petitioner has been made to feel she is to be used as a scapegoat."

She also accused her defenders of "going through said proceedings as a matter of formality" and decried a "total breakdown of communications."

As the judicial process ground on slowly, Samuel Lee Green was also having some second thoughts. During a suppression hearing on August 14, 1988, Green, through his defense attorneys, denied that he signed the police statements that he had made earlier. The motion to suppress was denied.

The time before trial also enabled FBI print examiners to complete their work. They found that the latent prints found on the screen outside Bowser's apartment, on the telephone and on the wall in his bedroom, matched latents found within the bloody handprint inside the car and also prints found within the Chevy van. Green's prints were at all three locations.

At Green's trial in January of 1989, the jury in Northampton County seated at Easton, Pennsylvania, found Green guilty of murder, kidnapping and conspiracy. In the penalty phase of the trial, after the January 24th guilty verdicts, the jury also concluded that there was one aggravating circumstance and there were no mitigating circumstances. Under Pennsylvania law, Samuel Lee Green was sentenced to death.

According to one courtroom observer, Green was so shaken by the sentence that his pants were wet.

Bonnie Sue Pflugler didn't go to trial. Just before it began, on May 16, 1989, she entered a guilty plea to third-degree murder, kidnapping and conspiracy. She received a sentence of 20 years on the third-degree murder charge, five years for kidnapping, to run consecutively to the murder charge, and three and a half years for conspiracy, to run concurrently with the others.

When he was quizzed on the discrepancy between the penalties given the two defendants, Assistant D.A. John F. Spirk, Jr., a prosecutor with Northampton County for 10 years, said that there was no evidence linking Pflugler to Bowser's apartment, where the crime originated.

Mr. Spirk acknowledged that Green's statement that he brought Pflugler back to the Harrisburg area for the second phase of the crime, as he described it in the statement "was theoretically possible," but not likely. He noted that it is an hour-and-a-half trip from the two locations, and Green would have had to have traveled in both directions twice during that time to have done it in that way.

More likely was that "Pflugler said she was never in Harrisburg, that Green showed up with Bowser in the car. There was no physical evidence to put her in the apartment."

Mr. Spirk said that he believed that the abduction and kidnapping was done by Green alone, and that Bowser cooperated initially because he would have had his 9-mm. pistol in the trunk of the car. However, apparently Green prevented him from getting the pistol before Bowser got into the trunk.

"At Green's trial it seemed . . . he was the principal actor," Mr. Spirk said. While there was no evidence to show that Green was trying to settle an old score with Bowser, once it was discovered that Bowser was a police officer and he apparently awoke during the burglary, his fate may have been sealed.

Although Green received the death penalty, the sentence may not mean any more than that he will be incarcerated for life. There are numerous death row inmates and none of them have yet been executed.

In any case, Green may never experience the terror that Richard Bowser felt as he traveled for two hours in the trunk of his car, trying feverishly to light flares, monkey with the taillights, tear away insulation, while at the same time squirming around in his own blood and excrement with no clothes on, while dreading the final stop of his own car that could mean only one thing.

"Certainly he knew he was on his way to die," said Mr. Spirk. "He'd understand there's no reason to take him in his car" unless it was to his own execution.

"LETHAL STING
OF THE 'SPIDERMAN' "
by Julie Malear

Whistling a happy tune as he dressed for work that hot, bright morning of August 22, 1988, West Palm Beach Police Officer Brian Chappell made a mistake — the most devastating mistake of his entire life. He neglected to wear his bulletproof vest beneath his shirt. The Florida sun was simply too hot that day for the cumbersome, weighty piece. He'd taken a chance it wouldn't be needed.

The likable five-year veteran was a motorcycle officer assigned to the traffic division. As always, before leaving for the station, Officer Chappell added the finishing touches to his uniform, attaching his small gold nameplate, his insignia, and his badge — number 826.

Chappell was good-looking in a Tom Selleck way, with his strong 31-year-old body, his smiling eyes, and his dark hair and mustache. Chappell spoke to several of his fellow officers while signing in and checking for messages. The following week his vacation was coming up. He was going to Mexico with a friend, Officer Don Wesson. They were both looking forward to it.

Chappell had many friends. He was also close to his parents and siblings. He was engaged but not yet married.

Chappell liked to joke around, never griping or complaining, and was a popular man with his co-workers. Mentioning that he planned to get some fishing in before summer was over, he put on his helmet, climbed on his motorcycle, and cruised the West Palm Beach streets feeling relaxed but alert.

Around 10:30 A.M., as the relentless sun chased a trickle of perspiration down Chappell's forehead, the radar on his bike indicated a "speeder" in the vicinity. Chappell was driving on Southern Boulevard, a state highway that traverses the south side of Palm Beach International Airport. When he turned onto Dixie Boulevard (U.S. Highway 1), he saw a pickup truck charging through traffic at excessive speed with no apparent regard for pedestrians.

When the truck, a silver-gray Mazda, braked for a stop sign and made the turn off of Dixie onto Malverne Road, Officer Chappell signaled for it to remain in place. The pickup pulled over and stopped. Because traffic prevented the lawman from going up to the vehicle, he motioned the driver to pull forward a little. He then put the kickstand down, removed his helmet, and approached the open window of the pickup.

The driver, a young man, was glaring at him with hate in his dark eyes. Chappell noted a menacing tattoo on the man's neck — the realistically portrayed image of a three-inch spider.

Suddenly, Chappell saw the driver raise his hand. Something was in that hand. It was a gun.

The move was so fast, so unexpected, there was no time for the surprised officer to escape. A bullet from the driver's 9-mm. semi-automatic tore through Chappell's chest with devastating force, then ricocheted against the curb on the other side of the street.

"Oh my God!" the lawman cried out. Chappell's training prompted an almost unconscious reaction. He stumbled back toward his motorcycle, losing blood fast. Once he was down on his back on the pavement, he turned to his handheld microphone. "Officer down. Officer needs help," he managed to call into his shoulder mike. Mortally wounded, Chappell could speak no more. Life ebbed from his body in a scarlet flow as the killer sped away.

Back at headquarters, horrified officers heard the wounded man's SOS on the police radio. Who was the officer in trouble? Where was he? The transmission ended before those questions could be answered. One of their brothers was down, but they had no way of helping. The hairs on their arms rose. Adrenaline pumped. Frustration grew. The station erupted in frantic, helpless chaos.

Nearly two agonizing minutes passed before a resident on Malverne Road called, her voice taut with emotion. A policeman had been shot by her house, she told dispatchers.

At last, police had a location—the 400 block of Malverne Road. Cruising nearby, a uniformed officer heard the message, swung around the corner, and arrived at the scene within 15 seconds, immediately calling for paramedics. Based at a fire station barely a block away, the EMTs wasted no time. They started CPR and maintained an artificial heartbeat as they rushed the victim to Good Samaritan Hospital in West Palm Beach.

Interviewing the woman who made the phone call, the first officer at the scene learned several details. He got a description of a silver Mazda pickup truck with a lone male driving. The truck, she said, was a late

106

model with a black pigtail-type antenna—the sort usually connected to cellular telephones—and a trailer hitch. The Mazda also had whitewall tires and tinted windows. The driver, dark-haired according to the resident, shot the policeman as he walked up to the driver's window of the truck. The officer managed to stumble back toward the motorcycle where he fell down.

When the call came, Lieutenant John Conklin was transporting his invalid father to a doctor's appointment. Although the lieutenant, a slender man with dark blond hair and mustache, was not due at the station until 3:00 P.M., he learned the bad news when he answered his beeper. He headed immediately to the crime scene.

By the time Conklin reached the 400 block of Malverne Road, Officer Chappell had already been removed to the hospital, where he was soon pronounced dead. The bullet had traveled straight through his heart. Lieutenant Conklin surveyed the scene with a sick sensation. For a guy to have shot an officer over a traffic violation didn't make sense. Dope dealers regularly shoot other dope dealers, he thought; but speeders do not usually shoot traffic cops—unless they have something to hide.

Chappell's motorcycle was still on its kickstand. One spent 9-mm. shellcase lay on the street.

Lieutenant Conklin, who was in charge of major crimes investigations, assigned various tasks to his investigators, then reinterviewed the woman who had phoned the police station. She'd been on the telephone, she told him. She could see out her window and saw the officer pull the truck over. She heard the gunshot, saw the officer fall, and saw the truck speed away. So the police knew what the perp was driving, but they knew little else. Lieutenant Conklin recalled all the homicides he'd investigated in which he'd known who did it within minutes. Sometimes he and his men would take a couple of days and then pick up their suspects. At the start of this case, however, they had a policeman dying in a hospital, one spent shell casing, and a description of the perp's truck.

A heavy smoker, the lieutenant lit a cigarette. As he sped back to headquarters, he had the uneasy feeling that this would be an extremely difficult case.

Once at the station, he began to set up a bank of telephones. Fortunately, he found a vacant room that was being converted into a new dispatch center but wasn't yet completed. There was a great deal to do — round up tables and phones, get telephone people to install the wires, assemble volunteer officers to man the phones 24 hours a day, figure a way to log the calls, then get the news people to put out the special TIPS phone number — 637-4013.

There was no time for Conklin to bring his men in for a brainstorming session. This was no time for reflection. Conklin knew police had to act quickly to get the facts.

Three of Conklin's detectives became the central figures in the search for their fellow officer's killer. Detectives K.C. Myers, Mark Anderson, and John Johnson, who, as they termed it, "hit the ground running." For the next four days they ignored the luxury of even a single breather.

On Tuesday, the second day of the investigation, an adult called to say a boy had witnessed the crime — a 13-year-old who'd told the adult all about it. The detectives soon met with the boy and learned he'd been standing at the intersection of Malverne and Dixie and had seen the whole shooting. Probing further, they learned that he'd been fascinated with the motorcycle policeman and his Kawasaki. He had watched atten-

108

tively as the officer pulled up. The youth had been standing in the middle of the street and had to wait for the truck to turn off U.S. 1. He got a good look at the driver right through the windshield and the open window as the truck turned. He saw the driver's hand come out the window with an automatic pistol and fire one shot. He knew he'd be able to identify the perp, he told the detectives.

The TIPS line paid off, but not immediately. First, people had to get a newspaper; then they had to read the newspaper and determine if they really saw what they thought they saw. But within two days valuable information started to pour in, specifically from people riding on the Florida Turnpike. They had seen the news in the paper and had observed a truck being driven into a canal within approximately half an hour of when the crime was committed. The TIPS line was receiving 50 calls a day regarding silver Mazda pickup trucks. The team had to check into each one. In addition, law enforcement agencies statewide sent teletypes to the West Palm Beach PD about people they had stopped.

Lieutenant Conklin appointed one desk-bound officer to sort out all the information, to separate leads that could wait from those that had to be taken care of immediately. It wasn't until the night before the slain lawman's funeral that the paperwork was finally put together. But before then, as well as afterward, things kept rolling. There was never a time the detectives could sit down and say, "What do we do next?" Whenever they saw a "warm body," they gave that person the next chore.

A man from Ft. Lauderdale and another driver from Palm Beach Gardens—one northbound and one southbound—both phoned to say they'd seen the truck go into the canal. One of the callers had even stopped at the nearest toll exit and called the Florida Highway Patrol about "an accident." Although the highway patrol investigated, they were unable to locate the truck.

Using the Palm Beach County Sheriff's helicopter, the police team checked the canals along the turnpike from the air. At 100 feet up, the pilot finally spotted the pickup. No wonder the highway patrol had missed it. Not only was it completely submerged in seven feet of water in the canal, but it also didn't actually go off the turnpike where the highway patrol could find tire tracks. The turnpike has a canal on both sides. The detectives saw that the pickup had been sunk into the canal from the opposite side — from a dirt road. It had plunged in from the west side about 500 yards north of Lantana Road.

Detectives Myers, Johnson, and Anderson were all at the firearms lab when Sergeant Guillermo Perez and his men pulled the silver Mazda pickup truck out and secured it for crime scene investigation. The sleuths had been checking out the lone casing from the Chappell case along with several casings from a gun taken during a burglary. The missing gun, along with rolls of coins and a camcorder, had been stolen from Pat Kutlick, a sheriff's deputy whose house in nearby Riviera Beach had been burglarized shortly before Chappell was killed. Comparing casings Kutlick had saved from the stolen weapon, the detectives discovered that hers matched those from the murder weapon. Ironically, Officer Chappell had been killed by another law enforcer's gun.

Myers, Johnson, and Anderson had a suspect in mind for the burglary and began to work from that angle. This individual had been committing burglaries in certain areas of town. Convinced that such a crime was definitely involved in the cop-killing case, they spent a full day keying in on the person they suspected. Before they actually found the man, however, a number of events conspired to turn the investigation around.

Theresa Domingo, a young woman who lived in Palm Springs at the south end of West Palm Beach, phoned the police department in that small residential city to give them "some information" on the cop killer. Palm Springs police quickly called the West Palm Beach police, who interviewed the woman at once.

The trio of sleuths had been listening to Theresa Domingo only a few minutes when they realized this was the real thing. Nervously admitting that she believed an older relative of hers was involved, she poured out her tale. Actually, she knew a great deal — enough to change completely the direction of the probe.

Her relative, 25-year-old Norberto Pietri, pulled into her driveway Monday morning and picked up her teenage brother, Juan, and his bicycle. Norberto, she told the detectives, was driving a silver Mazda pickup. He told Theresa he wanted Juan to help him dispose of it. The two zoomed back out of the drive and headed west.

After a while, they returned to her family's Palm Springs house in a taxicab and, once inside, phoned to have a pizza delivered from a local shop. When the man brought it, Norberto paid him with several rolls of coins.

As they ate, they told Theresa how they had disposed of the pickup. They said they drove it beyond the turnpike overpass on Lantana Road and turned onto a dirt road that ran along a canal. Then, while Juan Domingo waited with his bike by the narrow east-west highway, Pietri drove the truck about 500 yards north on the dirt road, stopped, and pushed it into the canal. He trudged back to join Juan. They

111

rode double on the bike down Lantana Road, intending to pedal back to Palm Springs. The summer sun turned the ride into a sweaty chore.

"Forget this," Pietri told Juan. They stopped a mile down the highway at a business and phoned for a taxi. When the cab driver pulled up, he helped them load the bike in the cab before taking them home.

After Theresa Domingo finished her account and left with the detectives' thanks, the trio's next step was to put all the pieces together and verify that what she'd said was accurate. With Lieutenant Conklin's approval, they contacted the pizza delivery man. He still had some of the rolled coins Pietri had given him as payment. When he showed them to the detectives, they realized they were the same rolls that had been taken from Sheriff Deputy Kutlick's house.

The sleuths interrogated people at the business where Pietri had used the phone, as well as the cab driver who'd answered their call. Both supported Theresa Domingo's story. It was all fitting together.

Delving into the identity of Norberto Pietri, the lawmen discovered that he was a man they'd known simply as "Spiderman" because of a spider tattoo that graced the side of his neck. Pietri was 25 and had been at odds with the law since he was 17. In addition to his spider tattoo, he was also known for a 1978 Cadillac Eldorado he drove and for his typical mode of burglarizing. Due to his muscular build and extreme agility, he predictably entered a house by crawling through a window.

Pietri had pleaded guilty to a Lake Worth burglary in November 1986 and was sentenced to seven years in prison to run concurrently with sentences for several other burglaries. After doing time elsewhere in the state, he'd been serving the latter days of his term at the minimum-security Lantana Community Correctional Center (LCCC). The facility was a work-release center, a complex where inmates are held on the honor system. No bars were on the windows, no gates to lock. Despite the freedom, inmates seldom leave the prison grounds. On the other hand, they don't always return from the jobs they hold in the community.

On August 15th, Pietri had gone to his construction job. That evening, he failed to return. Although the center notified the Lantana Police Department, he returned to the LCCC of his own volition the following afternoon. He was reprimanded, but not severely. On August 18th, four days before Officer Chappell was killed, the LCCC held a disciplinary hearing over the incident and Pietri was given an additional 180 days on his sentence plus room restriction. Because of this and an earlier demerit for possession of drugs, Spiderman probably knew he might end up in a more restrictive facility. A half-hour after being confined to the center's dayroom, which is not locked or guarded, Pietro walked away from the complex and didn't return.

Now, on Wednesday, August 24th—day three of the murder case—the detective team saw that everything was breaking at once, and it all pointed to Spiderman. Witnesses had seen a man fitting Norberto Pietri's description in the neighborhood where the Monday burglary had been committed. TIPS began getting calls telling the investigators where they'd seen Pietri, where he might be, and where they thought he'd go. The busy police checked each reported sighting, but the suspect was fast and elusive.

Sergeant Laurie Van Densen suddenly spotted Spiderman near Palm Springs. He was driving a Toyota Starlet, which had been stolen the night before from the daughter of a sheriff's deputy who had parked it at the Florida Atlantic University's campus in Boca Raton, 30 miles south. Racing after him, the sergeant called for backup as she chased Pietri through an apartment complex and right to his relatives' house.

Sheriff's deputies responded, as did the West Palm Beach team, some of the K-9 staff who were on their way into the city, and a sheriff's helicopter. Excited and determined to catch the cop-killer, the lawmen played a desperate game of hide-and-seek as the wiry fugitive bolted from his relatives' house when the police closed in. Dressed only in baby-blue shorts, Pietri scrambled from tree to shed to shadow, staying just out of the lawmen's grasp.

A neighbor saw a bare-chested man creep around the corner of a house as a helicopter hovered above. She thought she saw him slip into a storage shed across the street. He was gone, however, when police arrived.

Spiderman's next stop was two doors away, near an airboat repair workshop. A witness saw him there talking to a man in red shorts. When the latter left, the suspect hopped on a bicycle and pedaled toward Kirk Road. Police sped after him, searching one street after another with photographers, reporters, and residents following. Pietri ran from yard to yard, climbing fences, hiding in bushes, as elusive as a feather in a breeze.

Finally, with the threatening helicopter seeming to spot him, Spiderman climbed a tree outside a church. An off-duty Lake Worth motorcycle police officer was inside, attending the Wednesday night service; noticing the crowd, he came out and asked, "What's going on?"

Someone answered, "They're looking for the guy that killed that cop."

Another person said, "There's someone over in that tree."

Recalling that police were looking for Pietri, who'd

been described during morning roll call, the officer, Roger Palmer, walked over to the tree and looked up. He didn't have his gun. He'd left it in his car, not wanting to carry a weapon into church.

Pietri yelled down at him, "Get away from there or I'll shoot you." With that the fugitive jumped on Palmer. A scuffle ensued. Pietri ran. Palmer and another man chased him, but Pietri was able to escape.

The suspect reappeared at a Palm Springs house where a man and wife were getting into their brand-new Honda Accord. They'd already strapped their five-year-old boy into his car seat in back when Pietri rushed up, aimed a gun at them, and yelled, "Get out! Get out!" Pushing the woman out, he slid into the driver's seat.

The woman screamed, "Let me get the baby! Let me get the baby!" The child, hearing Pietri tell his mother he'd shoot her, started to cry.

While the father frantically struggled to rescue his son, the fugitive turned the ignition. The parents had barely freed the boy when Pietri blasted off, seconds ahead of the police hot on his heels. He was able to lose his pursuers by chasing through backyards and over two fences. He ditched them completely by turning south on Davis Road as the lawmen sped north.

Faulty communication further hampered the capture. Officers from West Palm Beach, Palm Springs, and the sheriff's office were each working on different radio frequencies. Adding to the confusion were reports from residents that placed Pietri in different locations at the same time.

Within the hour police in Delray Beach, a resort city 17 miles south of West Palm Beach, were flooded with bulletins telling them the suspect was in the Germantown Road section of Delray, an area known for its crack cocaine sales.

When one of their members is killed, a miraculous bonding takes place among the brotherhood of law enforcement officers. So when the word reached Delray Beach police around 9:00 p.m., Wednesday night, that Pietri might be in their bailiwick, the officers there were just as anxious to catch the fugitive as were police in the West Palm Beach area.

Five of the 15 members of the TACT team, a group formed in 1985 when drugs became a decided problem, cruised toward the Germantown Road neighborhood in various vehicles. Dressed in their black TACT outfits, the men were hyper, ready, alert to every shadow in the semidarkness. After scouring the area for nearly an hour, Sergeant Mike Swigert, with Officers Charles Hoeffer and Tom Quinlan, returned to headquarters in their unmarked black car to pick up another officer.

Just as they drove up to the station on West Atlantic Avenue, they heard fellow officer Bart Donovan transmitting. His excited voice on their police radio said he had spotted the stolen four-door Honda Accord on Southwest 10th Street.

Following the car west, Donovan threw on his lights and saw Pietri stop at the railroad tracks just beyond the I-95 underpass. The fugitive parked his car at an angle. As the officer started to get out of his car with his gun down, Pietri turned off his headlights and sped away.

When Donovan's broadcast began, the Swigert-Quinlan-Hoeffer team gunned their unmarked car back out of the police station. No time to pick up the fourth officer. Barreling south to Lowson Boulevard, a continuation of Southwest 10th Street, the three lawmen raced west in pursuit of the suspect, who by now was traveling at speeds of more than 100. Pietri was far ahead of Officer Donovan and the other TACT men, hurtling toward Military Trail, a north-south highway at the western boundary of Delray Beach.

Just before the trio from the station reached Homewood Boulevard, a residential road running parallel to Military Trail, Officer Hoeffer called out, "Turn here!" It was only a hunch, and he prayed it was a good one as Sergeant Swigert twirled the black car northward on Homewood. As a matter of fact, the hunch was perfect. By the time the three lawmen reached Atlantic Avenue, the main east-west street of the city, Pietri had already raced north on Military then east on Atlantic Avenue. The excited officers could see the Honda Accord zooming toward them at 120 miles per hour and hoped against hope the wild fugitive wouldn't hit anyone.

As the black TACT car caught up and other police cars approached, Pietri lost control of the Honda. Dust flew as the spinning car rolled onto a golf course. Spiderman staggered out, running south across the sand traps with Sergeant Swigert, Quinlan, and Hoeffer on his heels. Then, dodging cars, Pietri dashed across busy Atlantic Avenue onto the grass of a Jewish temple.

"Stop!" yelled Sergeant Swigert. Spiderman did. He then reached into his shorts. Thinking he had a concealed gun, Swigert released the safety on his 9-mm. semi-automatic, but before pulling the trigger he saw the suspect put something in his mouth. Seeing that what he was trying to swallow was cocaine, Swigert, Hoeffer, and Quinlan tackled the man, rolling him onto the grass and cuffing him.

The Delray police charged Pietri with possession of the drug and drove him to the station. It was finally over. They had nabbed their cop-killer.

It was not over for the West Palm Beach team, however. Picking up Pietri shortly before midnight, the detectives took him to their headquarters. To Lieutenant Conklin and Detectives Myers, Johnson, and Anderson, it was "such a relief to have him in custody." Two public defenders showed up at one o'clock in the morning demanding that the detectives not talk to Pietri. It became a legal issue, but the West Palm Beach police won.

The sleuths booked Pietri and fingerprinted him. Now it was up to them to firm up the Chappell case so the perp wouldn't walk when they took him to trial. For three months they worked on the case. Loose ends left dangling when everything was so hectic now had to be tied together. The three days spent rushing to catch the perp had their adrenaline flowing; the next three months, while extremely important, consisted of the mundane work of acquiring evidence. It had to be done, but this time no adrenaline surged to make the duties easier.

The sleuths went back and reinterviewed witnesses. They did paperwork. They did crime scene work. Going over the pickup truck, which had been towed out of the canal, crime scene detectives found a good thumb print. In spite of the hours the vehicle had been submerged in the water, the window tinting film had retained the oil from his hands and thus preserved the print. When it was compared to Spiderman's thumb print, it was a definite match.

After the tan Toyota Starlet that Pietri had stolen at the University was recovered, an RCA camcorder found on the seat helped the team link Pietri to the Riviera Beach burglary. The camcorder had been stolen, along with the murder weapon, when he broke into the deputy's home.

The 13-year-old boy who'd seen Pietri shoot the motorcycle officer had already identified the suspect in photos. Now he and other witnesses, including the

118

woman who had first phoned in about the murder, were given the chance of picking the killer out of a live lineup. This took time to prepare. The detectives had to choose stand-ins of approximately the same weight and height as the suspect, then dress everyone in identical clothes and turn the collars up to hide their necks so that Pietri's spider tattoo wouldn't give away his identity. It was strange that not one witness had seen that spider tattoo originally. If they had, Lieutenant Conklin mused, "We'd have had him immediately." Even without the spider, the witnesses easily picked out the perp.

In spite of that, Pietri refused to confess, and Conklin and the three detectives knew they'd have to have overwhelming evidence before a jury would pronounce the suspect guilty. Plodding on, they collected that evidence. The detectives had been so thorough that when the trial was held in early 1990, the prosecution was able to use only a fraction of the material the detectives had worked so diligently to acquire.

Pietri's lawyer told the jury in his opening statements that his client did, in fact, shoot the officer and kill him. For Pietri he was using a "cocaine defense." There was a "cocaine psychosis," the lawyer claimed.

In court was the first time the lawmen heard Pietri confess to killing Chappell. When the defendant took the stand, he said in effect that he did it because he was an abused kid, his father was an alcoholic, and he lived with 14 other children in a one-bedroom house. Pietri blamed the crime on his poverty-stricken childhood in Puerto Rico—on anything but himself.

The trial didn't last long. The defense was mainly working to keep Pietri out of the electric chair. Hearing the vast amount of insurmountable evidence, however, the jury determined otherwise. They found Pietri guilty and recommended death. At the present time, Spiderman is in prison. The cop-killer is waiting for his execution.

EDITOR'S NOTE:

Theresa and Juan Domingo are not the real names of the persons so named in the foregoing story. Fictitious names have been used because there is no reason for public interest in the identities of these persons.

"... IN THE LINE
OF DUTY"
by Joseph McNamara

NEW YORK, N.Y., OCTOBER 6, 1975

It was 9:10 on the waning summer night of September 16, 1975, when Sergeant Frederick Reddy approached the battered red Plymouth convertible on debris-littered East Fifth Street on Manhattan's Lower East Side. To casual observers it looked like any other spot check for a possible traffic violation. The police cruiser had cut in at an angle in front of the convertible; its emergency lights flashing and double parked because of a solid line of cars lining both sides of the one-way street.

Patrolman Andrew Glover began to slide from behind the wheel of the patrol car and join his partner as the sergeant moved to the side of the Plymouth. Reddy, 50 and a veteran of 28 years service on the force, had gone through the procedure so many times it must have seemed like second nature. But the usual words—"Let's see your driver's license"—never were uttered.

With a creaking protest, the door of the red car flew open and a young man stepped out with a blazing pistol in his hand. The gun barked twice as streaks of flame pierced the darkness.

Sergeant Reddy staggered and reeled from the impact of bullets, but managed to clear his gun from its holster as he went down. By that time, the deadly gun had been turned toward Patrolman Glover and it spat twice more.

The first slug caught the police officer in the left side of the face, spinning him around. The second tore into his back and sent him headlong to the street.

Reddy, wounded in the left side of the chest, got off three shots in a heroic effort before he collapsed. One of the bullets smashed the glass in the convertible and sent it flying.

The gunman immediately took to his heels as residents of the red-brick tenements that loomed grimly over the scene raced to their windows to investigate the noise. Several of them quickly ran back to their phones to call police.

The fallen officers were rushed to Bellevue Hospital, where they were pronounced dead on arrival. Despite that assessment of their conditions, a team of 15 surgeons labored valiantly to restore the pulse of life to them.

"We used open-heart massage; we looked for any signs of life," one doctor said later. "But it was to no avail."

One witness told police, "I knew one of them [the officers] was dead when they picked him off the street. He was bleeding from the head."

Meanwhile, out over the police radio, went the message every man in uniform dreads but knows someday may refer to him. "Two wounded officers being removed to Bellevue by radio car."

More than 20 police cars immediately converged on the entrance to the hospital's emergency room at the foot of East Twenty-ninth Street, just off the East River.

"Where do I go to give blood?" was the repeated question.

As the surgeons labored fruitlessly in the operating theater, four lines of men, at least ten deep, waited outside in hopes of being needed. They weren't. At 9:45 P.M., a supervisory nurse told them Sergeant Reddy and Patrolman Glover were dead. A police captain moved along the lines, gently telling the men: "Go home . . . Resume patrol . . . There is nothing more you can do."

Reddy, who headed a police team that worked to improve area community relations, had been shot through the lungs and heart. Glover, 34, and a member of the department for six years, had been hit in the head and heart. Both had been blasted at very close range.

While a detective gathered the bloodsoaked clothing of the slain officers into a plastic bag and carried it from Bellevue, scores of other detectives already were swarming all over the scene of the tragic shootings, East Fifth between Avenues A and B.

"Actually, this is one of the quieter streets in the worst part of this precinct," one officer noted to a reporter.

Under the glare of emergency lights detectives searched for clues — slugs from the weapons fired in the fatal gun duel, for Glover's service revolver which was missing, for a telltale sign that might lead the way to the killer.

It was a dismal scene. On the sidewalk, a few feet from where one officer fell in the gutter, garbage was heaped against a tenement wall. Someone had printed at one time the words "May Day" in large block letters on the stone facing. Heavily grilled windows spoke eloquently of how safe some tenants considered the place.

Overhead fire escape ladders soared toward the sky, while underfoot lay the scattered litter of a city fighting its way back, not entirely successfully, from a recent garbage strike. It was Tuesday, September 16, 1975, a day that would be remembered in precinct history. All days are when a policeman is murdered in the line of duty.

Reddy, white, and Glover, black, became the fifth and sixth police officers shot to death in the line of duty in New York City in 1975 and they met their fate just six blocks from where another black-and-white team—Police Officers Gregory Foster, 22, and Rocco Laurie, 23—were gunned down January 27, 1972. Ironically, Reddy had been their commanding officer.

"You know," said one patrolman at Bellevue as he thought back over the years, "Reddy was in tears when Foster and Laurie were killed."

Two hours after the blazing shootout and following intensive questioning of area residents who massed on the street a police radio issued an alert for three people reported by witnesses to have fled the scene.

The killer was described as an Hispanic, 20 to 25 years old, with a large Afro haircut and a goatee and wearing a *dashiki* (or a loose African-type shirt) which was vari-colored but mainly red. His companions were described as a white, or Hispanic, male about 5 feet, 10 inches tall, slender, but with a "beer belly," and a white woman, 29 or 30, about 5 feet, 1 inch, wearing a coat, beige slacks and a low-cut blouse.

The alert launched one of the most intensive manhunts for a killer in the recent history of New York City and it brought more than 100 investigators into the probe, many giving of their own time. At one point, a high-ranking police officer said, "There's no telling how many men are involved. We have no account of those working on their own."

Mayor Abraham Beame hurried from the executive Gracie Mansion to the murdered officers' precinct house, arriving after midnight. "All New Yorkers join me in expressing shock and anger at the wanton slaying of these two men, slain in the line of duty," Beame said. The mayor added that he had been assured that "an all-out manhunt now is underway to apprehend the killers and bring them to justice."

That assurance had come from First Deputy Commissioner James M. Taylor, who had rushed to the hospital, as had Kenneth McFeeley, head of the Patrolmen's Benevolent Association. The PBA promptly offered a $10,000 reward for information leading to apprehension and conviction of the murderers.

Louis Cottell, chief of detectives, took charge of the investigation personally, working from the offices of the First Homicide Zone at the East Twenty-first Street stationhouse. In addition, officers from the Narcotics division were called into the case because of a suspicion that illicit drugs might be involved in the slayings.

Police Commissioner Michael Codd cut short a visit to the convention of the International Association of Chiefs of Police in Denver and rushed back to New York City. He told reporters:

"I am outraged by the wanton killings of these policemen and the public should be too."

Commissioner Codd said the main topic at the IACP convention was the fact that, between 1963 and 1973, 613 police officers had been killed by guns in the United States. "We need better regulations to curb guns and Congress should stop holding hearings and do something about it right now," Codd declared.

Mayor Beame echoed that plea, especially lashing out at the cheap "Saturday-night specials" that proliferate in large cities.

Both Reddy and Glover had been slain with the same .38-caliber pistol. At first, it was theorized that maybe a second gun had been used, but, the next day, ballistics tests proved that one weapon killed both officers.

Bullet fragments found at the scene also convinced the investigators that only the killer's weapon and Reddy's pistol had been fired. It was assumed that the slayer picked up Glover's service revolver as he fled.

Exactly why the officers had stopped the red convertible was not ascertained. One witness told authorities he had seen the car make an illegal U-turn shortly before heading into one-way Fifth Street. It also was thought possible that the car was being routinely checked because it bore out-of-state plates. The tags, from Pennsylvania, were 26Z908, the police alert noted. For more than an hour after the shootings, the old car had stood in the street with its emergency lights blinking. An investigator finally shut them off, after the instrument panel was dusted for fingerprints.

At dawn, a police alarm was broadcast for a two-door green Pontiac sedan with Pennsylvania license 26Z909. A witness who had run out of a social club on the street when he heard shooting told investigators that he had seen a gunman standing next to such a Pontiac. Other witnesses, though, contradicted this report. Police felt that since both license numbers were but a single digit apart, there had been some confusion by the latter witness. Nevertheless, the alarm was sent out.

"We're passing up nothing on this one," a desk lieutenant explained to newsmen.

Within minutes of the arrival of detectives at the

scene, several investigators were checking with Pennsylvania motor vehicle authorities as to ownership of the battered red Plymouth that the killer had been driving. They learned that it had been bought in Langhorne, Pa., by a man who gave the name E. Ralph Hernandez and listed a Trenton address.

Detectives immediately sped to Trenton to try to locate the car owner. They discovered that the address listed in the car sale papers was fictitious. That was a blow to the probers, but they felt, nevertheless, that the name, or one quite similar to it, was that of the actual owner and that he lived somewhere in the area. A check of the traffic division showed that the name had picked up several parking summonses in recent weeks. And several residents acknowledged that they had seen it on local streets.

While the investigation proceeded, the families of the slain officers made the preparations for the burials. Reddy was the father of six children, aged 9 to 27, five girls and a boy. Glover had a seven-year-old daughter.

Both officers were extremely well liked. Reddy, who lived with his wife Marie and family in a white clapboard house in Levittown, L.I., was described by neighbors as friendly and generous. "He was always ready to help neighbors with their plumbing and electrical projects and was a robust, athletic father to his kids," one neighbor said. "Sometimes he'd drive four kids on a bicycle, laughing all the time."

Reddy reportedly had been thinking of retiring, but fellow officers pointed out he already was eight years past the time he could have retired, in point of service.

"He loved the job too much," a fellow officer said. "He didn't just put in the time; he lived the job."

Reddy had set up store-front police stations and had been instrumental in establishing athletic programs to try to help kids.

"He called me Chico," said one youngster with tears in his eyes. "I called him 'Man.' It was just great."

One neighbor told how he had had trouble getting work since a marijuana arrest and said that Reddy had helped him land a job driving a taxi.

Glover was taking courses almost full time in a special liberal studies program for police at Brooklyn College. He once said that if he lived to retire from the New York police department he would like to go into teaching.

"Andy's rapport with people on the street was a sight to see," one of his fellow officers in the precinct said. "He never had a problem with people. He could talk with them, identify with them."

Glover loved basketball and often returned on his own time to play the game with neighborhood kids on the Lower East Side. He and Sergeant Reddy had helped organize a Puerto Rican street fair. Reddy used to attend block association meetings, listen to problems, get things done.

Because the officers were so well liked, the neighbors made good use of two telephone numbers set up by police—one, answered in English, and the other in Spanish—for anyone with information about the crimes. The calls poured in and the questioning of just about everybody who lived on the block continued.

On September 18, two days after the two policemen were slain in a flurry of bullets, the police announced they had a "good solid eyewitness" to the crime. The investigators were questioning the man they identified only as Chino Conception and named him a robbery suspect. He was not being held at the jail or the precinct, where he would come to the attention of reporters. It was presumed he was being interrogated in

128

a hotel somewhere in Manhattan.

At the same time, the authorities issued a plea for a cabby who had picked up two men near the murder scene to contact headquarters. The two, investigators said, were the suspect and an accomplice. They had been sighted entering a taxi at Avenue B and East Sixth Street, a block and a half from the shooting, at 9:15 P.M., just moments after the twin slaying.

Through good solid police work the investigators had identified the pair of suspects, but they declined to name them or release their pictures for fear they would jeopardize any future court case against them. "We've got hard stuff on these guys, but we just can't go with it yet," one official told reporters. "In the old days, the investigative evidence would have been okay. Now we need more."

While police refused to disclose their "evidence," it was noted by veteran newsmen that announcement of the knowledge was coupled with a "good, solid eyewitness" was in hand. Also, it was reported, fingerprints had been lifted from the red convertible left at the death scene.

It next was learned by the press that detectives working the case had photographs of the suspected triggerman. That led to speculation that he had a record and a mug shot was on file. Police subsequently did identify him as a small-time dope pusher.

About that time, one reporter asked Chief of Detectives Cottell why no composite drawings of the suspects had been released. "We don't need them," Cottell said. He declined to amplify on the statement.

Quietly, however, detective teams had been combing every hotel around the area in hopes of catching up to the suspects. Finally, just after midnight on Saturday, September 20, they got a tip that a man they were seeking was in a hotel at Madison Avenue and East

129

Twenty-ninth Street.

He was Frank Segarra, 24, who was short and slender with rather tight-cropped hair and a black goatee. Detectives descended in force on the hotel room at 1:30 A.M. and arrested Segarra without resistance. The young man was staying at the hotel with his common-law wife.

Segarra reportedly admitted being a close friend and partner in crime of the suspected triggerman and told the detectives where their quarry was.

Immediately, a raiding party was assembled to pick up the alleged gunman. At 2:10 A.M., some 50 policemen, carrying shotguns and wearing bullet-proof vests, used a battering ram to smash down the door of a tenement apartment at 40 Clinton Street on the lower East Side. The detectives missed their man by minutes. He had slipped away not long before they arrived, it was said.

Whether someone had tipped him that Segarra had been busted, the authorities were not sure. But, at daybreak, they announced to the news media and the public the identity of the man they were seeking in the murders of Sergeant Reddy and Patrolman Glover. His name was Luis Serrano Velez, 25, who had the nicknames "Blackie" and "Angelo."

Velez was to be considered armed "and extremely dangerous," the alarm sent to all precincts and across the nation read. It noted that Velez—listed as 5 feet, 6 inches tall and weighing 130 pounds—was wanted not only for the police killings, but for bank robbery.

In fact, both Velez and Segarra were wanted for a series of bank robberies, but it was not known whether the two slain policemen had tried to question them on the fateful night. Velez' photo, it was said, had been plastered on "wanted" boards in precincts in connection with a bank job. It was surmised that the murder suspect might have feared he was being stopped for questioning about the armed heists.

Velez and Segarra were described as drug users with a record of arrests for minor narcotics violations. Velez also had been picked up for robbery and Segarra for burglary. Public knowledge that he was being sought would, police theorized, put pressure on Velez. And efforts, already intense, were stepped up to apprehend him.

Later that day, some 3000 people, including Mayor Beame, filled the streets outside the Convent Avenue Baptist Church at 145th Street for final services for Patrolman Glover. During the "inspector's funeral," the highest honor the department can bestow, Richard Reddy, son of the slain sergeant, sat with Glover's widow, Dolores, and daughter Keishe, 7.

After the services, the casket was taken between the lines of an honor guard of policemen, some in the uniform of state and suburban forces and even from other areas of the nation, to a waiting hearse. Sixty motorcycle patrolmen escorted the cortege to a cemetery in Butler, N.J.

The next day, September 21, police amended the nationwide alarm on Luis (Blackie) Velez to include the information he "may be suffering from cuts." Several witnesses were found who had told police that the gunman had been bleeding from a face wound as he fled the scene and investigators theorized he might have been grazed by one of the three bullets Sergeant Reddy triggered off before he died. Or, possibly, the killer had been cut by glass from the window shattered by one of those same slugs.

Detectives began checking hospitals and doctors' offices on the lower East Side to determine if anyone answering Velez' description had sought aid for a face wound since the twin murders. Investigators believed that Velez still was in the area and 35 detectives spent that Sunday afternoon touring the Lower East Side, showing residents pictures.

According to the probers, Segarra and Velez were suspected of pulling at least three bank heists in Manhattan and Brooklyn in September. After questioning, Segarra had been booked in the $10,000 robbery of a First National City Bank branch at 170th Street and Broadway on September 11. Police said that Velez also took part in that robbery.

Sources close to the probe revealed that Segarra admitted being with Velez the night the policemen were slain, but he denied having anything to do with the slayings. His common-law wife was held as a material witness in the killings.

When pictures of Velez appeared in the city's newspapers and on TV sets, telephone calls began to deluge police stations in the area.

"We have received more than 100 phone calls today," A First Homicide Zone detective told newsmen late Sunday. "Detectives have checked them out, so far without success. But we'd rather have any lead than none at all." Many of the detectives following up the unproductive leads were working on their own time that day, it was noted.

Monday, funeral services were held for Sergeant Reddy on Long Island. Some 6000 police officers, mostly uniformed, from across the country were there to render tribute — accompanied by muffled drums and pipers' dirge of the department's Emerald Society Band — to their fallen comrade.

Every seat was filled for the mass at St. Bernard's Church in Levittown when the cortege rolled up with the police escort of a radio car and 26 motorcycles.

Overhead, four helicopters also flew escort.

When the services got underway, members of the Reddy family participated. The sergeant's oldest child read, from the lectern, from St. Paul to the Romans: ". . . a good man has the courage to die."

But Mayor Beame wondered why it was necessary for good men to die so tragically. After the Communion, in which two other Reddy daughters presented the wine and bread, the Mayor spoke.

"How long," he asked, "must we have the dubious distinction of being the only civilized society in the world where a criminal or a mentally deranged individual with a few dollars can buy a handgun as easily as he might buy a bar of candy."

While navy veteran Reddy was being interred in Long Island National Cemetery at Pinelawn, on Manhattan's Lower East Side, the massive manhunt for Velez continued. Tremendous pressure was building up on "the street," men on the fringes of crime, the petty punks and an army of informers. Everyone knew that the heat would get no better until Velez was caught.

Shortly before 11 P.M. on Wednesday, September 24, Lieutenant John J. Yuknes, commander of Homicide Zone 1, and a team of detectives piled into cars and went to an apartment house on West Nineteenth Street in Manhattan's Chelsea district. Among those with Yuknes were Detectives Edward Gomez, James Grant, and Edward Dahlem and Sergeant William Taylor, the latter two from the robbery detail. They were acting on a tip that originally said only that Velez could be reached at a certain telephone number, the address unknown. A check with company officials showed that the phone was in the building on West Nineteenth. On the way there, however, enthusiasm was not too high among the officers.

"Since the murders, we had been to 13 other apartments without finding Velez," Lieutenant Yuknes later explained. "But Jimmy Grant kept saying, 'This is it!' "

The detectives weren't sure which apartment might hold their quarry, but they believed it was on the ground floor of the well-kept building. Yuknes decided on a ruse to flush out Velez, if indeed he were there. From a phone in another apartment, the lieutenant dialed the number and, without disguising his voice, said:

"Velez . . . The cops are coming to bust you. They'll be there in five minutes. I don't want to get involved."

Yuknes heard only a polite "Thank you," then the phone was hung up. He ran back to his men, who had flattened themselves along the wall of the hallway on the ground floor.

Thirty seconds later, an apartment door opened and a man burst out.

"Police! Freeze, Blackie!" someone yelled.

The man reportedly jerked a handmade grenade from his belt and went to pull the pin, but Detective Grant grabbed it.

"The only thought I had was to get it away from him," Grant, attached to the Manhattan Homicide Task Force, later told reporters who asked how he felt clutching the grenade.

As other lawmen pounced on the man, he shouted, "I'm not Blackie, I'm Jose Santos."

But he wasn't. He was Luis Serrano Velez. And there was a .38 pistol holding six cartridges stuffed into his belt, police said.

Velez had shaved his Afro-cut hair, but he was wearing a red *dashiki* similar to that which witnesses had said the cop killer had worn.

Inside the apartment from which Velez had bolted,

detectives nabbed Edward Colon, 25, without resistance. He later was booked for bank robbery. Almost $10,000 in cash was discovered in the flat, too, police said.

Velez was taken to the East Twenty-first Street stationhouse and questioned. Several hours later, detectives raided an apartment on East Fifteenth Street in Brooklyn, where other members of the holdup mob were reportedly holed up.

Augmented by machine gun-wielding members of the Emergency Service Division, the detectives gained entrance to a second-floor flat and arrested E. (Eddie) Nelson Hernandez, 26. Police said Hernandez, who also used the name Fernandez, owned the red Plymouth that Reddy and Glover had stopped on September 16.

Another man, Azul Amante, 26, and two women were arrested in the apartment, which also yielded up an arsenal that included a hand grenade, a .357 Magnum pistol, a sawed-off shotgun and a rifle. The women were Gwenn Richardson, 30, wanted as a fugitive from Clinton Reformatory in New Jersey, and Lillian Cora, 26. All four were charged with possession of weapons and explosives.

Velez was booked for the murders of Reddy and Glover and held without bail by Manhattan Criminal Court Judge Michael Dontzin. Shorn of his goatee hair, Velez stood silently before the judge at his arraignment, dressed in a brown leather jacket and jeans. Assistant District Attorney Louis Kelpon told the court Velez had a record of at least six previous arrests and had served prison time on a felonious assault rap.

Police Commissioner Codd said the group was suspected in at least ten robberies, including banks, supermarkets and Off Track Betting parlors. Its members, interchangeable on different strikes, have amassed more than $50,000 in loot, police said.

According to investigators, a live hand grenade left on the floor of a bank stickup in upper Manhattan was similar to the one brandished by Velez when he was arrested. The explosive was described as homemade and resembling the type of device used by the German Army in World War II.

After Velez' picture was published, Stacy Loren, 57, notified police from his hospital room that the suspect was the same man who shot him and killed his brother, Alexander Loren, 53, in a robbery of their Manhattan fur shop on West Twenty-ninth Street on September 19. At that time, Velez was being sought in the extensive manhunt. Ballistics tests later reportedly showed that the fatal slug dug from Mr. Loren was fired from the gun Velez had on him when arrested.

The investigation continues, at this writing, into other robberies during what officials called the six-month crime spree of the stick-up mob.

As for the night of the fatal shooting of the two police officers, authorities told reporters they believe Velez was alone in the red car when Sergeant Reddy approached and that he feared the policeman wanted to question him about the heists.

After the barrage of deadly slugs, the killer raced down the street, spotted Segarra on the street and asked his help in the getaway. The two men grabbed a taxi around the corner and escaped, investigators say. They have ruled out the possibility that three persons were in the car, despite original reports to that effect.

The two men and a passing woman had been spotted on the street and witnesses assumed all had come from the car, it was believed. Thus, Velez was expected to face the homicide charges alone.

Patrolman Glover's service revolver never has been

found. Probers felt certain that a passer-by probably picked it up from the street. If so, there may be another chapter yet to be written on the tragic killing of two of New York's Finest.

During the first week in October, a grand jury handed down a four count indictment against Velez in connection with the double slaying.

Two of the counts were for first degree murder and two for criminal possession of a dangerous weapon.

"ALEX MENGEL'S ONE-MAN CRIME WAVE!"

by Joseph Pedreiro

YONKERS, N.Y. MAY 2, 1985

Sunday evenings are generally a peaceful time of the week. The weekday hustle lies ahead and the weekend festivities have been left behind. The police officers who patrol Westchester County would probably tend to agree. The roads are quiet, traffic is light, and the problems are routine. It certainly must have seemed so to the officer manning the dispatch and communications desk at police headquarters on the evening of February 24, 1985.

It had been a quiet Sunday — typical in many respects — as was the first radio transmission received from Officer Gary Stymiloski. Officer Stymiloski, 27, who was patrolling the Saw Mill River Parkway in Yonkers, had stopped a blue, 1973 Mercury Capri on Stratton Street, near the southbound Palmer Avenue exit of the parkway. He had stopped the car for a minor traffic violation and requested standard information.

A few minutes later the patrolman sent another message with a request for further information. After a short interval, at 7:25 P.M., Stymiloski again contacted headquarters, this time to request that a tow truck be sent to impound the car because the driver did not have a driver's license and a current registration for the vehicle.

Any lingering notions in the dispatcher's mind that this situation might be routine were dispelled by the next (and last) message received from Officer Stymiloski at 7:45 P.M. The final call to headquarters was for a backup unit because Stymiloski had discovered shotguns in the trunk of the car and was requesting assistance.

A backup unit was dispatched immediately. As it proceeded up the northbound lane, the officer glimpsed what appeared to be another police patrol car headed southbound. Thinking that this might be Officer Stymiloski's vehicle, the backup car attempted to contact it by radio but received no response.

When the backup unit arrived a few minutes later at the reported location, the Capri and Stymiloski's patrol car were gone. Understandably worried, the officer reported the situation to headquarters and requested further assistance in locating Officer Stymiloski. A search was undertaken immediately, and, approximately 30 minutes later, it bore grim results. The missing police car was located near the intersection of Prescott and Van Buren Streets, a few blocks from the next southbound exit of the parkway. Inside, slumped in the front seat, was Officer Gary Stymiloski — unconscious and bleeding heavily from a wound to the head. He was rushed to St. Joseph's Hospital in Yonkers where, despite diligent efforts to save him, he died at 10:10 P.M. without regaining consciousness.

Despite their sorrow and anger, the efficient machinery of investigation snapped into action. Although scanty, there were some leads available for immediate follow-up. Foremost among these were the description and license plate number of the Capri, which had been noted by Officer Stymiloski.

Detective Michael DeRosa was assigned to the case. He immediately issued an A.P.B. for the car, alerting all police and law enforcement agents that the occupants were wanted in connection with the shooting of an officer; they were known to be armed with shotguns at the very least, and were considered to be very dangerous. Stymiloski had reported that there were four occupants in the vehicle: three men and a woman. This fact was noted, and officers armed themselves and prepared accordingly.

Detectives were dispatched to the presumed scene of the shooting, on Stratton Street, to search for any evidence that might have been left behind. Lacking sufficient light to work effectively, they secured the scene as best they could until the next morning's light would permit them to continue.

Other probers, checking the license plate number of the blue Capri with the Department of Motor Vehicles, were informed that the last owner of the car was a woman, Fiona Gerano, and the given address was located on the 2200 block of Grand Avenue, in the Morris Heights section of the Bronx. The detectives proceeded immediately to the address they had received. There, they found Mrs. Gerano at home and, after detectives explained why they had come to speak to her, the woman assured them that she would cooperate fully.

Knowing that a woman had been reported in the car, they questioned her carefully as to her whereabouts earlier that evening. Mrs. Gerano said she had not used the car for a few days and explained that several relatives had keys to the car and would sometimes borrow it. It was for this reason that she had not reported the vehicle stolen; it always turned up after a few days, and she had gotten used to this impromptu arrangement.

Detectives from the New York City Police Department had now joined in the investigation, and they fanned out — some to check out Mrs. Gerano's alibi for the time in question; some to question the list of people she had supplied them with that were most likely to have keys. Other sleuths began to canvass the area to see if any witnesses could be found that could tell them who had been the most recent person or persons to "borrow" the car.

Meanwhile, detectives from the Yonkers area were checking the two primary sites — the location where Officer Stymiloski had been shot, and the place where he and his car had been abandoned — in the hope of finding a witness or witnesses to the events in question. Both the presumed location of the shooting and the street where the fatally wounded officer was found are generally residential.

The Bronx detectives were the first to have some luck. They were proceeding down Grand Avenue when an alert detective pointed to one side. A blue Capri. Pulling up behind it, they checked the license plate number. It matched. They approached the car carefully and examined it, but there was no one in the car. They called for a tow truck to take the car into the nearest police garage, where fingerprint and evidence technicians could search the car carefully for clues.

In the meantime, the press began deluging the police information number, attempting to discover the pertinent facts and whether or not a suspect had been identified. Police officials explained that the investigation was just beginning, and that they would present what little they had found out on Monday, at which time they would also present an appeal to the public.

The next day, true to their word, the police department called a press conference. Dr. Louis Roh, the Westchester deputy medical examiner, explained how Officer Stymiloski had died, saying that, "He was shot once in the head."

Also responding to questions was Captain Owen McCain, of the Yonkers Police Department, who had been placed in charge of the investigation. He said that the fatal bullet might have been a nine-millimeter or a .38-caliber. Or, he explained, "he could have been shot with his own gun." McCain said that the officer had been alone in his patrol car and had been shot at close range.

He added that the murder weapon had not been found, but would not say whether Officer Stymiloski's service revolver, a .38-caliber weapon, had been recovered. He stated that the detectives were questioning witnesses from both sites in Yonkers, but had not had much luck: "We're having trouble with their descriptions because some of them are diametrically opposed to each other."

With regard to the owner of the car, Captain McCain said that, "she came forward voluntarily and is not a suspect.

"She's only a part of a large puzzle. It appears other people have had use of the Capri in the past, and they still have keys to it."

Also revealed at the press conference was the fact that evidence technicians had found shotgun shells in the car, but they had determined that they were not connected to the slaying. Investigators said they had no suspects in the slaying, and they requested that the public lend whatever assistance it could provide.

In response to questions about the slain officer, reporters were informed that Officer Gary Stymiloski, age 27, had lived in Yonkers with his family, and had been planning to get married in November. He'd joined the Westchester County Department of Public Safety in 1982. He was the eighth police officer to have been killed in the line of duty in Westchester County since 1974.

Detectives concluded the press conference by saying that investigators from three agencies: Yonkers, Westchester and New York City, would be working closely on the case.

Meanwhile, investigators continued to carefully search the presumed area of the shooting, Stratton Street, with metal detectors, looking for spent rounds of ammunition.

One by one, the persons on the list provided by Fiona Gerano had been found and questioned. Only a few remained to be checked, especially a relative, "Alex," who she explained had "borrowed" her car most frequently. As investigators questioned more people, the name "Alex" came up over and over until the sleuths were very eager to speak with Alexander Jerome Mengel, age 30.

Mengel, described as an "unemployed security guard," was a Guyanese-born legal alien. His current address was on Grand Avenue in the Bronx, not far from where the Capri had been found. However, he was not at his apartment and could not be found.

Detectives continued to investigate other leads but began to wonder whether Mengel might not have "borrowed" someone else's car.

Tragically, this speculation would prove to be all too accurate, but for the time being, only the family of Beverly Capone would be nervously wondering about her whereabouts.

On Tuesday, the police received more tips identifying Alex Mengel as the driver of the Capri. Then, someone in a social club in the High Bridge section of the Bronx called the 44th Precinct and told police, "If you want the guy who killed the cop, he's here." Dozens of uniformed officers and detectives converged on the club and questioned nearly 50 patrons, but the suspect was not among them.

Later that day, the evidence and testimony gathered up to that point by sleuths was presented to the district attorney's office for evaluation. They presented this information to Justice James R. Cowhey of the State Supreme Court, who issued a warrant for the arrest of Alex J. Mengel.

Mengel's photograph was subsequently circulated to the New York City Police Department and to law enforcement agencies in the county and beyond.

At a news conference, County Executive Andrew P. O'Rourke made it official, identifying the suspect as Alex Mengel and saying that he "is being sought in connection with this death." He said that the other occupants of the Capri were also being sought.

With a suspect now clearly identified, police began to question Mengel's family members, friends and casual acquaintances. All his known hangouts were checked, and every tip, no matter how trivial, was run down. They knew Mengel would need money to live on, a place to hide from the ever-widening dragnet and, if he had not left the city, someone to get him out or procure a means of transportation.

This painstaking effort paid off in the discovery of the other occupants of the car on the night of the shooting. When detectives advised them that they could also be charged as accessories to the murder, they cooperated with police.

They explained that all four of them had been returning from a weekend vacation of hunting and target shooting in upstate New York. Alex had been driving the car when they were stopped by a patrol car. The officer (Stymiloski) had asked for Mengel's license and registration, which he was unable to produce. The officer returned to his patrol car, used his radio, then had returned to ask further questions.

Mengel had gotten more and more agitated, they said, and, after the cop had discovered the shotgun and had informed the foursome that the car was going to be impounded, Mengel seemed to snap. His companions in the car claimed that he turned to them in the car and said, "I'm going to kill him. If you hear a shot, you better get out of here. It means I killed him."

With that statement, Mengel had gotten out of the car and walked over to the patrol cruiser. Moments later, they had heard a shot, and they obeyed his instructions and left in the Capri.

Each of the passengers had been interviewed separately and had given a consistent story that agreed with the others and matched all of the known facts. They were asked for the location of the shed or cabin where they had spent the weekend and were questioned closely regarding any possible locations or persons with whom Mengel might try to find refuge. After furnishing detectives with this information, authorities decided that, while they would not be considered suspects, two of them would be held in protective custody as material witnesses. They were then taken to the Westchester County Jail in Valhalla.

As detectives redoubled their efforts to find the suspect, a seemingly unrelated report was received by Mount Vernon police. The family of Beverly Capone, 44, a resident of Mount Vernon, was reporting her missing. She had last been seen at 7:45 P.M. on Monday, February 25th, as she left her job in the payroll department at IBM in Dobbs Ferry. Family and friends all described her as a "conscientious career woman"—someone who would never abruptly take off without notifying someone. They gave police a detailed description of the missing woman as well as the description and license plate number of her car, a new, white, 1985 Toyota Tercel that she had bought two weeks earlier.

Investigators assured the Capone family that they would do everything possible to find the missing woman, and they distributed her description and that of the car and license plate number to all of their units.

A clue to her whereabouts was unknowingly discovered the next day, as state police searched the areas of upstate New York where Alex Mengel often hunted and camped, in their efforts to find clues to his whereabouts.

As they were examining a summer cabin in rural East Durham, the troopers came across unmistakable evidence that the cabin had been broken into. Speculating that Mengel might have broken in to look for supplies and money, they summoned technical aid.

Specialists soon arrived and confirmed that the cabin had been burglarized. As they examined the place, the investigators found several items of clothing belonging to a woman in the burglarized cabin. They found an IBM employee identification card. The I.D. card was that of Beverly Capone.

This evidence was carefully tagged, bagged, and noted, but the linking of the two cases — the missing Beverly Capone and the alleged cop killer — would not be made until later, when more evidence became available.

While the state police were engaged in examining the cabin, something unusual had occurred in Skaneateles, a small community located between Syracuse and Auburn, New York. A young girl had run frantically to a house and cried for help, claiming that someone had tried to kidnap her. The police were summoned, and she told them that she had been delivering newspapers on her regular paper route when a white, late model car had pulled up to her, and the occupant had asked her for directions. As she looked at this person, she started to feel that something was fishy. His hands and arms looked like a man's, but he had a wig and some lipstick on. The girl became nervous and started to turn to walk away when he pulled out a gun and pointed it at her.

She said that the driver had said something like "Get in the car or I'll kill you." She fled towards the nearby house, and the car sped away. When questioned further, the girl said the man had been asking for directions to Auburn.

Although puzzled by the strange story, a description of the occupant and car were distributed to law enforcement officers in the area.

On Thursday, February 28th, an estimated 5,000 police officers from around the country came to the North Yonkers Community Baptist Church to pay their last respects to Gary Stymiloski.

"We all know the reality and violence of how he died," said the pastor of the church. "Any one of the police officers in and outside of this church could have been Gary. That's why they're here, to show this oneness at the precariousness of their vocation."

Joining the grieving family in the church were nearly 200 of Gary Stymiloski's fellow officers in the Westchester County Department of Public Safety — some of them weeping openly, as they looked at the flag-draped coffin resting in front of a wide window behind the altar.

There were over 400 mourners filling the church, while outside, lined up along Route 9, were scores of officers from police departments in the metropolitan area, from other cities in the tri-state area, and still others from Houston, Chicago, and as far away as Los Angeles.

The minister traced the life of the 27-year-old officer, who had grown up in Yonkers and was to have been married in November.

He described Gary's career in law enforcement, having served in the town of Sloatsburg, in Rockland County, before joining the Westchester police force. He had served as an undercover agent in a narcotics investigation, and as a result of that work, was named "Cop of the Year" by the Police Pulaski Association of Westchester County in 1983.

The pastor went on to say that, "His life has been shortened, negated by a violent act committed by someone who, in one moment, changed a destiny." He spoke of the "never-ending violence in our society" and concluded by saying that he hoped the murderer "is found and that justice is done."

The service ended with the singing of "Amazing Grace." The hymn travelled far beyond the church, as steeple bells and police bagpipes took up the music. As the coffin was carried from the church, the two brothers of the slain officer, themselves both police officers, walked slowly behind the casket. One of them was carrying Gary's badge, cap and gloves. They escorted the coffin to Hastings-on-Hudson, where it was interred in Mount Hope Cemetery.

Whenever someone is murdered, surviving family members and proponents of the death penalty usually join forces to call attention to the problem of violent crime and stress that capital punishment is the only fate that will deter certain criminals. In the case of a law enforcement officer or public figure being murdered, the media devotes even greater attention to this debate.

Gary Stymiloski's death was no exception. New

York Governor Mario Cuomo, who had previously placed Alex Mengel on the state's "Dirty Dozen" list of most-wanted fugitives, was the recipient of numerous letters and petitions asking that he move to restore the death penalty. The New York State Assembly has passed a death penalty bill each year for the last nine years. In each case, the bill has been vetoed by the incumbent governor. This year again saw the passing of the same bill, and Governor Cuomo had said that he would exercise his veto for the third straight time.

In an attempt to change his mind, a relative of the slain officer personally wrote to Governor Cuomo. She asked him to restore the death penalty by not vetoing the current capital punishment bill that was due to come before him shortly.

In her letter to Governor Cuomo, the relative said she believed if New York State had capital punishment, Gary "might not have been killed. I think it might have made a difference." If Gary, she wrote, had died of "an unavoidable accident, carelessness or a disease, I could have accepted his fate." But, to lose Gary to Mengel, whom she described as "a fiendish individual who apparently couldn't give a damn about human life" was something she would never be able to understand.

"Governor Cuomo, how many more police officers and citizens must die before you enact and enforce the death penalty?"

A spokesman for Governor Cuomo, when asked about the letter, stated that, "The Governor's position on the issue of the death penalty is clear. While the concerns "of the officer's family are understandable, it is the governor's view that the death penalty does not prevent crimes, and may in fact encourage them."

Speaking at her Yonkers home, the relative said that she had decided to write to Cuomo after she received a letter of condolence from the governor.

"It was nice of him to do that, but I feel he has a responsibility to okay the death penalty. I think we need it. I have to deal with this the rest of my life. I'm taking it one day at a time."

There were many police in attendance that day at the victim's funeral, but there were still other officers who had not been able to attend due to their duty schedule. Others continued to press the manhunt for Mengel, thinking that bringing Gary's killer to justice would be the best tribute they could give him.

Tips continued to pour in from all parts of New York State and neighboring states. Each of these was carefully checked out. Although a great many tips prove to be totally worthless, every veteran cop knows their value. Because one may sound strange, or the person making the tip may not be your normal, average citizen, this does not mean that the tip is not a good one. Thus, the detectives patiently and carefully sifted through the information gleaned from those calls, waiting for the right one to come through.

Meanwhile, a student at the State University of New York at Buffalo was deeply troubled. Finally, he decided to speak to some of his friends. He told them that the man the police were looking for, Alex Mengel, had been staying with him and had recently left. He explained that Mengel was related to him by marriage, and that he had shown up asking for help. He felt he should call the police, but was uncertain about what to do, partly because the man was a relative, but primarily because he was afraid of what Mengel might do to him if he found out.

The friends counseled him to call the police immediately, but the student remained hesitant and nervous. After leaving him, his friends discussed the situation at length and finally decided that the circumstances were serious enough to warrant a breach of confidentiality.

While they were deciding on how to go about this, a white, 1985 Toyota Tercel was approaching the Canadian border. It entered the crossing point, which is the Peace Bridge, slowed and came to a halt. Canada and the United States have very close ties, and, as a result, travel between the two countries is informal. To enter either country, a visitor need only show some form of acceptable identification. The border guard approached the car and waited politely while the passenger, a woman, searched for some identification.

Moments later, the motorist produced a driver's license and gave it to the guard. As he accepted the card, the guard glanced at the woman briefly. He saw a woman with long, dark hair, wearing a scarf and dress, waiting patiently to pass on. He examined the license, found everything in order, and returned the license to its owner, Mrs. Beverly Capone. The driver nodded her thanks and drove across the bridge and into Canada.

As the afternoon of March 1st wore on, the police switchboard received still another call from someone who wished to speak with an investigator connected with the recent cop slaying. The call was transferred to a detective assisting on the case. He asked the callers (there seemed to be two of them), for their names, but they said they would rather remain anonymous. They explained that their friend (a student) was too scared to call police, so they had decided to call themselves. The detectives asked them their friend's name and address and questioned them briefly for more particulars. Then he thanked them for calling. This was just the type of lead police had been waiting for. Detectives were immediately dispatched to interview the student.

When the officers arrived at his apartment, the student was visibly surprised to see them. Presented with the details of the call, the student admitted it was true. His relative, Alex Mengel, had recently been there seeking help. Mengel told him, "I'm in trouble and I need money." He had made no actual threat, but the student said that he felt his life would be in danger if he did not cooperate.

Mengel told the student that he had killed a cop, and he showed the relative the gun he had used—a nine-millimeter pistol. When the student asked him why he had done it, Mengel replied, "Because the cop was harassing me."

At first, the student thought that Mengel was kidding him, but the gun and the news stories he had heard changed his mind. Mengel had asked him for some clothes, but the only things that would fit him were a sweater and some sneakers. When asked for some money, the student had given him $300, which, he told lawmen, he owed Mengel for a small television set that he bought from him when he had stayed with him briefly during the summer.

Detectives questioned him closely. What were Mengel's plans? Where was he going? What kind of a car was he driving? The student answered these questions as best he could. Mengel had told him he was going to try to cross over to Canada and stay there awhile. He had been driving a white, 1985 Toyota Tercel, which, when the relative had asked him where he got it, Mengel had replied, "I stole it from somebody's garage."

After completing their questioning, the detectives immediately sent out a bulletin advising the Canadian authorities that a suspect in the recent murder of an officer was believed to be heading for their country, and requested their assistance in the apprehension of the suspect.

The Canadian authorities pledged their complete

cooperation, and immediately alerted all border crossing points to be on the lookout for the fugitive.

Back in the United States, detectives began to carefully check all reports of stolen vehicles and missing persons to see if they could uncover further leads in the case. The description of the car was found to match one belonging to a woman who had been missing since Monday, February 25th, the day after Officer Stymiloski had been shot.

As the available information was correlated, including the finding of the woman's identification in an area that Mengel was known to be familiar with, detectives began to theorize that he had kidnapped the woman and had stolen her car. They ordered a search to be conducted in the area of the cabin where the identification card had been found.

The student had not reported seeing anyone in the car with Mengel, and they began to fear that the woman, Beverly Capone, might already be dead. However, the investigators again notified Canadian authorities, advising them that the owner of the Toyota might be a prisoner of the fugitive—perhaps being held as a hostage to insure his safety. They also sent the license plate number of the car to aid in the identification of the vehicle.

The family of Beverly Capone was also afraid. Capone had last been seen walking towards her car in the employee parking lot of IBM in Dobb's Ferry, New York. From there she had disappeared, and the agony of waiting had begun.

After several days passed and no clues as to her whereabouts were forthcoming, the frantic family members turned to a psychic friend of the family for help in the search effort. The psychic, Carol Jason, had assisted in police investigations in the past—most notably in the notorious "Son of Sam" murders.

She told police about an old mill and a red barn type of structure which she described in detail and said figured in the disappearance of Beverly Capone. She concluded her findings by telling detectives that she saw the stolen car going north over a bridge, headed toward "Falls"—perhaps Niagara Falls.

The diligent efforts of many law enforcement officers and individuals like Carol Jason were about to be rewarded.

The latest available information of Alex Mengel had been transmitted to Canadian authorities. These persons, in turn, began the process of disseminating this information to all the rank and file of the Canadian police departments nationwide.

On Saturday, March 2nd, seven days after the shooting of Gary Stymiloski, that information arrived via telex at the Forty-First Division stationhouse in the East Toronto suburb of Scarborough. That it did not become just another routine bulletin can be attributed to the attentiveness and diligence of one individual. That Saturday afternoon, Constable Clive Richards arrived at the stationhouse for his tour of duty at four P.M.

He examined all of the communiques and bulletins which had arrived that day and then left to commence his one-man patrol assignment.

A short time later, Richards was cruising past a store located about a half-mile from the stationhouse. He decided to pull into the parking lot to check if everything was in order there.

As he passed by one of the parked cars, something about it struck a chord in his mind. Abruptly, his memory made the connection: the telex message he had read earlier that day. Rolling slowly past the car, Constable Richards saw the New York license plate and realized that the man sitting in the car was the missing fugitive, Alex Mengel. Moving out of range so as not to attract suspicion, Richards now radioed his headquarters immediately, reporting on his find, and requested backup units.

In a few minutes, Constables Peter Howarth and Herbert Lawrence arrived. They attempted to surround Mengel's car with their vehicles and box him in, but, as they approached his car, Mengel, no doubt highly suspicious and wary of anyone, stepped on the gas and raced away. A high-speed chase ensued as Mengel frantically tried to escape, with the constable right behind him.

Turning into a side street about half a mile away from the store, Mengel suddenly realized he had made a mistake. A big mistake. He had turned into a dead-end street. Looking frantically around, he spotted a car dealership parking lot. Mengel sped into the lot, hoping to be able to twist his way around and emerge before the pursuing cops. As he tried to make a tight turn, his car was thrown up against a snow drift; then it crashed into a pole and stopped.

As the pursuing officers pulled up around his car, Mengel got out and started to run. He had a gun in his hand—a .38-caliber revolver. As he began fumbling with the gun, apparently in order to take aim at the constables, Mengel dropped it. Before he could recover it, Constable Richards informed Mengel, in no uncertain terms, that an attempt to do so would be his last, whereupon Mengel surrendered.

Taking him into custody, the officers recovered the .38 revolver, which was fully loaded, and a nine-millimeter pistol that still had two live rounds. Several knives were also found in his possession.

As they searched their captive and secured him, the constables took a good look at the man who had slain a brother officer in America. They all noticed something very odd. For some reason, Alex Mengel had shaved off about two inches of his hairline all around his head. His eyebrows were also partly shaven off.

Speaking later to the media, Sergeant Howard Kiddie of the Scarborough Division Unit explained that the .38-caliber revolver which had been recovered was identified as Stymiloski's missing service revolver.

The nine-millimeter automatic pistol which had also been found on Mengel was believed by authorities to be the murder weapon. Kiddie added that Alex Mengel had been alone when he was arrested. When asked whether Mengel had made any statements to police, Kiddie replied, "He didn't say much." Responding to one newsman's expression of surprise that he had surrendered so easily, Kiddie told the reporter, "He was staring down the barrels of three .38's. That'll stop anybody."

The following day, Alex Mengel was charged with Canadian weapons felonies and ordered held without bail, pending extradition proceedings. Mengel stated at that time that he would refuse to waive extradition. The judge ordered arraignment proceedings to be held on March 4th.

Investigators spoke with Mengel to ask his cooperation in the search for Beverly Capone. He made several statements to authorities at this time, admitting that he had indeed killed Officer Stymiloski, but he insisted that he did not kill Beverly Capone, and he refused to help in the search.

Meanwhile, state troopers led a massive search in the upstate New York areas that Mengel was known to be so familiar with. Detectives from the Westchester County Police Department travelled to the East Durham cabin to examine the clothing and other articles found there which had been identified as belonging to Beverly Capone. Chief among these was an IBM identification card. A pocketbook, belt, and several other articles of clothing had been found, which were also subsequently identified as belonging to Capone.

Police technicians carefully checked everything within the cabin, while other crews searched outside and nearby areas. The search parties were having a difficult time of it, caught as they were in a fierce winter storm. Detectives felt that Capone might have been brought north with Mengel when he fled upstate, not only because of the articles that had been found there, but also because of the fact that he had been hunting in that same area shortly before killing Stymiloski.

The confirmation that Beverly Capone had indeed been abducted by Alex Mengel brought feelings of anguish and dread to her family. Night after night, relatives and friends kept vigils around the telephone, hoping for news, yet fearing what that news might be. Family members said they could not understand how this could have happened to her.

"She didn't go out that much. She led a quiet life, worked a lot of overtime, and stayed at home on weekends. She just got a promotion. She was going to get a new office very soon and was very excited about that. She was very happy with her job and her life."

Said another relative, "She was not the kind of person to pick up a hitchhiker. She would never just run off. I'm afraid something happened to her. I just hope the cops find out what."

Sadly, the next news that relatives would receive regarding Beverly Capone would be horrifying in its implications.

If one believes in omens, the fifth of March did not get off to an auspicious start. Four more inches of snow had fallen during the night, and it gave no signs of letting up.

Sergeant J.S. Kievort, of the State Police, said,

"We've been out there looking for her for three days—with dogs, helicopters, and on foot—and so far we've come up with nothing.

"With the new snow, I don't think we'll be able to get much done today," he explained.

Meanwhile, evidence technicians had made some important findings. Captain Harold Turner, also of the State Police, summed up the latest information.

"We know proof-positive that Mengel was in the Cairo area last Tuesday night, and we have strong circumstantial evidence that Beverly Capone was here at the same time."

As for continuing the search that day, they noted that that was not too likely. Said Kievort, "We couldn't put a copter in the air if we wanted to. It's very foggy and hazy." Kievort and Turner said they would be meeting with other state troopers to map out search strategy, but said it was very unlikely that they would be able to do very much.

While this aspect of the investigation was meeting with delays, evidence technicians in Canada were about to make an important, though chilling, discovery.

After Alex Mengel had been captured, the car he had been driving was taken to the nearest police garage to be carefully examined by experts.

When a car is processed, pictures are taken, the contents of the car are noted and carefully catalogued, and latent fingerprints are checked for and lifted. Everything is taken into consideration during this evaluation. The interior is vacuumed to recover and preserve evidence that normally might be too minute to see, such as hair and fibers from clothing. Very often, the smallest shred of evidence can be valuable in tracking down suspects, and instrumental in convicting them.

In this instance, the technicians were also hoping that the getaway car would yield additional clues to Beverly Capone's whereabouts.

Among other things, the investigators found several dresses, a scarf, a handbag, and several identification papers — among them a driver's license.

Looking under the seats for possible concealed items, one of the investigators found something hidden under the front seat. Carefully extracting it, the technician thought at first that he had found a wig. Upon closer examination, however, the searcher felt a twinge of horror as he realized that he was holding a human scalp — not a wig. Given the circumstances, the description of Capone, and the coloration, length, etc. of the hair and of the scalp, the police were forced to conclude that the human scalp they had found most probably had been that of Beverly Capone.

By now, Canadian authorities had discovered that Mengel had entered the country by showing Beverly Capone's driver's license at the border crossing. They now began to investigate the possibility — given the facts of the scalp, the clothes, Mengel's shaved hair and eyebrows — that Alex Mengel had worn her scalp and clothes to disguise himself as a woman so that he could enter Canada.

Informed of these developments, the police sent the clothing found in the burglarized cabin to Toronto so that forensic experts could compare them with the dresses found in Beverly Capone's car. Several New York State forensic specialists also travelled to Toronto to aid in the examination of the scalp and of the automobile.

The news of the grisly find served to intensify the efforts of state authorities to locate Beverly Capone — or, what was by this time felt by most of the searchers, the body of Beverly Capone.

An intensive search was conducted, with some 25 state troopers using helicopters, bloodhounds, and German shepherds to search the wooded areas, streams, lakes and cabins in this resort area of East Durham. Scuba divers were brought in to search lakes, ponds, and creeks where Mengel had been known to go fishing.

Privately, the searchers began to despair of ever finding her body. As one said, "It doesn't look promising at all."

That Wednesday, Mengel was brought before Judge Isabel Soltar of the Canadian Employment and Immigration Department. The strain of incarceration and the knowledge that the scalp had been found in the car had evidently unnerved him. As he was being driven to his court appearance, Mengel pressed his face against the steel-mesh window of the police van and screamed, "I'm innocent! I'm innocent!"

This struck the lawmen driving him as an extremely ludicrous thing to say, considering that Mengel readily admitted to murdering Stymiloski and still bore the evidence of his disguise on his body, in the form of the shaved eyebrows and hairline, which had not yet had time to grow back in.

Appearing before Judge Soltar, Mengel told the court he was applying for refugee status, and that he would seek permission to remain in Canada. Toronto Prosecutor Ken Anthony called this effort a "delaying tactic" to avoid deportation. He revealed that Mengel had confessed on videotape to killing Stymiloski. Indeed, he had said that he had done it because the officer "was giving me trouble." The attorney requested that Mengel be sent back to the United States immediately.

Judge Soltar adjourned the proceedings until Tuesday to give Mengel an opportunity to secure a lawyer to represent him.

Late that night, Detective Sergeant John DeMascio, of the Mount Vernon Police Department, returned to Westchester with the scalp and the other items of evidence. Further tests would have to be conducted before the scalp could be positively identified.

Meanwhile, during another interview session with Mengel, he again refused to discuss Capone's disappearance with authorities. Even when two Toronto friends of Mengel's relatives tried to talk him into helping the search effort, he repeatedly maintained he was not responsible for her abduction, claiming he had just stolen the car from a garage.

Knowledge of his confession to the killing of Gary Stymiloski brought varied reactions from Mengel's family, friends, and acquaintances. His family thought that, "He must have snapped." They explained that this was probably because Mengel had marital problems. Then he lost his job as a Yonker's mechanic. Finally, Mengel had been evicted from his apartment.

Said a former co-worker, "If Alex thought the cop was gonna take his car, too, well, that might have been the last straw."

However, another former co-worker said that Mengel had a violent temper. "If he didn't like the way the cop talked to him, he'd do something about it. He was that way."

The characteristic that most of his friends and relations probably found hardest to deal with was Alex's extremes.

He broke his wife's jaw (for which he was arrested) then said that he tried not to hurt her. He also loved hunting and owned a shotgun and a .22-caliber rifle which he used primarily to hunt deer. Yet relatives said Mengel loved animals. He found a seriously injured squirrel once and had taken it home and nursed it back to health. He called it Squeaky and kept it as a pet until it eventually escaped.

Asked what he thought Mengel's biggest fault was, a relative replied, "He lied and exaggerated."

On Monday, March 11th, Mengel appeared in court, represented for the first time by a lawyer. Mengel sat behind a partition of bulletproof glass, securely handcuffed. The hearing was adjourned for one week, until March 18th, so that his lawyer, Michael Smith, could have time to familiarize himself with the case.

Mengel was again questioned regarding the abduction of Beverly Capone and the human scalp found in the car, but he refused to cooperate. As he was taken back to his cell, his questioners speculated on Mengel's lack of cooperation regarding Capone. One of them pointed out that Alex Mengel was considered something of a "folk hero" among fellow prison inmates because he had killed a cop. In the mentality of the inmates, this made Mengel a real hero—a real tough guy. But if it got out that he had mutilated a woman just to escape, the prisoners might have turned on him. Therefore, it made sense to admit to the crime that gave him status, but not to the other.

The next day, March 12th, Onandaga County officials announced that they were considering whether to charge Mengel in connection with the attempted kidnapping of the 13-year-old girl from Skaneateles. When asking the girl for directions, the driver had indicated he "she" was looking for Auburn. In the search of the car, a map had been found with Auburn circled in pencil. The authorities said they had not yet learned Mengel's motive for wanting to go there.

Search teams continued their operation as best they could during this period, often unable to continue due to more snow or unmanageable conditions. The troopers were on the verge of giving up on the search when, on March 15th, they finally located the missing Beverly Capone.

A volunteer searcher and his German shepherd named "Flash" were approximately one half mile from the burglarized cabin, moving along a stone wall, when the dog began to paw a section of the wall. One investigator started to remove some stones, then stopped when it became apparent that a body was, indeed, hidden there. As a sleuth would say later, the body was covered "real tight so that she looked like she was part of the stone wall."

Crime scene technicians were summoned to remove the body and properly preserve any evidence found.

The body was that of a woman. It was found to be wearing a bra and a flowered housecoat. Not unexpectedly, though still shocking, the woman's body had been scalped and the skin removed from the victim's face.

The victim was taken to the Albany Medical Center for an autopsy and positive identification.

The next day, the Greene County Medical Examiner's Office announced that the scalped body had been positively identified as Beverly Capone. The victim had been stabbed three times, and the cause of death had been hemorrhaging in the chest cavity caused by a stab wound near her heart. No sign of sexual abuse had been discovered.

Family members, informed of the discovery, felt numb and sad. When the police had called that Friday evening, one family member said he knew that the waiting was over, and he felt relieved that the ordeal of waiting was over and that at least the body could be given a decent burial.

On Monday, March 18th, Greene County District Attorney Seymour Meadow filed a second-degree murder charge against Alex Mengel in connection with the death of Beverly Capone. A burglary charge was also filed at that time, relating to the upstate cabin. A first-degree murder charge in New York State is possible only for the killing of a police officer.

Meanwhile, a crowd of 250 relatives, friends, and neighbors gathered on Wednesday, March 20th, to bid farewell to Beverly Capone. The minister spoke warmly as he eulogized her, saying, "Beverly Capone is not gone forever. She lives in another dimension."

A letter from one relative was also read at the ceremony, saying, "I'll always remember your beautiful smile, your love of life, and, especially your love for me. You will be part of me forever."

Following the service, Beverly Capone was buried in Beechwood Cemetery, in New Rochelle.

Six days later, on March 26th, Mengel was ordered deported from Canada by Judge J.D. Benning, who ruled that Mengel had "been found in contravention of the Immigration Act on two counts: entering the country with false identification and possessing insufficient funds." Mengel's lawyer said he would not appeal the ruling, stating that his client was resigned to returning to the United States.

Upon receiving this information, Westchester D.A. Carl Vergari's office immediately initiated grand jury proceedings to formally bring a first-degree murder indictment against Alex Mengel in the murder of Gary Stymiloski.

The Canadian authorities had said they would return Mengel as soon as possible and, true to their word, Mengel was deported the very next day, March 27th. Arriving in the U.S., he was taken to Yonkers City Court, where he was ordered held without bail. Arraignment was scheduled for April 8th.

On that date, Mengel's lawyer, John F. Ryan, entered not guilty pleas before County Judge Nicholas Colabella to murder and ten other charges. Bail was not requested and Mengel was returned to the county jail, pending a hearing on motions, set for May 28th.

But Alex Mengel was not fated to attend that hearing. On April 26th, Mengel was being transported to Westchester after an arraignment in Greene County. Investigator Robert Stabile was driving the car, while senior Investigator Godfried Grunwald sat in the backseat with Mengel, who was handcuffed. The cuffs were attached to a restraining belt around his waist.

Suddenly, Mengel erupted with a flurry of biting and gouging as he sought to take Grunwald's gun. Stabile immediately pulled over and drew his service revolver, preparing to force Mengel to surrender. He realized that Mengel had gotten hold of the gun, so Stabile reacted quickly, firing once.

Shortly thereafter, they drove Mengel to Highland Hospital in Beacon, where he was pronounced dead at 3:38 P.M. of a gunshot wound to the head.

Reactions to the news of Mengel's death were mixed. Gary Stymiloski's family expressed relief, saying that Mengel had been "a vicious murderer who would stop at nothing."

Mengel's family reacted angrily, charging that Alex had been set up.

Beverly Capone's family expressed regret because now they "would never know what really happened to Beverly."

Later that evening, when asked if it had been necessary to shoot Mengel, Commander Stanley Hook replied, "There was no other choice. He had the other officer's gun." Hook added that the officer had been taken to St. Francis Hospital in Poughkeepsie, for treatment of multiple bite wounds.

At a subsequent hearing, the shooting of Alex

Mengel was found to be justified. District Attorney William Grady said that no charges would be filed against the officers, who were acting according to proper procedure. However, a report recommended a review and upgrading of procedures used in transporting prisoners.

On Thursday, May 2nd, Alex Mengel was buried in Queens in a private ceremony. The reign of terror was over.

EDITOR'S NOTE:
Fiona Gerano is not the real name of the person so named in the foregoing story. A fictitious name has been used because there is no reason for public interest in the identity of this person.

" 'BEAST MAN' AND
THE BURNING COP!"
by E.E. Gilpatrick

Rudolph Schaffer, age 39, had been on the Chicago
police force for 12 years. From basic patrol work, he'd
progressed to a position in electronic maintenance, a
unit which affects the continued efficient, effective operation of the thousand and one different electronic de-
vices so essential to the smooth, continuing operation
of any modern law enforcement agency, large or small.

It was Friday afternoon, January 31, 1986, at about
four o'clock when Officer Schaffer arrived home where
he lived with his wife and three young daughters. It
was a pleasant little house in the southwest suburbs of
greater Chicago.

Schaffer flopped for a moment to collect his
thoughts, then rose and announced to his wife that he
was going to run out to his favorite tobacconist to get
some cigars. He said he'd be back before long.

She had a good idea how long that would be. She
went to the kitchen, pulled open the refrigerator door
and, in the glow of the little white light, stood contem-
plating supper. She paid no attention to the sound of

Rudy's dark green van backing out of the driveway and pulling off down the street.

It was after six o'clock. Supper was beginning to get cold. She called Rudy's brother. He was a policeman, too. Perhaps Rudy had stumbled onto something. A cop is always a cop. He and his brother were very close, and if Rudy Schaffer wanted to confer with another lawman, his brother would probably be the first he'd turn to.

No. The brother was as mystified as was Rudy's wife, but he said he'd make a few calls.

Rudy had bought his cigars, chatted a bit with the tobacconist and some regulars of the shop as was his custom, and left. No significant comments had been made by anyone. Nothing seemed out of the ordinary. He simply left the shop. That was at about six o'clock.

It can happen to any wife—all night long, no husband, no word. For most wives, it comes totally by surprise, a complete shock. For a police officer's wife, there can be many such nights of fear and loneliness. Will it be tonight? For Officer Schaffer's wife, that night was the worst night—no husband, no word, no trace.

The official report would state: "His wife called his brother who is also a policeman. In turn he checked with friends. When he (Officer Rudolph Schaffer) did not turn up by Saturday afternoon, a missing-person report was filed."

The brother suggested the missing-person report. She was startled by the suggestion. To file a missing-person report is to admit one has a problem requiring outside help. Certainly, her brother-in-law knew best.

It was about ten o'clock on Saturday morning, February 1st, that a pumper thundered up to a van burning in an alley in the 6900 block of South Peoria Street on the south side of Chicago. It was a few moments before that hour that two young people had seen the van blazing and reported it.

The call appeared to be routine. Both the circumstances and firemen's noses indicated a gasoline fire which the pumper crew was entirely ready to deal with. They had faced such fires many times before.

What they weren't prepared to deal with was the body they found in the van. It was burned beyond recognition.

The find was immediately pointed out to the drivers of the light blue and white Chicago police cruisers which came to back up the firefighters. The patrol officers put in a call to the Brighton Park Violent Crimes Unit in whose area the discovery was made.

The deputy coroner of Cook County, in which Chicago is located, was no more successful in establishing the identity of the body in the van than the smoke-eaters had been. Because portions of the skin had been burned away from the skull, the deputy coroner was able to determine that the victim had suffered a gunshot wound to the skull. The body, the deputy coroner established, was not primarily a burn victim. The apparent cause of death was a gunshot wound to the head. The deputy coroner tentatively classified the death as a homicide. The county coroner's man ordered an immediate autopsy.

For his own part, the Chicago Fire Department battalion commander filed an immediate request for a detailed arson investigation.

His own professional experience led the commander to believe several things: the fire had not started in the engine compartment; neither had it started in or around the gas tank, nor along any gas line. Burn patterns suggested that it had started in the rear portion of the interior body of the van.

Slowly, painstakingly, the deputy coroner attempted

to find out as much about the victim as he could while detectives from the Brighton Park Violent Crimes Unit now at the scene began their crime scene investigation, working in concert with Chicago Fire Department investigators.

The body was unrecognizable and bore no identification. The dental structures were all there; evident was some dental work which had been done in the past. There was no wallet on the victim, no keys and none of the other metal trinkets one might logically expect to find on the person of any victim.

The victim carried no weapon of any type. From the few hair and skin samples available, the coroner's representative guessed that the victim could have been anywhere from the early 30s to the mid-40s. In scorching heat, the body tends to double up the thighs and the stomach protecting the genitals. The victim was a Caucasian male.

The possibility existed that the wound may have been self-inflicted, even though no weapon was found in the van. If so, it wouldn't be the first time some alley scavenger stole a gun from a corpse, thinking perhaps the theft was from a passed-out dope-head or an armed, exhausted wayfarer. Using fire to cover crime is common.

Other evidence tended to refute the suicide hypothesis. The license plates had been removed from the vehicle. As soon as the van was cool enough, and the rest of the truck had been carefully processed, the crime scene investigators would get at the van body number and engine number in an attempt to determine current ownership. Although the fire had been hot, some portions on the corners of the metal body suggested that the van had been a dark green, or what might be called emerald green.

Early on Saturday afternoon, as the arson and crime

scene investigations continued, a police clerk in the Brighton Park Area headquarters who'd been culling missing-persons reports was alerted to the fact that a new missing-person report was coming in over the printer at that moment. The clerk was momentarily startled by the fact that the newly reported missing person was a Chicago police officer. His name was Rudolph Schaffer; he was 39 years old. It was noted on the missing-person report that when last seen, Schaffer was driving his dark green van.

The clerk assembled all the available pertinent data to have it ready when the detectives returned from their crime scene investigation. Going over the report, the clerk also noted that the complainant on the missing-person report and the officer taking the report were the same person — a relative of the missing officer's.

While the crime scene investigation was in progress, occupants whose quarters faced the alley were questioned. That done, the canvass for information was expanded to include both businesses and homes in an area centered roughly by the intersection of 70th and South Peoria Streets, not many miles from the home of Rudolph Schaffer.

The two young men who'd summoned the fire department were questioned at length. There was, among the investigators, a nagging feeling that the pair may well have known more than they were telling, but none of the sleuths had any reason to believe that either of the two young men was intimately connected with the crime. Whether they'd seen more than just a van burning in the alley seemed to be an open question.

That was part of the enigma of this arson-murder. The arson squad readily agreed with the battalion commander: the fire had been set. The body and the inside of the van had been doused with gasoline and ignited. What made this crime an enigma was some of the statements the canvassing investigators were getting from residents whose homes overlooked the alley.

When asked if they'd seen who drove the dark green van into the alley, several residents expressed surprise. They were early risers. They'd gone to the alley to empty waste baskets into the trash barrels there or walked down the alley to a favorite coffee spot early that morning. There was no van in the alley then. Yes, they'd seen the fire and heard the fire engines and wondered where the van had come from.

A woman who lived on the alley off the intersection of 70th and South Peoria Streets didn't know anything about any van that had burned in the next block over. There's been a dark-colored van parked in her alley all night long, but someone must have moved it, because it was gone when she came out to see what all the commotion was about in the next block. There were fire engines, police cars and even a black station wagon with gold lettering on the side. It was too far away to make out what the gold lettering said.

Upon completion of the first phase of canvassing and questioning, Detective Sergeant George Owen of the Brighton Park Area could say only, "Right now we have more questions than answers." It seemed that the search for information to resolve the questions had only created more questions. Some valid evidence was discovered at the crime scene, but the witness testimony, rather than resolving any questions, seemed only to complicate and contradict what information the detectives could uncover.

Before the end of Saturday afternoon, the autopsy on the burned body was completed. John Stibich, Brighton Park Area commander of detectives, asked the pathologist to do all he could in an attempt to determine time of death. It seemed that the victim had been killed, doused with gas and set on fire, but something wasn't adding up.

The pathologist reported that the victim had been shot twice. One bullet entered his skull in the area of the temple. This shot caused massive trauma and brain damage, resulting in death almost immediately. There was another bullet wound, this one in the victim's side. It went straight into the victim's chest from the side and would have quickly proved fatal had not physiologic processes been shortstopped by death from the head wound. The victim had been shot first in the side and then in the head in rapid succession. The bullets had been fired from two different guns. The Chicago PD was looking for at least two assailants. The head wound had been inflicted with Rudolph Schaffer's own service pistol.

The dental comparison was done at the same time as the autopsy, working from medical-dental records in the CPD personnel file of Officer Rudolph Schaffer. The burned victim found in the back of the dark green van was indeed Rudolph Schaffer. Motor vehicle records listing the motor number of the burned vehicle indicated that it was Schaffer's van.

The pathologist's time of death report confirmed what a number of detectives had began to suspect. Schaffer had not been killed, doused and burned — one, two, three. Normally, the pathologist explained, he would be able to state the time of death under these circumstances without a fire to within about a half hour. Considering the fire, the pathologist could say only inexactly that Schaffer had been killed 14 to 16 hours before his body was discovered or sometime on Friday evening or the earlier part of Friday night. Schaffer had been killed, one, but it had been some 14 hours later when he'd been doused, two, and burned, three.

To these seasoned investigators of the Chicago PD, a workable hypothesis was beginning to emerge. As both Schaffer's wife and brother confirmed, Schaffer, like any other law enforcement officer, always carried his gun and his badge. Somehow he was lured into an alley where he was robbed and killed. The attackers had no way of knowing that he was a cop. He was off duty, out of uniform, and driving his own van. Only after the assailants had killed Schaffer — probably when they found his gun and badge — did they learn that they'd killed a cop.

They knew they were in big trouble, for they knew as well that the detectives wouldn't rest until the cop-killers were caught. But, the killers dreamed up a way to avoid getting slapped with the label of cop-killers. To arrest someone as a cop-killer, there had to be a killed cop. The way Schaffer's killers had it figured out, if they ditched the gun and the badge, no one would ever know the body was that of a police officer. Bums burn themselves up every winter in Chicago. The lawmen do their best to check out each of these bum burnings, but it's usually an impossible investigation.

Giving the devil his due, the sleuths of Brighton Park genuinely believed that the killers probably didn't know they'd killed a cop until Schaffer was already dead and was being robbed. They probably took all night to hatch their scheme of how to change a murdered policeman into a "nobody". The location in the alley of the 6900 block was less likely to cause a major fire, so the van was moved from the scene of the killing across 70th Street to the scene of the burning, the alley in the 69th Street block.

The canvassing probers hit the bricks again. This time their major targets were gasoline service stations

174

in the area. If the plan was hatched Friday night and executed Saturday morning, it was distinctly possible that the accelerant, as the arson investigators called it, had not been purchased until Saturday morning.

Two investigators walked up to the cashier at a self-service discount service station. It was already dark on this chilly Saturday afternoon in February. The sleuths asked the cashier if she recalled two people coming in that morning to buy gas in a can. Taking a clue from information provided by the arson squad, the questioners ventured that it was probably a five gallon can of some sort.

The cashier recalled no such customers. The detectives proffered their business cards and asked for the name of the owner of the station and where they might reach the manager. After noting the information, they turned to go. The cashier stopped them, suggesting that they might want to talk to the day cashier who came in to work that morning. He was in the back, washing up to go home.

There are a lot of nuts in this world. That's why he remembered. Only one guy came in to buy gas in a five-gallon can that morning, but the can he had looked more like an old oil bucket than it did a gas can. He warned the guy that it looked pretty cruddy — putting gas in that can might cause engine problems.

The gas customer seemed to grunt disinterested acknowledgement. He paid for the gas and headed off across the station yard toward the corner of South Peoria and 70th Street, slopping gas as if he were lugging a bucket of well water.

The day cashier was able to give a sketchy, general description which might fit many young-adult black males. Yes, he thought he could identify him. Now it remained for the detectives to find a suspect with a face to be identified. The rest of the canvassing operation turned up nothing.

The night shift team at Brighton Park Headquarters reviewed all the investigatory data, but no new ideas presented themselves. Potential witnesses not contacted during the day were contacted on Saturday night. None had anything significantly new to offer.

Part of police work is working your share of weekends and holidays. Only retirement brings relief from doing one's fair share. Detective Sergeant Owen had pulled the day watch on that Sunday morning.

An operator flashed a red-light call to the seasoned sleuth, who was sitting at his desk in the violent crimes unit. The voice of the caller sounded female.

The woman said she'd been sitting at her kitchen table on Friday after supper, cup of coffee in hand and staring out her back window onto the alley, daydreaming about nothing in particular. She really wasn't aware she was looking directly into the alley until she saw the Martin girl who lived right there off the alley, leading a man driving a dark green van into the alley.

At a certain point, the girl stopped him, and he opened the driver's door. In a few minutes two young men—the one called "Beast Man" and the one he ran with—came down the alley. The two guys got into the van. The caller was startled when she heard a noise from the van in the alley like the heavy thump of a door slamming in another room. Then, it sounded again. She didn't want to believe the noises were gunshots. There appeared to be a commotion in the van and the two young men got out and ran off.

Sergeant Owen thanked her profusely both for himself and on behalf of the people of the city of Chicago. She hung up abruptly.

But the trace went through. The call had come from a phone booth in the 7000 block of South Peoria

Street. When a squad-car officer took a look, he saw no one in or near the phone booth.

Several neighborhood residents immediately knew who the Martin girl was. She was 17-year-old Ann Martin, who lived in the immediate area and was well known by many of the neighbors.

Sleuths quizzed her and, Martin told them that something had gone all wrong. She had no idea that someone was going to be robbed and killed. She'd been told that the guy in the green van was going to buy a small quantity of marijuana—all she had to do was to lead him into the alley to set up the deal. Martin was not told that robbery and whatever else it took had been the original intent and continued to be the motivating thrust of the crime. A car payment had to be made, or a car would be repossessed.

A canvassing investigator had knocked on the door of her apartment and talked to her previously. She'd denied any knowledge of anything connected with the death of Officer Schaffer.

Now Martin was advised that whether she realized it or not, she'd acted as an accessory to murder before the fact. As such under Illinois law, she might be prosecuted as a full and equal participant in the crime. This could result in a long prison term. Murder was serious business, and it would be in her own best interests to tell the probers just what happened, and who was involved.

Martin said that she "enticed him (Schaffer)," into the alley as she'd been instructed by her boyfriend. Once in the alley, the off-duty officer got into a conversation with two young men who were lying in wait there.

Schaffer didn't know it, but they were Ann Martin's boyfriend and the boyfriend's sidekick. The girl said that the two finally announced, "This is a robbery!"

Schaffer reached for his gun, and one of the men shot Schaffer in the side of his chest. The other man grabbed the gun Schaffer had tried to draw and shot the officer in the side of the head.

At the time, Schaffer and the two men had been standing beside the van. The side door of the van was open, and the officer stumbled backward, falling into his van. The killers then jumped into the van to strip Schaffer of his money and any valuables he might have. They robbed him of his wallet, which contained $73, his wedding ring, his pistol and one other significant item in his wallet—his badge. They were terrified to discover they'd killed a cop—they knew what that meant.

Rattled, they ran off, leaving the body in the van. At that point it was in the alley off the intersection of 70th and East Peoria Streets, almost under an overhanging wooden porch.

That night, the two robber-killers agonized over the quicksand problem they'd blundered into. When daylight came, the body would most certainly be discovered and identified. When it was learned that a cop had been killed, their futures would look bleak.

As they batted their problem back and forth, the thought came to them: what if no one ever finds out he was a cop? What if it looked like a bum who crawled into a van, lit up a little canned heat for warmth, and it got away from him? Just a bum, unidentifiable—who cares?—just as the investigators had theorized.

Martin explained that she wasn't there for the planning and what happened afterward, but her man told her about it. The next morning, Saturday, after nine o'clock, one of the killers went to a nearby gas station to buy gas. As he did, the other perp drove the van across 70th Street to the more open alley in the 6900 block of South Peoria Street. They didn't want to start another Chicago fire, but they did want a good, hot, roaring fire that would destroy all the evidence and identification.

The questioners asked her if her boyfriend was "Beast Man." She nodded. She said his real name was Calvin Trice. He was 21 and lived further on down South Peoria Street. She went on to say the other man was Sylvester Henderson, 20. He lived over on South Normal Avenue.

As soon as the questioning was done, special tack units went to the two residences the girl had mentioned. As the tack unit assigned to South Peoria Street approached Trice's residence, they saw a man answering Trice's description come out of the house, get in a car and start to pull away. The police pulled the car over to question the driver. He identified himself as Calvin Earl Trice and was placed under arrest without incident on a charge of suspicion of murder. It was now Monday night.

The detectives read Trice his Miranda rights, and he acknowledged that he understood them. It didn't make any difference. He had nothing to say.

On South Normal Avenue, there was no answer at the door of Sylvester Henderson. The police waited. It was not long before the peace officers saw a man answering Henderson's description walk down the street. Plainclothesmen casually strolled up the sidewalk toward him. Henderson, like Trice, was placed under arrest without incident on a charge of suspicion of murder.

Henderson was read his Miranda rights, which he acknowledged. At first he disclaimed any knowledge of any shooting and any arson coverup. He was advised of the results of the questioning of the Beast Man's girlfriend. The sleuths knew it all.

179

Faced with the specific knowledge that the Martin girl had provided, Henderson made a complete confession, which varied from the story the girl told only in minor details. He was able to provide some specifics as to the chain of events which transpired on Saturday morning.

Both Henderson and Trice were indicted on charges of armed robbery and murder. From a possible charge of being an accessory to murder, the charges against the Martin girl were reduced to concealing a homicide and aiding fugitives.

As the April 1987 trial of Henderson and Trice approached, Henderson recanted his confession and said that the police beat it out of him. While Henderson and Trice were being held without bond and Martin was free on her own recognizance, Martin wrote letters to her boyfriend in which she stated, "Listen, I love you. They think I'm going to testify against you, but I'm going to shock the damn court. . . . I swear to God I'll be at your trial to tell the truth. You deserve your freedom."

And, Ann Martin did swear to tell the truth at the trial. Neither prosecutor nor investigators were shocked or surprised at her testimony in court. Her testimony was essentially the same as it had been in an interrogation room some months earlier. The jury listened to the recorded voice of an unknown caller who'd talked to Detective Sergeant George Owen on a previous Sunday morning. The Henderson confession was played for the jury, and the defense was given every opportunity to refute or discredit the recorded statement. There appeared to be no uncertainty among the jury. Both accused men were quickly found guilty as charged.

On Wednesday, June 10, 1987, at a sentencing hearing, the prosecution requested that the court impose the death penalty on both convicted killers. As neither had a previous record, the judge chose to sentence both to life imprisonment.

EDITOR'S NOTE:
Ann Martin is not the real name of the person so named in the foregoing story. A fictitious name has been used because there is no reason for public interest in the identity of this person.

"REQUIEM FOR A GOOD COP"

by Richard Shrout

The two rookie Miami patrolmen had just started routine patrol on September 2nd. When they saw the Volkswagen Bug going the wrong direction down a one-way street at 9:45 A.M., they made a U-turn and followed. Strictly routine.

Officer Terry Russell, 26, was just two months out of the police academy. He was driving. Officer Nathaniel Broom, 23, had been on the job a little longer. They were the kind of bright, eager cops the department justifiably boasts about.

Within minutes Officer Broom would be dying in a rat-infested alley in Overtown, a black ghetto not far from sparkling downtown Miami.

When the officers turned to follow the Bug on a routine traffic matter, the car sped away down the one-way street. The occupants, two black men and one white man, ignored the officers' signal to stop, and the chase was on.

The VW turned into an apartment house parking lot, and the three occupants bailed out and ran. Officer Broom jumped from the patrol car and dashed after the nearest one, the white man, and chased him across the busy NW Third Street intersection.

His partner wheeled the patrol cruiser around, but lost sight of Broom, who was pounding down the pavement of an alley in hot pursuit of the suspect.

The chase led down two blocks on NW 11th Street and turned south onto NW 3rd Avenue. The fleet-footed suspect ducked behind a fenced-in apartment building and darted through a small, grassy backyard and into an alley on the other side of the building where it was a dead end.

The fleeing man tried to run through an adjacent shop. An employee saw him with his gun and yelled to another worker. The cornered man dodged away from them and back into the alley.

The 120-pound, six-foot suspect with the long blond hair was trapped. There was no way out. He crouched behind a wall and waited, hoping he had lost his pursuer. He hadn't. The policeman was young also, and in better physical condition. He had outrun fleeing suspects before.

Broom reached the backyard and stopped, gun drawn. The suspect was nowhere in sight. Broom stood in the grass about five feet away from the concealed man behind the wall, his gun pointed at the ground, unaware he had reached a dead end, unsure if the fleeing suspect was armed.

Officer Russell immediately grasped the fact that the other two men had escaped, so he had concentrated on keeping track of his partner, hoping to intercept the suspect or serve as backup to Broom. He reached Third Avenue and screeched the car to a stop when he heard five shots.

It took several minutes for Officer Russell to find his partner lying in a clump of weeds behind the building.

Two City of Miami Police Department officers, Homicide Sergeant Ernest Vivian and Detective

Richard Bohan were en route to a 10 A.M. meeting, when their car was flagged down by a young woman. "She was frantically waving at us," said Bohan. He backed up the car. "She was on the second story landing of an outside staircase and she was pointing down. But a fence blocked the view and we couldn't see anything."

He stopped the car and ran toward the woman, who shouted: "A policeman's shot!" Bohan vaulted the fence and when he saw Broom lying face down in a clump of weeds, he took charge. He yelled for Sergeant Vivian who was right behind him: "Get the rescue squad. A policeman's been shot!"

He rolled Broom over and saw the dark red stain growing on the dark blue uniform shirt over the center of the chest. Broom wasn't breathing and no pulse could be detected. Detective Bohan began mouth-to-mouth resuscitation. Another arriving officer applied heart massage in spite of the chest wound. Broom's heart wasn't beating anyway. There was always a chance. Seconds counted.

The Fire Rescue Squad arrived in less than two and a half minutes. The quick actions appeared successful. Broom was now breathing and there was now a slight pulsebeat, maintained artificially. Broom was rushed to Jackson Memorial Hospital where a team of doctors and nurses, alerted by the paramedics' radioed description, tried frantically to save him.

It was several hours before Nathaniel Broom was pronounced dead.

Broom's mother, who had proudly pinned on his badge at the police academy graduation in December, sobbed at the emergency room where he was pronounced dead.

"The bullet struck his heart," Dr. Joseph H. Davis, the Dade County Medical Examiner later explained.

"When they got there he was beyond all help, but they tried in the emergency room. They immediately opened his chest and tried to clamp the aorta but when they did, it was very apparent that there was nothing that could be done."

A 125-gram steel-jacketed hollow point bullet from a .38-caliber or .357 handgun had pierced the officer's heart. As the impact hurled him back, a second slug slammed through the sole of his shoe. A third had grazed his belt buckle. The wounded officer had managed to fire two shots at his assailant.

In the instant the first radio call had gone out that an officer had been shot, the police response was fast and enormous. More than 150 Miami police officers were joined by more than 50 Metro officers, who searched buildings and fields with helicopters and dogs, and stopped dozens of suspects.

There were witnesses, each of whom saw a small part of what occurred. It would take time to put it all together into a coherent whole.

The alley where the shooting took place stretched west between an ancient church, Miami headquarters for the Southern Christian Leadership Conference, and a two-story building with businesses on the street level and apartments above.

"In this neighborhood, the gunfire is so common," said a police spokesman, "they just duck down on the floor and wait until it's over. This is Vietnam. It's by far the most dangerous area. At least three Miami policemen have died in the Overtown area."

"I looked in his face and he looked in mine," said a shaken witness who had been in the shop where the suspect had run. "He saw me, turned around and pulled out a black revolver. He fell back behind the building for cover. He had the gun in his right hand. He balanced it with his left, took his time and aimed.

Then he fired. I was astonished that in five or six seconds it was over. I haven't seen anything like it since Vietnam. Then he jumped the fence and ran south."

From his vantage point, the witness hadn't seen the gunman's target, but was sure from his reaction that the victim had fallen. The witness rushed to the street and heard someone shout: "Somebody just shot a black policeman."

The witness first asked that his name be withheld, but added: "If they catch him, I'll testify. I still believe in the justice system. I wish they'd catch them all."

"He looked nervous, like, he didn't know the area," the other man who had been in the shop said. He said the man took a shooting stance, aimed and fired at his pursuer, then he vaulted a fence and vanished, the witness concluded.

Other people who were on the street, or looking from windows, or driving cars had been stopped by the army of policemen. They verified that the skinny subject had jumped the chain-link fence, ran to the Interstate-95 overpass a few blocks away, and raced across its four lanes of busy traffic. A lot of people had seen the man. Everyone agreed he was in his 20s, very tall and thin, and had long blond hair.

The intensity of the investigation bordered on the fantastic. Shoulder-to-shoulder, dozens of officers carefully walked over the crime scene area, hoping to find a discarded gun, an article of clothing, a footprint or any type of clue. The neighborhood for blocks around had been cordoned off, drivers and pedestrians stopped and questioned. Every door in every dilapidated tenement was knocked on, and every inhabitant was questioned by the army of cops who had suddenly occupied Overtown.

The mayor and city manager arrived, along with a platoon of media reporters.

But the police maintained a businesslike order in what threatened to turn into chaos. Rookie officer Russell was understandably grief-stricken. "He wasn't taking it well," a police sergeant explained. He was distraught, nauseated and unable to talk, even to superiors. Russell was whisked away and scheduled for a visit to a police psychologist.

"It's a very sad and horrible thing," the mayor told reporters. "It's doubly tragic. He's only eight months out of the academy, he is black, and we're trying to recruit more blacks."

He took the opportunity to explain that the City of Miami PD had 814 officers and would soon expand to 1,000. There were currently nearly 130 black officers, the highest number that had ever served the city, and a vigorous campaign had been underway to recruit more.

"We need more police and stronger backing from the community," the mayor said. "We're the Number One murder city in the country and we have to do everything in our power to turn things around—even if it means increasing taxes. We'll just have to bite the bullet. This was a police officer doing his job."

Why, reporters demanded, were two rookies assigned to patrol Miami's most dangerous district?

Police spokesman Michael Stewart said that it wasn't unusual for two rookies to be paired on patrol. "With our shortage of personnel this is inevitable," he said.

The police chief explained that Broom, in spite of his brief time on the force, wasn't really considered a rookie. As a 15-year-old youth, Broom had served as a Police Explorer Scout. He'd also served as a military policeman and had attended a Savannah, Georgia police academy before joining Miami PD.

"He was a fine young officer," the chief said. "To have him killed was a tragic loss to the department, his family, and the community."

Nathaniel Broom had been a Police Explorer Scout, a former Army military police officer and a graduate of Jackson High School. Broom was described as a quiet, dedicated man who "wanted to be a cop most of his life. After Broom became an officer fourteen months ago, he wanted to go back and encourage other young Explorers with his story of police work. Only he never lived to tell it."

His short career had been so outstanding that he was scheduled to become a training officer in the next academy class.

"He was a good cop, one of the most progressive black officers that we've had," a spokesman said.

TV and newspaper accounts that day reported many comments of his fellow officers: "It's something we know can happen any day, but you're never prepared for it," said one. "You never expect it to happen, especially at 9:30 in the morning."

"When it's another police officer who's shot, you know it could have been you," said Metro Officer Jack Stevens. "All of us feel bad, especially for a young officer, when we're trying to recruit new officers."

Another officer had a solemn thought: "If any good comes out of this kid dying, it will be that he saved some of these young guys because other cops will critique and learn from it."

As Broom lay dying at the end of the Overtown alleyway, his bulletproof vest hung in his locker at headquarters seven blocks away. Had he worn it, it could have saved his life.

Vests are available to all Miami officers but wearing them is not mandatory. Most officers on patrol in the heat of the day find them extremely uncomfortable. In Miami's heat, said the chief, "It's like wearing a rubber workout suit."

While all these statements were being given to the press, the multitude of officers were busy doing their duty. The VW Bug was gone over for latent prints. The other men who had escaped were described only as black men, possibly Jamaicans due to their Rastafarian hairdos, and were being sought. They left behind drug paraphernalia in the car.

It was soon discovered that the car had been stolen from the son of a well-known former Justice of the Peace.

Within five minutes of the shooting, a call had been received about another stolen car. The suspect had fled across I-95 to a laundromat where he pointed the gun at the head of the driver of a Delta 88 Oldsmobile and ordered the driver out and fled in the car.

A small black revolver was found in a dumpster outside the apartment house where the VW was stopped and another handgun was found blocks away near an expressway embankment.

"Finding guns in that neighborhood is not unusual," a police spokesman said. It was unknown if they were linked to the suspects. Dramatic events would later determine that they were unrelated to the shooting.

The entire Miami community was outraged at the murder of the young officer. Reporters interviewed Officer Broom's friends and neighbors. "Just the other night we were standing here talking," one said. "He knew there were people out there who would do anything. I would always tell him to be careful." He told how a few weeks earlier, Broom had to arrest a neighbor's son on robbery charges. "He felt bad but it was his job. He went and talked to the father so that he understood that."

Nathaniel Broom was three years old when his family moved into a neighborhood of neat, modern little stucco houses and after 20 years, everyone knew "Nay" Broom. "I've known him for eleven years," said a neighbor when she heard the tragic news. "He was a good boy. Oh my God, not Nay. I loved that boy like a son."

Major credit for the quick identification of the suspect went to a half-million-dollar Rockwell computer system put into service by the Miami police six months earlier.

Forty-eight minutes after the shooting, fingerprints lifted from the interior and exterior of the Volkswagen Beetle originally stopped by Broom were fed into the computer. It instantly compared the prints with literally hundreds of thousands on file.

In minutes, the computer spit out the name of Robert Patten, arrested the previous March on auto theft charges.

Such a feat would be "a lifetime task for a fingerprint technician who compares prints by hand," the chief said. "That machine is phenomenal. There is no way ID technicians could have searched out that information and got it."

With the name of the suspect, it was a simple matter for sleuths to show Patten's photo to witnesses who identified the skinny six-foot, 120-pound suspect as the gunman.

In the hours that followed, more witnesses came forward and talked freely to police. As many as 20 to 25 others walked into police headquarters unsolicited to offer information. "They were absolutely terrific," said Lieutenant Robert Murphy.

"From them we were able to put together the story of how the officer was killed and how the killer got away," the chief said.

Knowing the suspect's identity, appearance, and former arrest record plus the fantastic cooperation of an incensed community, it would be only hours before the police captured the killer of one of their comrades.

What kind of man was Robert Patten? It would be hours before they really understood the man they looked for.

Patten was three when his father died and he moved to Miami. The mother remarried and Robert went to live with his grandparents. He resented the separation, but the grandfather treated him well, flying him to Mexico City or to Disney World to celebrate birthdays. When the child was six, the grandfather died.

At eight, Patten's hip bones began to deteriorate. He spent a year confined in a body cast from the rib cage to his feet, unable to move. "He couldn't do anything," said a relative who was afraid to be named because of the community outrage over Broom's murder. "It definitely affected Bobby."

He was popular in junior high school but with the wrong crowd. Relatives say he was involved with drugs and he was brash, reckless, often in trouble. "He liked to swipe cars," the relative said. "When he was sixteen and they wouldn't let him get a driver's license because of the trouble he was in, he got worse."

Court records show when he was 14 he used drugs excessively, including LSD, heroin, cocaine, and STP; he also sniffed glue and transmission fluid.

In 1975, the 17-year-old Patten and a friend held up a store using an emergency flare gun. He was caught, convicted and received a suspended sentence.

When he was sentenced to eight years in prison for armed robbery when he was 18, court records say he escaped from a road gang in Gainesville, was caught three months later in Homestead, Florida driving a stolen car. At that time he was found not guilty by reason of insanity and was committed to South Florida State Hospital. Records show he wasn't released until early in 1980.

"They let him out," one of his friends said, "but he wasn't cured. He was never right."

Patten then got a job as an electrician with a construction company in Palm Beach but went off to a rock concert in Miami one day and never returned to work. One rainy day while hitchhiking in Miami, he got picked up by a struggling rock musician who introduced him to his drummer. The drummer invited his new friend to live with the family, his mother and sister. "There's been nothing but trouble ever since," said the mother. Her divorced daughter was lonely.

The daughter said: "Yes I was lonely, and I felt drawn to him because I felt he needed somebody to take care of him. He was romantic. He would write love songs and sing them to me and accompany himself on the guitar." She described him as a gentle man who went to the park and played John Denver songs on his guitar for the children. "And he seemed so aware of everything going on around him, but I guess that was just his paranoia."

Over the past four years, doctors described Patten as suffering from "a chronic major psychiatric illness" and an "anti-social personality with immature-dependent characteristics."

Basically that meant that without warning and without provocation, Bobby Patten would explode. He pounded doors. He smashed mirrors. He hurled his black dog against the wall across the room. He fought his friends. He beat his lover.

And just as suddenly, he would grow quiet.

"He'd go crazy and the next minute, he'd be sorry," said his girlfriend. He brought medical books home. "He tried to psychoanalyze himself but you can't do that," she said. "He was sick. He needed help.

"He was taking a lot of drugs in all kinds of combinations," said the girlfriend. "He started getting paranoid. He'd come into the house and close all the windows and blinds. He'd have these flare-ups of anger and he'd be hollering at everybody, and we'd fight about nothing right out of the blue. He had this terrible fear of being confined. He'd get picked up for traffic violations and he'd always run from the police. He told me that when he was little, he had this disease that made his bones soft, so they put him in a body cast. The only thing he could move was his hands, and that's when he learned to play guitar. That could be why he was so afraid of being penned up."

A year before Broom's shooting, Patten got worse. He became aggressive and mean. "My daughter's a religious woman, and we kept praying that he would change," the mother said. "We watched religious television programs and listened to religious radio stations. When she had their little girl, we thought that might change him."

It didn't. The daughter noticed other troubling tendencies. "If a policeman tried to stop him, even if everything was legal, he would run," she said. "He was more afraid that he would be locked up than anything."

Patten indeed made a habit of running from the police. Sometimes he escaped, but a year before Broom's death, he was arrested for fleeing a police officer, resisting arrest with violence, aggravated assault, reckless driving, carrying a concealed weapon and leaving the scene of an accident. The cases had not been adjudicated.

Patten's emotional state grew uglier during the four months prior to Broom's killing. "Something clicked," a relative said. "I think he still knew right from wrong, but he just didn't care what happened to him anymore. He just didn't care."

Patten's 23-year-old girlfriend later said: "All I can

say to that officer's family is that I'm sorry. I had nothing to do with it, but I hope God blesses the rest of that family. I read in the paper that his sister wanted to be a police officer. I would tell her not to get involved in that. It just seems like things are getting worse and worse and worse. There are sick people all over."

She said Patten was one of those sick people, and the courts had agreed. But psychiatric illness is not necessarily the same as legal insanity in a homicide investigation.

Shortly after the suspect was identified and shortly before the huge manhunt ended in an arrest, the police chief expressed his "heartfelt appreciation and personal thanks to the community" for overwhelming assistance during the manhunt.

Then the chief broadcast this message over police radio 45 minutes before the suspect was arrested:

"I implore all officers to exercise care and prudence in the discharge of their duty. For this above all shall be the most symbolic way to memorialize the loss of a fallen comrade."

Patten had given motels in the southwest section as addresses at the time of previous arrests. The most recent was for grand theft when Patten was charged with stealing a van and leading police on a 100-mph chase on Florida 112. He was arrested when he overturned the van at the toll booth.

Investigators had checked out several motels where Patten had stayed at various times, one where he and his lover had been evicted just two weeks previously.

"I told him he had to leave," said the manager. She said Patten was in a rage, had ripped the furniture and walls of the little apartment, and had broken doors and windows. "And he beat everyone. We were afraid he was going to kill the girl's brother. He was a crazy man. He didn't look normal. He would walk all night around and around and then he would start running like crazy. Sometimes he could be a very nice person, and then his personality would change, right away in a minute."

The sleuths checked the latest address and learned Patten's girlfriend had tried to break off the relationship.

They'd checked with the motel manager. "He came to visit his family, I guess, or to get drugs he had hidden there," she said. "I kicked him out last year. He stole things and damaged the furniture. I tried to help him, but I didn't want him around.

"The police came and showed me his picture and asked if I had seen him. I said, 'Yes, I have his family in 212.' "

Early that morning, he'd come by the family's new apartment and had beaten her. He hadn't stopped until her brother and another man threatened him. "Then he just wanted to go inside and sleep like nothing had ever happened," a witness commented to them.

The manager said Patten came by the motel after the shooting a few hours before his capture. "He looked normal. He didn't look like someone who had just killed a man."

"If he killed the policeman, I don't think he did it to kill a man," the girlfriend said. "I think he did it because he was afraid that this time he couldn't get away. He was so worried about his freedom."

Police staked out the building, hoping he would appear. At 5:15 P.M., the stakeout paid off.

Fifty undercover and uniformed Miami police armed with shotguns and snarling German Shepherds were waiting for Patten at the motel when he returned to visit his girlfriend and infant daughter.

"There were at least 50 policemen pointing their shotguns at him," said a businessman who witnessed the capture from his office next door. "He came around the block with his dog. At least 15 officers surrounded him with their guns drawn. He continued to struggle and they threw him on the ground. Plainclothes police were waiting in the building across the street. They were everywhere."

"He tried to run and they tackled him," said Sergeant Jack Sullivan. "We felt good about the arrest and lucky. It was a combination of the cooperation from the community and the fingerprints found in several places in the car."

Another gun was found in weeds near the motel where Patten was arrested. It later proved unrelated to the crime. The stolen Oldsmobile was found at 7:00 p.m. at an apartment building several blocks from the motel where he was arrested.

Police had already ascertained that Patten was well-known to Overtown drug dealers. "We believe he and the other two men were there for a drug transaction," said Lieutenant Robert Murphy.

The two men who had left the scene were located. Police determined that they should not be charged as accomplices in the killing.

"I was satisfied we had the killer," said Murphy. "We had people who recognized him and saw all portions of it, including Broom's partner, Terry Russell, who identified Patten. We felt very confident about the case." Patten was charged with first-degree murder, armed robbery, and gun violations in what Murphy called a "picture perfect case."

"We have several witnesses who saw the guy running and heard the shots," said Miami policeman Mike Stewart.

The suspect was under arrest within eight hours

after the murder of Officer Nathaniel Broom, but there were loose ends to tie up. The major one was to locate the murder weapon, identified by tests as a .38 Smith & Wesson.

Since it was such a "hot" gun due to the massive publicity which surrounded the case throughout the day on local TV, the police surmised the culprit might have sold it, or tried to. Because of the outstanding co-operation they were getting from citizens, the detectives had even offered to reimburse anyone who might have purchased it after the slaying. Their offer was widely publicized in the media and on the streets through every cop on both the Dade County and City of Miami police departments.

"I'm sure whoever bought it did not know it was just used to murder a policeman," Miami Homicide Sergeant Ernest Vivian announced to the public. "You have a chance to turn in the weapon, get your money back and do a service to the community by giving us the weapon. I'll definitely see that they are reimbursed for the funds they spent."

It was especially fitting that Homicide Sergeant Ernest Vivian and Detective Richard Bohan, the detectives who found Officer Broom dying and tried in vain to save him moments after the shooting, were the same men who found the gun. They had relentlessly pursued the case from the start.

In retracing Patten's footsteps between the time of the Overtown shooting and his arrest, the detectives learned that Patten had stopped at his grandmother's home.

"He came to the house, changed his clothes, got cleaned up, then left," Sergeant Vivian said.

Judge James Henderson met the detectives at the Metro police building during the night and signed a search warrant they had prepared.

The woman "was cooperative and concerned about the events of the last couple of days," Vivian said.

They diligently searched the room used by Patten whenever he stayed with her. They took some clothing as evidence but found no trace of the missing gun.

Then the alert investigators noticed something odd as they walked out of the room. "We felt a difference in the flooring," Sergeant Vivian said. They lifted a throw rug. Beneath it was a piece of cardboard which covered an old heating vent. "And inside, underneath the grating was the gun silently sitting there, waiting to tell its own story," recalled Bohan with satisfaction.

The five-shot revolver had been wiped clean but it still had two live rounds in the cylinder. Three shots had been fired at Officer Broom and he had been hit twice. The third grazed his belt buckle. That left two. They were still in the gun, which lab tests proved to be the murder weapon.

"We're all extremely happy to be able to put the last piece in the puzzle," Vivian said. "Now it's just up to the courts."

On September 23rd, Patten appeared in court, dressed in green baggy trousers, a T-shirt and plaid work shirt, in leg irons. The courtroom was packed with blue uniforms but he didn't turn to look at the policemen. He faced a robbery charge stemming from the taking of the getaway car found within three blocks of his grandmother's home. According to Assistant State Attorney David Waksman, Patten stole the 1978 brown Oldsmobile at gunpoint from its owner a few blocks and a few moments after he had fired the fatal shot that felled Broom. Patten pleaded not guilty to the armed robbery charge while awaiting action by the Dade grand jury for the first-degree murder of Broom.

On February 3rd, the grand jury indicted Patten for Broom's murder.

On the third day of the murder trial, on February 19, 1982, witnesses told of seeing Broom chasing Patten and of seeing Patten flee the alleyway across Interstate 95 to a laundromat. There he held up a washer-dryer repairman and stole his brown Oldsmobile.

Waksman called more than 30 witnesses to piece together the incident. There were more than 85 exhibits, ranging from the bullet fragment that passed through Broom's heart to blown-up aerial photos of the location.

The defense conceded Patten carried the gun with the intention of selling it that day to buy drugs, but claimed that there was no time for Patten to premeditate the murder; that he shot Broom in the heat of the moment. The State contended Patten shot the policeman because he was on probation and facing five years in prison if captured driving in a stolen car and carrying a weapon.

On March 4, 1982, Robert Lester Patten was found guilty of the first degree murder of Officer Nathaniel Broom. He was given the death penalty.

Then the justice machine slipped a cog.

The judge made a mistake when the jury, after finding the defendant guilty, couldn't decide on the death penalty and he told them to continue deliberations. This was not required by the law in such cases, and Patten's case was appealed.

A higher court reviewed the matter and upheld the guilty verdict but set aside the mandatory death penalty. The claustrophobic defendant who "couldn't stand to lose his freedom" was sentenced to a lifetime behind bars in a prison cell with no parole.

"THE BLOOD OF
FOUR COPS!"
by Krist Boardman

Little did Officer Robert F. Pyles suspect that September 18, 1986, would be his last day alive. The possibility of a life-threatening incident dogs every police officer during the waking hours of his career, but Officer Pyles had less reason to be concerned than most officers — he worked for a specialized force in Maryland called the Toll Facilities Police. For such officers, work is usually a specialized form of traffic patrol. Something highly unusual would have to happen for that kind of routine to be changed.

Something highly unusual did happen.

The Susquehanna River Bridge on U.S. Route 40, only recently renamed the Thomas J. Hatem Memorial Bridge in honor of a recently deceased politician, spans the Susquehanna River and connects Harford and Cecil Counties in Maryland. It's an aging structure, and because most of the interstate traffic crosses on nearby I-95, it's a secondary thoroughfare for mostly local traffic.

Unexpectedly at about 8:15 P.M., a white step van rolled out into traffic from a parking area on the northeast-bound side of the bridge. It careened cross the two lanes and struck a concrete median barrier and stopped. Immediately it attracted the attention of local police, who arrived to investigate.

Havre de Grace Patrolman Dennis Rittershofer was the first to arrive at the scene of the step van. He was joined immediately by Harford County Sheriff's Deputy Stephen O. Wagner, who was serving civil papers at the time and stopped by to assist. Both officers noticed that the van was unoccupied by anyone at the time. They ran a check on the van's New York plates and discovered that it was listed as a stolen vehicle.

A closer examination of the van also revealed that ignition wires had been torn out.

At another point on the span, Officer Pyles was driving westbound. He had heard the radio report of the step van accident and as the officer with jurisdiction, he was going to the scene. But on his way he noticed a slightly built young man walking across the bridge. Because there is no pedestrian walkway on the bridge and it is illegal to cross on foot, Pyles suddenly changed his immediate plans. He might also have thought that the pedestrian had something to do with the abandoned vehicle.

Since the man was heading in the opposite direction, Officer Pyles swung his patrolcar around and drove up behind him. He told the pedestrian to get into the patrolcar, since walking was not allowed. The man got into the rear seat of the vehicle. At this time Officer Pyles' vehicle was approached by one driven by an Officer Squires, who asked Pyles if he needed help. Pyles replied that he did not, but Squires assisted the pedestrian into the rear of Pyles' car and then he left in his own car.

At this point there is some question as to what happened, as the main witness, Officer Pyles, never got a chance to give his version. The pedestrian said that he heard a report over the officer's radio that the step van was listed as stolen; however, interviews with numerous officers involved fail to confirm that a single one recalled this information being radioed. Whether the pedestrian simply came to this conclusion himself, whether he decoded a cryptic radio code broadcast by the police, or whether he was simply anticipating what would soon become general knowledge anyway — is not known.

The pedestrian decided that the free ride across the bridge was not exactly what he wanted, and opted for his freedom. This was not quite so easily attained because there were no door handles inside, and because there was a wire screen separating the front and rear seats. The pedestrian then drew a gun and held it to the back of Officer Pyles' head, through the screen, telling him to keep driving. As Pyles was attempting to make a U-turn on the bridge, the gun was fired.

Officer Pyles' car smashed into the concrete barrier, and because it was still in gear, it continued to roll along the barrier. Bleeding profusely in the head, there was nothing that Pyles could do to control the car, nor was there anything that the pedestrian could do.

Soon after, Havre de Grace Patrolman Dennis Rittershofer pulled up in his car. He was joined by Deputy Wagner, who had an auxiliary police officer and another civilian in his car. Because of the blood and the accident, initially these officers thought that Pyles had had a heart attack, causing him to crash, or that he had crashed and was injured. At the same time the passenger was screaming, "Get me out of here!"

Deputy Wagner unlocked the screen between the two seats, and as he and Officer Rittershofer unlocked one of the rear doors, the passenger banged it open with his feet and jumped out of the car. He surprised both Wagner and Rittershofer by opening fire. He shot Rittershofer in the head and Wagner in the arm before fleeing into the night.

Soon after, Sergeant Rimel from the Havre de Grace Police Department arrived. Two eyewitnesses who were in Wagner's car told him what happened and the sergeant radioed for backup assistance and medical help. Soon after, Maryland State Police helicopters arrived to evacuate Officers Pyles and Rittershofer to the Maryland Shock Trauma Unit in Baltimore. Wagner, meanwhile, was taken to a nearby hospital in Havre de Grace.

By this time the discovery of the stolen van was beginning to yield additional information about the possible suspect. Frank Green, 27, was employed by the company that owned the van when both he and the van were suddenly absent.

The Far Rockaway, New York resident was also no stranger to law enforcement circles. Earlier that same year, in January, Green had been released on parole from Attica Prison where he had served five years of an armed robbery sentence. At the time of this incident, he was also wanted for questioning in connection with the brutal daylight rape and attempted murder of a woman in Far Rockaway.

Three weeks earlier, a woman had been attacked in daylight, dragged under the boardwalk, raped and assaulted. She sustained five stab wounds to the abdomen and her throat was slit, and she was left for dead.

But miraculously she survived. And Frank Green was wanted by New York authorities in connection with this crime, too.

If police knew who the suspect was most likely to be, they had less idea of where to find him. After dashing off into the dark, he was last spotted near a fast-food restaurant. And then he disappeared into the deserted streets of Havre de Grace.

Police barricaded the few approaches that there were to the 350-year-old town by road.

The police had the advantage of geography, and knowledge of the terrain and town. They also had the advantage of superior numbers, for by this time the forces of the Harford County Sheriff's Department, the Havre de Grace, Bel Air and Aberdeen town police departments, the Maryland State Police, and even officers from neighboring states such as Delaware and Pennsylvania, joined in the search.

For nearly 12 hours the chase through the streets went on — one against many. Hundreds of sightings were reported by Havre de Grace residents, who were terrorized by the prospect of a paroled convict with a gun, and who were hardly reassured by the constant activity of uniformed police. Overhead, police choppers circled incessantly, invisible but for running lights and never-ending search beams, their thwacking sounds reverberating throughout the neighborhoods. The town was as if it were in the heart of a war zone, as the lawmen literally beat the bushes for their elusive and highly dangerous quarry.

Once during the night, the Maryland State Police discovered that Green was still there, somewhere among them.

The police had called Green's father, a minister in North Carolina, and told him that his son was in trouble and that he should report his whereabouts to the authorities. Minutes later, young Green called and told his father that he had shot three police officers. This information was reported back to the police.

At the same time, the Harford County Sheriff's Department was doing a search of the road and surrounding area where the officers had been shot. These were not ideal conditions, as a light rain was falling and except for what light was manufactured artificially, there was total darkness.

The search on the ground did turn up a few things, but ultimately they were of little help. A spent bullet was found on the road; according to evidence technicians, it seemed to be the one that passed through Rittershofer's head. Then there was the van and Officer Pyles' car, and the blood on the asphalt . . . but still there was no Frank Green.

Patrolman First Class Charles Briggs III was the next of Green's victims to fall. He was searching the dark neighborhood not far from the fast-food restaurant where Green was last seen when suddenly Green bounded over a chain-link fence and shot him in the back of the head. Briggs fell without even seeing his assailant.

"I don't know what to think," one resident told a newspaper reporter. "I've never seen anything like this happen here before. I'm a Korean veteran, so I'm not scared. I'm just surprised something like this could happen here. In the twenty-two years I've lived here, we've never experienced something like this."

Havre de Grace Police Chief Earl Walker arrived on the scene and was shocked, particularly over the carnage of police officers.

"This is the saddest and worst day in all my years of policing," he said. "In my twenty-five years as chief here, no one has ever been shot."

Green had commandeered a Moped in the early hours of the morning before daybreak, but his efforts to get out of the town were thwarted by the bottling up of the exits by police units. So he abandoned the Moped and tried something else.

A handyman and his wife were up most of the night, listening to their police monitor. As dawn approached, the handyman went outside to his truck and was unlocking the driver's door when he saw the fugitive appear nearby with a gun pointed at him. The shirtless man put the barrel of the gun to the handyman's head and said: "I'm in trouble. I want to go to Baltimore. Drive me there."

The handyman drove him off in his 1984 pickup truck. The truck picked up speed and crossed two police roadblocks, but as it did the police began a hot pursuit.

Suddenly the handyman jammed his foot on the brakes, flinging Frank Green forward into the windshield. The handyman pushed the gun away and when the truck stopped, Frank Green was off and running, a hail of police bullets behind him and now he had no gun of his own.

Only a few minutes later another young man was interrupted in bed by the fugitive. Lying with his wife and young six-week-old daughter, the man found that Frank Green was trying to commandeer his car and a shirt.

"I didn't have time to be scared," said the man. "I just did what he said because I wanted to get him out of there."

He followed Green outside to his 1973 Plymouth Satellite and watched him start up the car, but not after being invited to join in the ride.

"I said I didn't want any part of it and he took off."

It was almost 6:30 A.M. on Revolution Street, near Juniata, when Green rammed through a police roadblock.

"I was near my house and I saw the blue car come up to police," said one nearby resident. "Then I saw police step back from the car and it sped away with them firing at it."

The police firepower was enough to kill the car, but the suspect kept fleeing. The car rammed into a sign, its windshield blown out and otherwise a total wreck.

But the end of the road for Frank Green was near.

Surrounded by police officers in all directions, Green dashed through a house, again eluding a hail of police lead. Then he went out the back door. He was spotted again, and another police blast felled him. He was trapped on the ground beside a pile of leaves. His hand was under the pile and he was told to remove it slowly. This he did, and when he did, his hand was empty.

He was cuffed and taken away.

Under the pile of leaves, Frank Green's gun was found. There were no bullets in it.

Unbelievably, there were no bullets in Frank Green. His only injury was a superficial wound to one of his legs. Even Green was amazed when it was all over.

Soon after, in the Harford County Detention Center, Green confided to a reporter that Havre de Grace confused him so that sometimes he found himself running after police cars that were supposed to be chasing him.

"I didn't know where to go," he said. "I was running and jumping and hiding. I was even following behind police cars to listen to their radios.

"I stopped a whole lot of times because I was tired. I stayed in a garage, in a truck, and in a car. I almost went to sleep (in the car) but something told me to get out."

When he found the Moped, "I never rode a Moped in my life. But I learned fast. I rode it for about two blocks and the police tried to run me over. I started running again."

After being disarmed by the handyman and escaping under a hail of gunfire, Green reflected: "I'm not trying to be smart, but (those) pistol experts and marksmen should have hit me a long time (before)."

Later, after fleeing from the blown-out Plymouth

and being cornered on the ground, he said he "wanted to get up and run, but everybody around me had real big guns. I thought they were going to kill me."

During the manhunt, he said he had wanted to die: "I think I wanted them to kill me. If I was dead, I wouldn't have these problems. I got to the point where I was so tired of doing everything. I even asked them (after his arrest) 'Why didn't you kill me?' I mean, that would have gotten things over with and we wouldn't have to go to court."

Frank Green's victims didn't get to go to court. One of them, Officer William Pyles of the Toll Facilities Police, died several days later in the hospital. He never got a chance to give his version of what happened.

Two other officers, Patrolmen Rittershofer and Briggs of Havre de Grace Police Department, miraculously survived despite head wounds. The more seriously injured of the two, Rittershofer, was assigned to civilian duty after recovering.

Deputy Stephen Wagner, injured in the arm, returned to work shortly after the incident.

In the days following the shootings, several more important details surfaced concerning Green's sojourn from New York.

In fleeing after his alleged rape and assault on the woman in Far Rockaway, New York, he had come to Baltimore looking for a relative. Though he never made contact with the relative, he drifted through the city.

"I really didn't do nothing around here," he told a reporter. "I stayed all over, most of the time in my (the stolen) van."

He said he was stopped by a policeman in Baltimore City after making an improper lane change. The officer let him go. Ironically, if the officer had checked out the vehicle, he would have found that it was stolen.

The gun he used in the shootings in Havre de Grace was arranged through a trade with a street person for some transportation. "I met this dude who wanted to go to New York to buy drugs. So I was going to drive him to New York and he was going to give me the gun.

"I never took him to New York, but I took the gun. It was so pretty. Real pretty."

On the night he started back, he was high on marijuana and he had only four dollars in his pocket, neither enough for gas nor for tolls.

Frank Green's trial was moved out of Harford County to Anne Arundel County, after his defense attorneys succeeded in winning a change of venue. In Anne Arundel County Circuit court, he was convicted of one count of murder and of kidnapping for Officer Pyles; use of a handgun in commission of a felony (murder); three convictions for attempted murder of the officers; plus a number of other charges.

In prosecuting the case, Harford County State's Attorney Joseph I. Cassilly pursued the death penalty for Green. The defense succeeded in having a separate jury selected for this purpose and also in having the sentencing phase removed to Anne Arundel County.

In January of 1988 a public defender attached to Frank Green's defense, Gary Christopher, contacted Mr. Cassilly to request that the death penalty bid of the prosecutor be dropped.

"As far as I'm concerned there has never been a defendant who deserved the death penalty more than this one," Mr. Cassilly commented.

But the defenders had gotten a ruling that prevented the specially seated jury from hearing anything except the details of Officer Pyles' murder. In late April 1988, the panel heard about the abused childhood of Green, but nothing about the other 25 counts on which he had been convicted.

Even so, the panel was divided and nearly hopelessly deadlocked on whether to impose the death sentence. Because of this, they voted for life imprisonment.

It was only after they had returned to the courtroom that they heard about the other crimes.

Some of the jurors appeared stunned by this development. The jury foreman commented, "I feel used."

However, it should be said that even where the death sentence has been imposed since Maryland's reinstitution of the supreme penalty, it has actually been carried out.

Frank Green received a series of extremely stiff penalties, in accumulated time. Judge Robert H. Heller, Jr. imposed four life sentences plus an additional 225 years on the 28-year-old convict. According to one tabulation, Green would have to be 101 years old to be eligible for parole.

"Mr. Green will be severely punished," said Jerome Deise, another of the defendant's court-appointed lawyers. "It is a civil death sentence."

On the prosecution side, Mr. Cassilly was still fuming. "Some day I'm going to get over this. Frank Green is going to wake up every morning and think that his lawyer screwed up.

"I can't think why keep a guy alive. The only thing I can think is we don't have the guts (to carry out the death sentence) . . . I'm sorry but I don't understand why we are saving these people.

"Prison is going to kill him slowly and surely. It may be harder initially to put the beast to sleep than to watch it happen slowly."

"MAN DOWN! AND IT'S A COP!"

by Bud Ampolsk

Once it had been a place of laughter and crowds and the spirited hijinx of high-spirited college kids. And there are still a number of senior citizens who remember it that way.

They can tell you about the autumnal Saturday afternoons when the crowds came rambling up the hill from the Jerome Avenue IRT elevated line and the East IND "D" Line. The smartly uniformed military band could already be heard inside the campus gates blaring out its spirited rendition of "Oh Grim Gray Palisades." The festive students, purple and white pennants held high above their heads, accompanied by their chrysanthemum-adorned dates hurried across the wide avenue. They dodged the yellow and red trolleys and made their way up the great stone steps, past Nichols Hall and into storied Ohio Field.

Soon their beloved "Violets" would race onto the gridiron to take such eastern juggernauts as Lafayette or Lehigh, or archrival Fordham.

Those who lived on University Avenue, a stone's throw away from the magnificent Stanford White-designed Bronx Campus of New York University, felt

211

their own pulse quicken. They felt very much a part of the educational community.

Those with long memories can even recall the torch-light parade which marked the end of the first half of the fall semester. It was quite an event. On that evening, hundreds of pajama-clad NYU freshmen would march down University Avenue, around the school's campus and through a gauntlet of paddles-swinging sophomores. There they would go through the time-honored rites of acceptance. These consisted of being completely immersed into the Fountain of Knowledge — (an ancient horse trough) and racing pell-mell and dripping wet through the lines of their anxious but good-natured upperclassmen tormentors.

Having survived the ordeal, the yearlings knew that all the tribulations of hazing were now behind them. From now on they'd be recognized as full-fledged scholars.

The event was not a campus thing alone. Literally hundreds of the residents of University Avenue came out to lend their vocal support to the quaking youngsters.

Then things changed, NYU could no longer afford the luxury of its Bronx Campus. The plant was sold off to the Bronx Community College (run by the City of New York). NYU consolidated its classes into its Washington Square branch.

University Avenue changed as well. The neatly kept six-story apartment houses which lined it became progressively more shabby. Although some of the old-timers continued living there, they now felt themselves under siege.

Where the long-term residents had never thought twice about going for evening strolls and mixing with the college kids, they now barricaded themselves behind locked doors in terror of the drug traffickers who

212

had taken over their streets.

Violence became an ugly fact of life.

For example, there was what happened at the corner of 181st Street and University Avenue on Thursday, May, 1986. It was at 11:00 A.M. on that day that the body of a "mystery woman," her life snuffed out by a bullet in her skull, was discovered in an abandoned park building just outside the Community College campus.

Nobody could be sure how the body of the slim and attractive girl had gotten there. All they knew was that she was dressed in a white sweater which was stained with blood, and a pair of light blue jeans. She was lying sprawled on a discarded bed in a debris-strewn room of the ramshackle house.

According to investigating detectives, witnesses had told them the woman had been chased into the area by three white or Hispanic men in the early morning hours.

The woman had been seen trying to get away from her assailants. However, her body had lain undiscovered for several hours before a passerby notified the police about it. The blotter showed the time of the notification to be 11:00 A.M.

Best estimates were that the unidentified woman had been dead for at least six hours prior to the time that the authorities arrived on the scene.

The neighborhood in which the grisly discovery was made was a known haven for drug dealers. But detectives working on the case refused to comment on whether narcotics had played any part in the girl's murder.

They did say, however, that robbery had been ruled out, despite the fact that the unidentified young woman's pocketbook had been found next to the bed on which her body rested.

213

The dead woman's assailants were described as wearing bright-colored clothes. One was said to have been wearing army fatigue pants, as well.

Despite an exhaustive probe into the slaying of the young woman, her murder remains unsolved at this writing.

The homicide, as well as numerous other drug-related violent incidents along University Avenue, pointed up the feeling of terror on the part of its residents and the sense of frustration that gripped lawmen assigned to the area.

Many of the young people who had moved away from the area could not enjoy their new and more secure surroundings. This, because they still had fears concerning the welfare of older relatives who remained behind. Although the various ethnic groups were mostly hardworking and live-and-let-live types who got along well with neighbors, the influx of drug dealers and their desperate customers cast a continuing pall over the streets adjacent to University Avenue.

Twenty-six-year-old Michael Reidy was one of those to whom family solidarity was a paramount consideration. A man of total loyalty and imbued with the spirit of family love, he recognized where his responsibilities lay.

Reidy had many reasons to be happy as he crunched through the season's first major snow drifts on the afternoon of Friday, January 24, 1987. He had just celebrated his first anniversary in the New York City Police Department. Eighteen days earlier he'd just received his permanent assignment to the 41st Precinct in the South Bronx. Now he was in a good position to look after his mother. He also now had a steady girlfriend.

The good times for the soft-spoken and caring young policeman had been especially welcome since they had followed a series of family tragedies which left an indelible mark.

There had been the accidental death of his sister, Eileen, two years earlier. Just two weeks before the day on which she was to have been married, Eileen had choked to death on a piece of food which had lodged in her throat. She had been buried on her 27th birthday.

Then, a scant year later, Michael Reidy's father had died of a heart attack.

Knowing the suffering his mother had undergone as a result of the two deaths, Michael had decided to move back into the Reidy family apartment on University Avenue. In that way, he would be in a position to look after her as well as to offer her the companionship which meant so much to her.

Friday, January 23rd, was a good day to be off duty. Just a day before, a howling northeaster had come swirling into the Metropolitan Area. It had dumped from 8 to 16 inches of wind-drifted snow, semi-paralyzing the city.

Undaunted by the deep freeze weather, Reidy had made the most of his day off thus far. In the morning, he'd dropped into the 41st Precinct stationhouse at Simpson Street to pick up his paycheck, which covered two weeks in salary, and holiday overtime. Then he'd returned to the University Avenue environs to cash the check and to tend to some weekend grocery shopping.

At 3:14 P.M., the outside chores completed, approximately $1,000 in his pocket (the proceeds of the cashed paycheck), carrying such items as the day's newspapers, and a supply of cigarettes, Michael Reidy turned into the lobby of the four-story University Avenue building where he shared a first-floor apartment with his mother.

Then it happened.

An elderly long-time resident of the four-story

building where the Reidys resided was in his first-floor rear apartment. He heard the sound of gunfire. Having become intensely aware of the way things happened in the West Bronx, he immediately went to his rear window in the belief that a drug firefight had erupted in the back alley.

To all who know their way around the neighborhood, the 80-year-old tenant's first reaction would have seemed entirely logical. Back yards along University Avenue offered cover for the comings and goings of the drug underworld. Here they remain free of the vigilance of anti-crime, anti-narcotics and quality-of-life patrols set up by the NYPD.

However, the witness saw no action through his window. Knowing that he hadn't imagined the afternoon gunfire, he made his way to the front door of his apartment and cautiously opened it.

Later, the unnerved octogenarian would recall, "I looked out in the hallway and saw a man crouched behind the door.

"He hollered at me, 'Call the cops! A man's been shot here!'

"So I called 911 (the police emergency number), but I didn't know who was involved. Then I went out and found out it was Michael Reidy, so I called back and told them it was one of their own."

Almost simultaneously, the police received a second call. This one came from another neighbor who was a nurse. The woman had arrived at the entrance to the apartment-house vestibule just moments after the shooting. She'd found her path blocked by a human body which was wedged behind the front door.

She gave this account of her immediate reaction: She tried to push the door open and in so doing had recognized the victim.

The nurse commented, "I thought to myself, 'Oh,

216

my! It's Michael. I'll call the police.' "

The "man down" alarm had now been amended to read "officer down" and brought an immediate response from units in the district.

Officers assigned to one of the first sector cars to arrive at University Avenue had but to take one look at the gravely wounded young cop to recognize what their prime responsibility would be.

As tenderly as they could under the dire circumstances, they lifted their unconscious comrade from the blood-drenched vestibule floor. They understood that time was of the essence and they could not afford the luxury of waiting for paramedics to roll up in a fully-equipped EMS ambulance.

They placed Reidy in their own police vehicle. With sirens undulating and red-and-white flashers gyrating madly, the police car raced towards the already alerted Emergency Room of North Central Bronx Hospital.

Meanwhile, plainclothes detectives, forensic specialists and uniformed officers crowded their way into the narrow confines of the crime-site lobby. They were under the command of Assistant Police Chief DeForrest Taylor and First Deputy Commissioner Richard Condon. Their task, tough as it might prove, would be to keep their own emotions under tight rein as they went about the grim job of determining what had happened and why it had happened.

As the chalk marks were drawn to outline the exact position where the 26-year-old probationary patrolman had fallen, it became immediately apparent that Reidy had had just enough time to draw his own .38-caliber off-duty revolver and empty it at his assailant before sinking to the floor.

Of course, at this extremely preliminary stage of the investigation, it could not be said with any finality that the perp had not wrested the revolver from the off-duty cop and turned it on him. Such evidence would have to wait a ballistics analysis of the bullet which had caused the grievous wound in Reidy's chest.

As they concentrated on assembling physical pieces of evidence, assigned officers to canvass potential witnesses and dispatched lawmen to the unhappy job of notifying Reidy's next of kin, they waited for late word as to the wounded young man's condition to come from North Central Bronx Hospital.

It came within the hour. Prepared as they might have been for it, the grim-faced lawmen felt the numb shock and sense of personal loss that came with it. Michael Reidy, aged 26, a quiet man with a sense of responsibility and values which could only be described as outstanding, had died while undergoing surgery for the single gunshot wound he had received to the chest.

After sorting out the bits and scraps of viable evidence discovered in the vestibule and its immediate surroundings and the added comments of shocked but eager-to-cooperate neighbors, those in charge of the early moments of what had within the hour become a murder probe, were able to come up with this sequence of events:

According to First Deputy Commissioner Condon, Reidy indeed had collected his paycheck at the Simpson Street Station. The slain patrolman had also cashed the check. However, none of the $1,000 which represented the two weeks' pay covered by the city check was missing.

Despite this fact, Assistant Police Chief Taylor felt robbery had been the murderer's prime motivation for having shot Reidy.

Said Taylor, "He (Reidy) was coming back from a store and we believe he was followed in. He had cigarettes and newspapers with him. He did not get into the apartment."

Manuel Salazar

Officer Brian Chappell

Funeral of Officer Brian Chappell

"Spiderman" Norberto Pietri

Officer Gary Stymiloski

Alex Mengel

Robert Patton

Officer Nathaniel Broom

Detective Brian Orchard

Trooper Philip Lamonaco

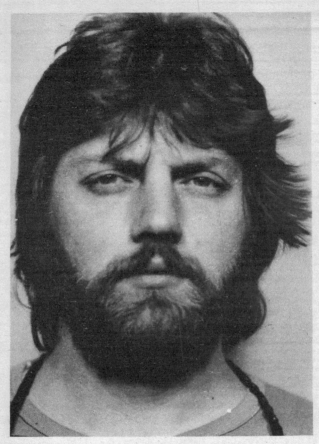

Richard Williams

Thomas William Manning

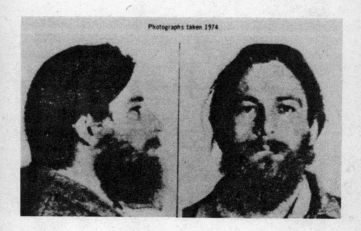

Photographs taken 1974

Eugene Gonzales

Thomas Martinez, left, with his attorney,
Paul Geragos

Trooper Mark Phebus

WANTED FOR THE MURDER
OF A TEXAS DPS TROOPER

5-12-83

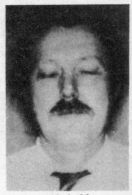

5-8-89

During the early morning hours of September 17, 1990, an off duty Texas Department of Public Safety Trooper noticed what appeared to be a traffic accident. The accident was an apparent domestic quarrel between a man and his wife. While attempting to assist the parties, the Trooper was shot in the head with a large caliber pistol.

Warrant number 0484, charging Murder (Willful Killing of a Police Officer), was issued on 9-17-90 in Montgomery County, Texas, for RICHARD LELAND JORDAN.

RICHARD LELAND JORDAN is described as a white male, DOB: 5-14-47, 6'0" tall, 190 pounds with black hair and blue eyes. JORDAN was last seen wearing a mustache, however, the mustache could be shaved at this time. He has Texas Drivers License number 0541 5209 listing an address of 22406 Sherrod Lane, Spring, Texas, and has a previous arrest in Harris County, Texas, for Murder.

JORDAN'S vehicle has been recovered and mode of travel is unknown at this time.

He has friends and relatives in the Houston, Texas, area and his family has a lake cabin near Carthage, Texas (Northeast Texas).

JORDAN should be considered <u>ARMED</u> and <u>DANGEROUS.</u>

Any information notify the Texas Department of Public Safety in Houston, Texas, at telephone number (713) 681-1761 or your nearest law enforcement agency.

FOR LAW ENFORCEMENT USE ONLY

Wanted poster for Richard Leland Jordan

From bullet fragments found on the entrance floor, it now seemed likely that Reidy had not been shot with his own off-duty five-shot revolver, but that whoever had killed him had been prepared for an armed robbery when he accosted the young officer.

Such a technique was not uncommon among the street perps who infiltrated drug-ravaged neighborhoods, it was said.

It could also be said with a feeling of assurance that Reidy had squeezed off all five shots in his pistol before losing consciousness. One shot had shattered the glass pane of the front door of the building.

What the investigating officers wanted desperately at this point was a meaningful eyewitness description of the wanted gunman. But none was available.

With summoned relatives arriving in a state of grief that touched the hearts of policemen and onlookers alike, what was being learned now was the enormity of the loss felt by those who had been associated with Michael Reidy.

Commented one cop who could not staunch the flow of his own tears, "He (Reidy) became a cop to help his mother to get out of here."

The officer, who preferred to remain anonymous, recalled that he and Reidy had attended the Police Academy together. The two young lawmen had lived within blocks of each other.

"He's (Reidy) a real street-wise guy, but coming from this neighborhood, he had to be," the officer noted. It was obvious that the grieving man felt it difficult to speak of his friend in the past tense.

Others recalled how much being a cop had meant to the slain officer. They talked of the day when he had graduated from the Police Academy.

Said one woman resident of the University Avenue building, "I remember his going to talk to my sister, saying he was so proud. He would say, 'I'm going to be a cop.' "

Others had known Reidy since he'd been a seven-year-old. That was when he and his family had moved into the building. They talked of his having graduated from St. Nicholas of Tolentine elementary and high schools, which were almost directly across the street from the eight-family building where he'd grown up. They said he'd gone on to college, but had dropped out because of his ambition to join the police force.

They said Reidy's life revolved around the police work. They pointed out that his girlfriend was a police officer who is assigned to the Police Academy. In addition a female cousin of the young patrolman was also on the force.

Investigating officers were now speculating as to whether any of the five shots which Reidy had fired had found their mark. It was possible that his assailant or assailants had been wounded in the vestibule crossfire.

With this in mind, word was flashed by the police to the admitting departments of all nearby hospitals to be on the lookout for anybody seeking treatment of an unexplained gunshot wound.

In hopes that someone would come forward to aid the lawmen in their search, the Patrolmen's Benevolent Association immediately offered a $10,000 reward for information leading to the arrest of Reidy's killer. Authorities set up two hotlines for handling incoming calls on the case. One was (212) 583-0144. The other was (212) 577-TIPS.

A civilian organization known as COPSHOT added its own $10,000 to the reward money being put forward by those seeking to bring Reidy's slayer to justice.

In the numbing cold of Saturday, January 24th, detectives prodded their way through mountainous snowdrifts which were the leftovers of Thursday's storm. The lawmen were using metal detectors in hopes of finding more fragments of shattered bullets.

Their interest in the ballistics aspects of the probe had been fanned by the findings of the Medical Examiner's Office.

An M.E. spokesman, in releasing the report of an autopsy performed on Reidy, noted that the patrolman's death had been caused by a single shot in the chest. The slug which had been recovered from the body was a .32-caliber bullet.

According to police spokesman Sergeant Edward Burns, authorities were now sure that Reidy had fired all five shots from his own off-duty .38-caliber revolver at the killer as the perp fled the murder scene on foot.

Said Burns, "We do know that the suspect fired one shot with his own gun and that the officer fired five shots. We don't know if the suspect was hit. We haven't found any trail of blood, but we still are looking."

The police alert to area hospitals to report anybody seeking treatment of gunshot wounds was still very much in effect. Thus far, cooperating medical centers had nothing to report.

The belief among detectives now was that the assailant had watched Reidy cash his paycheck and had subsequently followed the off-duty police officer to Reidy's University Avenue apartment. Because the 26-year-old victim's wallet had not been touched, it was thought that the robber had panicked.

Interviews of potential witnesses to the murder began to bear fruit for the investigators. As Saturday wore on, detectives began to put together a mental sketch of a young man whom passersby had put close to the murder scene around the time when Reidy had been mowed down.

Although at this point the police declined to characterize the man in question as either a suspect or a witness, they said they were interested in talking to him. Their feeling was that he might shed new light on the case.

Police artists were called in to prepare a composite sketch of the man. The drawing showed a Hispanic type, 20 to 23 years old, 5 feet 9 inches tall, and weighing approximately 190 pounds. The wanted man's build was stocky and he had brown eyes, black wavy hair, sideburns, a mustache and a dark complexion. He had been dressed in a black and green checked jacket, black jeans and white Reeboks with a red stripe when last seen.

For the moment, the cops were holding tight security on how they had developed the lead concerning the Hispanic.

However, it was recalled that on the day of the shooting, one resident of the University Avenue eight-family building had mentioned having seen a young man in the hallway who had told him that somebody had been shot and to call the police.

As the unrelenting probe into Reidy's murder went on, the family of the slain officer went about the sad task for making arrangements for his funeral. They remained in tight seclusion.

A funeral mass was scheduled for 10:30 A.M., Monday, January 26th, at St. Nicholas of Tolentine Church with burial to take place at Gate of Heaven Cemetery in Hawthorne, New York.

In nine-degree temperatures on Monday, more than 1,000 uniformed officers formed themselves into tight military ranks. They stood rigidly at attention in the slush of University Avenue as Reidy's casket was carried from the church. At a command, their white-gloved hands rose as one in a final salute to their fallen comrade.

It was noted that Reidy was the first cop to be shot dead during 1987 in New York City. But he was not the first to die. Officer Francis LaSale of the Emergency Service Unit had sacrificed his own life on January 10th of the new year when he'd braved a wall of flames to dash into a burning building in order to assist in rescue attempts.

Detectives assigned to the Reidy murder probe were now leaning to the theory that whoever had killed the officer probably had been out for a quick score in order to satisfy a craving for drugs. One investigator theorized that the man they were looking for might have been an outpatient at a Bronx hospital who had to augment the $500 a month Veteran's Administration pension he was receiving to support his narcotics habit.

The hoped-for break in the case occurred with startling suddenness just a few hours after Michael Reidy was laid to rest. It came with the strident ringing of one of the hotline telephones which had been set up.

The caller, who insisted on remaining anonymous, reported he had vital information to give.

Later, Chief of Detectives Robert Colangelo would describe the telephone conversation in these terms: "The caller said that a male known as 'Ski' was involved in the incident (The Reidy slaying). The suspect had gotten the nickname because of a series of robberies committed by a ski-masked stickup man."

Chief Colangelo would reveal how the suspect was identified by the informant as 23-year-old Angel Maldonado. Maldonado, the caller had said, lived with a family on West 190th Street.

A stake-out of the 190th Street address was hastily organized by Bronx detectives and uniformed officers.

Maldonado was taken into custody without incident.

However, the seemingly uneventful caller was to become something entirely different in the matter of a couple of hours.

The suspect was taken to the Cross Bronx Expressway stationhouse for interrogation.

At first, Maldonado appeared completely cooperative, according to police officials. He answered questions readily. There was nothing in his demeanor which caused any forebodings in the minds of the three detectives who were interrogating him. It is said that he made detailed statements. It is alleged that the suspect even went so far as to disclose where he had hidden the .32-caliber gun, which was considered as the key bit of evidence in the case.

(Later, Chief Colangelo would say that the weapon had been recovered in the apartment where Maldonado lived. Two other handguns were also found at the same location.)

So far everything was going according to routine. What happened next, according to Chief Colangelo, was anything but routine.

The high police officer noted that because the suspect had been so submissive and cooperative, interrogating officers had considered it unnecessary to handcuff him.

However, Maldonado's attitude allegedly changed when the detectives had asked him to repeat the statements he had already made to an assistant district attorney who was standing by.

The suspect is reported to have refused.

Taken aback by this development, three detectives, a woman police stenographer and the waiting A.D.A. met in the corridor of the Cross Bronx Expressway stationhouse, just outside the interrogation room.

Maldonado was said to have been momentarily

alone in the room, as the lawmen conferred.

Taking advantage of the lapse in security, the suspect allegedly raced for a nearby window. One detective made a desperate move to grapple with Maldonado, but lost his grip.

The agile suspect then leapt 13 feet through the window to a parking lot below. He landed on both feet running and took off.

Explaining the lapse in security, Chief Colangelo said, "He (Maldonado) had been cooperating and making statements. There was no reason to believe he would escape."

Others said the first inkling the police had that the suspect allegedly had escape on his mind was when they heard the interrogation-room window being opened.

All cops in the area were alerted to the police station breakout. They were told to be on the lookout for the wanted man.

It was some 25 minutes later when officers Steven Pandofelli and Gary Schmansky spotted Maldonado running into a building at East 178th Street, some five blocks from the stationhouse. The two officers gave immediate chase, following the suspect as he raced to the building's roof. They recaptured him there.

Brought back to the stationhouse, Maldonado was charged with murder, attempted robbery, weapons possession and the added charge of escape.

Outlining the case against Maldonado, police sources alleged that the suspect had first seen Reidy when the off-duty police officer had been at a neighborhood bank branch, cashing his check.

Maldonado is said to have followed Reidy into the University Avenue building where Reidy lived and pounced upon him there.

The police charge that when Reidy identified himself as a police officer, Maldonado apparently panicked and opened fire with his own .32-caliber pistol.

Chief Colangelo also alleged that Maldonado had a record of three other arrests and "may have been involved in other robberies."

At this writing, an investigation is under way as to the methods used in the Cross Bronx Expressway stationhouse which led to Maldonado's short-lived escape.

As for the suspect himself, Maldonado is now awaiting trial on the charges lodged against him. He has the constitutional right to be considered innocent of them, unless or until convicted by a jury of his peers.

"REQUIEM FOR A
BLUE KNIGHT"

by Bud Ampolsk

NEW YORK, NEW YORK
FEBRUARY 26, 1988

The last week of February 1988 was shaping up to be a good one for law enforcement officers and intrepid citizens who had committed themselves to an all-out war on the Big Apple's drug traffickers.

In the forbidding commercial corridor on Fulton Street between Franklin and Bedford Avenues, the coalition of Brooklyn North patrol command officers and Muslim activists appeared to be making substantial progress in reclaiming the neighborhood from the dealers and addicts who had plagued it for years.

The upbeat mood was best expressed by the president of the 79th Precinct Community Council: "A lot of people are becoming positive about what can happen when people work together. The Moslems, working with police, have done what no other group has been able to do. People feel there is a ray of hope here. If churches come and take a stand . . . the effort can be expanded to other areas."

Deputy Police Chief Thomas Gallagher, in charge of the combined operation, shared the council president's optimism: "I think the patrols are going well. We now have almost nonexistent drug activity in the locations that had been hard-core drug areas. This is a good example of what the public police and the community can do working together."

The spiritual leader of the At-Taqua mosque on Fulton Street, who had played a key role in mounting the citizen-lawman patrol, said, "We learned a lot of lessons doing this. The price you have to pay to fight against drugs is an ongoing struggle. We had to pay the price by standing in the cold and the rain, without pay, voluntarily, and after work. But the most interesting thing is that this has given people hope."

In the squadroom of the 115th Precinct in Queens, narcotics cops who had spent the past five years fighting to bring Lorenzo "Fat Cat" Nichols to justice had reason to be jubilant on Thursday, February 25th. That afternoon they got the news that Queens Supreme Court Justice Vincent Narro had sentenced Nichols to 25 years to life for 11 narcotics and gun convictions.

One 115th Precinct officer put it this way: "That's the death knell for Nichols' business. The Cat's nine lives are over. No one takes orders from a lifer."

In addition to the gun and narcotics-trafficking convictions, Nichols also faced a trial on second-degree murder charges in connection with the October 10, 1985 execution-style slaying of his parole officer, 34-year-old Brian Rooney. The state accused Nichols of having ordered Rooney's slaying in retribution for the parole officer's revocation of Nichols' parole because the drug kingpin had been consorting with known criminals. Of course, in accordance with the Constitution, Nichols must be presumed innocent of those charges until and unless proved otherwise by due process of law.

Nichols' sentencing followed by one day the conviction of his alleged henchman, Howard "Pappy" Mason, on a weapons charge. Mason faced up to seven years on that conviction.

Lawmen's feelings concerning Nichols were articulated at his sentencing by Assistant District Attorney Warren Silverman of Queens, who presented an impassioned half-hour argument for the maximum sentence. Silverman told Judge Narro, "The people of Queens County and the people of this state cry out that the defendant must be sentenced to the maximum."

Those who had probed Nichols' operations alleged that he was responsible for as much as $10 million — 10 percent of the county's $100 million drug traffic.

Defense Attorney David Cohen held that the stories of Nichols' drug activities were nothing more than "hysteria." Said the lawyer, "There is no evidence that he is a major narcotics violator. They claim it, they argue it, but they haven't proven it."

That the vast majority of hard-working and law-abiding citizens who live along such streets as Inwood between 105th and 107th Avenues in Jamaica had had enough and were now bent on taking back their territory from the army of drug dealers who poached there was exemplified by a 40-year-old resident of Inwood Street. The Guyanese immigrant was standing resolutely on the side of law and order in the face of repeated acts of violence and threats against him and his family.

Since November 9, 1987, the man had been under enormous duress.

On that date, the 40-year-old mechanic, who had just moved his family into a frame house on Inwood Street, had complained to the police about the number of drug dealers congregating on his block.

The cops moved. That very same day, they arrested a 20-year-old local man and charged him with possession of crack.

On the following morning, a Molotov cocktail was hurled through the mechanic's living room window. Investigating officers arrested 27-year-old Charles Johnson on arson charges.

Less than two hours after the arrest, two other men threw several more bombs into the house. One of the alleged bombers, 17-year-old Robert Webster, was nabbed on the following day. The police assigned a 24-hour guard to the mechanic's home.

On November 22nd, 50-year-old Robert Webster, Sr. was charged with tampering with a witness and harassment. The Guyanese homeowner told police that Webster, Sr. had approached him three times to coerce him into dropping charges against Robert Webster Jr.

On November 29th, the complainant was at a stoplight at 106th Avenue and Inwood Street when a man walked up to him and allegedly said, "If you and your family are not out of your house in three weeks, you'll all be . . . dead."

The mechanic was not to be intimidated. According to detectives, on January 12, 1988, he had identified a mugshot of Thomas "Mustafa" Godbolt as that of the man who had threatened him.

Godbolt, Johnson and Webster, Jr. were being held at Rikers Island pending court action on the charges against them. Webster, Sr. was released on $3,000 bail.

Meanwhile, the Guyanese homeowner put his house up for sale. He slept there alone, wishing to protect his relatives from further threats or violence.

The sale of the home was frustrated by the police presence.

When prospective buyers noticed the 103rd Precinct RMP parked at curbside, a uniformed patrolman at the wheel, they had severe second thoughts about owning property in such an environment.

For their part, the cops of the 103rd went about their guard duties with a sense of dedication and growing respect for the mechanic. They were well aware of the interdependence between lawman and upright citizen in the war to reclaim the city's streets.

While they had to fight off the discomfort and boredom of sitting alone in a patrol car hour after hour, their bodies aching from their immobility and shivering from the chill blasts of a New York winter, they recognized that this was what their job was all about.

For Patrolman Edward Byrne, the assignment was something very special. The 22-year-old rookie thought of it as a dream come true. The son of a retired police lieutenant who had gone on to a distinguished career in law, Edward Byrne had wanted to be a cop for as long as he could remember.

The young man had even done a hitch in the Transit Police while awaiting an opening on the NYPD. He'd gone through the Police Academy and been assigned to desk duty at the precinct house. But now he was on the kind of duty he had always dreamed about. He was here on Inwood Street to protect a man and the man's home. That was the ultimate service of any law officer.

For Patrolman Byrne, the last week of February had been a good one. He'd celebrated his birthday on Sunday, February 21st. On Thursday, February 25th, he put on his uniform and headed for his midnight-to-8:00 A.M. shift in the RMP in front of the courageous witness' home.

Patrolman Edward Byrne was seated behind the wheel of his RMP at 3:30 A.M. on the morning of Friday, February 26th. He was parked at the intersection

231

of Inwood Street and 107th Avenue. From this vantage point he was able to keep the beleaguered house under constant surveillance.

Eyewitnesses later described the sequence of immediate events . . .

An automobile, identified as a light-brown 1976 Oldsmobile Cutlass, pulled up alongside the RMP. (The witnesses believed that the car's engine had been turned off to maintain silence and that the vehicle had been coasting.)

Once the automobile was in position, one or two men, according to varying accounts, got out. One walked up to the driver's side of the RMP. Suddenly, the gunman began firing through the police cruiser's closed window. He got off five shots in rapid succession. Three of the heavy-caliber bullets drilled into Byrne's head, tearing away large segments of his skull.

Neighbors who heard the gunfire immediately called 911. Within minutes, the blocks surrounding Inwood Street were aswarm with police and emergency vehicles.

The mortally wounded rookie was rushed to Mary Immaculate Hospital, where he was pronounced dead.

Even as the first word of the cop-killing crackled through the NYPD's vast communications network, high police brass, city politicos, and a veritable army of detectives and uniformed personnel were converging on the 103rd Precinct.

In the eight days that followed, some 250 police investigators, working 12-hour shifts, blanketed the 103rd, 105th and 113th Precincts in southeast Queens. They conducted more than 200 interviews in almost as many locations. They carried out wide-ranging drug sweeps, interrogating the involved druggies as they went along.

In the eight days following Officer Byrne's death, the city seemed like a community under siege. Police organizations and private sources offered a reward, which quickly grew and reached the almost unheard-of sum of $130,000, for information leading to the arrest and conviction of Byrne's murderers.

At the very outset of the all-out murder probe, lawmen pooled whatever theories and information they had.

Sources inside the Queens District Attorney's Office said they felt the ambush had been ordered by the "drug lords of South Jamaica" in reprisal for the heavy sentence meted out to Fat Cat Nichols on the afternoon of February 25th and the conviction of his lieutenant, Pappy Mason.

At a hastily convened press conference at Mary Immaculate Hospital, the visibly shaken Police Commissioner Benjamin Ward told reporters, "The murder was a message to scare the witness out of testifying in another drug case."

Ward described the hit itself as having been "so lightning quick that he [Byrne] had no chance to do anything." He reported that the killer "got out of the car and got off five shots with a large-caliber weapon. The gunman then jumped into the car, and it took off. The officer had no chance to do anything."

The city's top cop vowed to spare "nothing and stop at nothing—and neither will my men—until we get this killer."

New York City Mayor Edward Koch added, "An attack on a cop is an attack on society. We're going to do more here because the killing was in connection with drug-trafficking. That's the added ingredient."

In announcing that the Patrolmen's Benevolent Association had already posted a reward of $10,000 in the case, the PBA president offered some criticism over Byrne's having stood his dangerous post all alone. "He [Byrne] should have had more protection," said the as-

233

sociation official. "He was placed in a life-threatening situation."

Regarding a possible conspiracy behind the murder, Commissioner Ward speculated, "It was very possible the hit was ordered from Rikers Island [where suspects awaiting trial and convicts awaiting transfer to state penal institutions are quartered], where people connected with this case are incarcerated. It happened so that the witness would get the word."

Sources inside the district attorney's office viewed the possible conspiracy as having been motivated by even wider and more grandiose considerations. They held that the witness himself could have been assassinated at any time, inasmuch as only his home was being guarded. The witness had not been under personal guard and had gone shopping by himself.

Said one source, "Ordering a cop killed sends a message that even if they put two heavyweights in jail, it cannot stop the South Jamaica drug trade."

Another source pointed out that the slaying had taken place just two blocks from Nichols' alleged headquarters.

With one of the largest concentrations of cops on a single case in recent memory about to take the field, a police hotline was set up under the grim call letters (212) COP SHOT. Public assistance was urgently requested.

The shock and grief of New York's finest over Byrne's killing was seen at a promotion ceremony for 91 persons that had been scheduled for Friday afternoon, the 26th, at police headquarters. A group of veteran officers and their families, standing with bowed heads in reverent memory of their fallen comrade, heard Commissioner Ward tell them, "What is normally the most joyous ceremony is overshadowed today by this event. Each of us goes out in the full knowledge of the apparent danger, but we don't expect to be gunned down in this manner."

Calling it "this heartbreaking experience," the commissioner told of having worked with Byrne's father, Lieutenant Matthew Byrne, who had been director of the NYPD's legal department from 1972 to 1976, when he had retired from the force.

The slain man had been one of four brothers — the eldest of whom was an assistant United States attorney in the office of Rudolph W. Guiliani, the United States Attorney for Manhattan. A second brother was a United States Marine Corps second lieutenant, based in California. A younger brother was a college student.

As the day wore on, those in charge of the probe moved to keep first theories from hardening and possibly misleading the investigation. For example, Commissioner Ward now said he didn't believe that Byrne's murder was connected to the sentencing of Nichols.

Sergeant Peter Sweeney, a police spokesman, declined to say whether those accused of firebombing the Inwood Street house and of other threats against the owner were now considered suspects in Byrne's murder.

"At this time," he said, "the investigation is getting off the ground, and we're looking into all suspects."

Ward had originally said that the killing might have been carried out on orders from inmates at Riker's Island. "They have access to phones and can give their orders right from jail," he had explained. Now he hedged somewhat.

At an afternoon news conference, Ward said, "We have not been able to confirm that the murder had been directed from Rikers. We know what is going on in southeast Queens, and we know we have some of the principals of the drug groups on Rikers Island."

That drugs had cast a pall over the territory in recent months was agreed upon by residents and police alike.

As far back as 1985, cops had mounted a major operation against drug trafficking. The September '85 operation in the 103rd Precinct had been known as "Operation Cleanup." In its first two years, it had resulted in 400 felony drug arrests and 225 misdemeanor collars. In all, 85 firearms and 30 pounds of cocaine had been reported seized in the course of the operation.

Based on the success of the 103rd Precinct project, the operation had been expanded to six neighboring precincts and renamed "Operation Queens." From October 1987 through January 31, 1988, it had resulted in 2,350 drug arrests and 12,871 issued summonses.

For their part, residents told of their own fears and expressed their sympathy for the witness whose home had been firebombed and for the officer who had died on their streets.

Said one resident, a middle-aged woman who had offered to help the hard-working immigrant mechanic, "He said he had nothing to do with it [crack]. He told me himself he was a hard-working man, and he wept when he told me that he had saved all his money to buy his house.

"Right after this [the arson] happened, he told me he was going to sell. I know he was scared.

"He was in the process of doing good work on the house. He was going to make a flower garden, but he got discouraged."

Then the woman asked, "How can people do such evil things for no reason?"

Recalling Patrolman Byrne, she commented, "I said hello to him several times because nobody wants to feel uncomfortable, no matter what color you are.

"Here's a young boy," she continued. "He had a nice face—a sweet boy, sitting there doing his job, protecting us. He didn't do anything to them. Why did they have to bother him?

"Somebody has to get to the root of this, because it's not fair," she said with a sigh.

One young man told of having heard the shots: "I didn't think anything of it. I didn't think things like this could happen. Who's going to be shooting with a cop on the corner?"

Another middle-aged woman noted, "We're living in times when your life don't mean nothing. And it's terrible in a place like the United States to live that way."

There was little doubt that crack was the cause of the desperate living conditions in the area. "There are nice people here," one woman said. "Most of these people work. Most have families."

However, that woman's daughter took a less sanguine view. The younger woman commented, "It was a nice neighborhood until they started with drugs on the corner."

A young man agreed: "Now this is a bad neighborhood. A lot of crack. A lot of bad stuff around."

By Saturday morning, the reward fund had reached the $30,000 mark with the New York *Daily News* adding $10,000 to the pool for information leading to the arrest and conviction of Byrne's killer or killers.

There were reports that more than 1,000 cops were now spreading a dragnet over the entire borough of Queens in search of the perps.

Ballistics experts now believed that either a .38-caliber pistol or a .357-caliber Magnum had been used in the slaying. The fact that Byrne's head had been partially blown off by the force of the slugs gave some indication that the bullets had been hollow-point.

Grim-faced lawmen called the assassination of their

237

brother-in-arms a declaration of war by the drug underworld. According to one highly placed source, "Byrne's execution was a statement to the police department, to the district attorneys, and to the judges that 'I am invincible.' "

Nevertheless, from the commissioner to the "portables" spread throughout the area, there was a resolution to see "law and order" triumph.

Noted one member of the top brass, "They [the drug dealers] may think they have won the battle. But they will lose the war."

To put their words into action, the police now began a series of lightning raids on crack dens. They also moved door to door, seeking witnesses to the actual murder.

It was reported that just seconds after the shooting, a man had called the 911 emergency number to report an officer down. The caller was said to have given an excellent description of the light-brown or tan Oldsmobile Cutlass that had silently drawn up alongside Byrne's patrol car.

An auto matching the getaway vehicle's description was located by detectives. It was parked on South Road about a half-mile from the crime site.

On the possibility that the automobile was the one used in the slaying, police set up a stakeout. When its owner appeared late on Friday night, the cops pounced on him, taking him into custody.

While the extensive questioning of its owner continued well into Saturday, the vehicle was impounded for an inch-by-inch examination by forensic experts.

As all this was going on, a number of side issues arose. One was Commissioner Ward's response to criticism by some rank-and-file cops who felt that Byrne might not have died had he been assigned to his post with a partner.

"Assigning a lone officer to a fixed post was a standard department practice," declared Ward.

He argued that having two officers in a patrol car would not have made any difference "if an assassin decides to arrive."

While crack dens were raided and doorbells rung, other backbreaking police assignments were being carried out.

Detectives at command-post precinct houses were sifting through hundreds of hotline phone tips. The callers fell into three main categories. Some were concerned citizens going all out to cooperate with the police. Others were members of the drug underworld seeking to settle scores with their enemies by linking them to the bloody doings on Inwood Street. Still others were motivated by the possibility of cashing in on the now-substantial reward being offered.

As for the owner of the impounded mystery car, a police spokesman, Sergeant Maurice Howard, revealed that the examination of the vehicle was still under way late Saturday night. He refused to divulge what, if anything, the cops had been told by the owner of the Cutlass.

High brass were going over and over whatever was known about the structure of the crack mobs.

According to those in the know, the drug menace had become acute with the arrival of the cocaine derivative on the scene. When the narcotic of choice was heroin, it was controlled by older, more established crime organizations, like the Colombian cartels.

Now, the spread of crack opened the Queens market to young punks who could set up kitchen operations for a few hundred dollars.

Those who had watched and fought against the crack culture noted that the ease of entry into crack-trafficking had resulted in previously unheard-of com-

239

petition among suppliers and dealers. It was all measured in the greater number of murders and shootouts that began in 1985.

"They're not battling the police," said Commissioner Ward. "They're battling each other."

Sterling Johnson, Jr., the city's special prosecutor for narcotics, agreed with the commissioner. "There's no monolithic structure here," he said. "There's a lot of independent organizations who are vying for the best locations and the best customers."

Although progress had been made, it had not bought peace, Ward reported. "We've come down rather hard on the leadership and took out their leadership rather rapidly," he said. "And while that sounds great, and we've gotten some convictions, and some of them will be sent upstate, that also has left the organizations in some disarray, causing them to scramble to put new leadership in place. And so the war will go on."

Special Prosecutor Johnson was equally pessimistic. "Drug dealers are like hydras," he said. "You cut off the head and another grows back."

It was against this intelligence that police speculation continued to center on what possible connection, if any, Nichols or his associate, Godbolt, might have had with the shooting of Patrolman Byrne.

As all this was going on, members of his family were sadly going about the business of preparing for Edward Byrne's burial. They recalled their family's close ties. Edward had not opted for the fast-lane life. He had continued to live in North Massapequa, Long Island, with his parents. His 22nd birthday celebration had been typical of the easygoing give-and-take that was so much a part of their lives.

At the dinner, Edward had regaled them with the lighthearted stories he had such a talent for telling.

Said a clergyman who had assumed the role of family spokesman in the family's hour of tragedy, "He [Edward] always kept the family entertained with his light stories. . . . He had dinner, perhaps for the last time with his parents."

Speaking of Edward's parents, the priest at St. James Catholic Church in Seaford, Long Island, commented, "They all feel a great loss. But they are able to chuckle at times about the funny things Edward did.

"The parents are proud of their son, and he was proud to be a police officer. He wanted to work in Queens and he did well."

One woman who had known the victim's family for many years observed, "He was a good boy, and whether you are twenty-two or forty-two, no one is prepared for this."

Relatives who had grown up with him said that Edward had always wanted to be a cop.

Young Edward had been a football star at Plainedge High School, where he'd worn the number 42 on his Red Devils jersey. He had completed 33 credits at Nassau Community College.

A brother officer, who had served with Edward Byrne in Transit District 53 while both had been transit cops, said of him, "He was a good kid. He went out of his way to help people. He would ask people who were asleep on the subways whether they needed help. He did his job."

And now, 22-year-old rookie cop Edward Byrne had become the first New York City police officer to die in the line of duty during 1988.

Questioning of the owner of the suspected "hit car" went on through Saturday night. It was reported that even though he was drunk when he was picked up, the man passed a polygraph test and was not considered a suspect in the Byrne murder. He told police that he'd loaned the car to somebody but could not remember whom.

Detectives made their first objective the apprehension of the actual assassin. They reasoned that once they had him in custody, they would have a better chance of determining who, if anybody, had hired him to snuff out the young patrolman's life.

There was also talk that one of the people being held on Rikers Island in connection with the Inwood Street Molotov cocktail firebombing and the harassment of the property's owner had been boasting to other inmates about a "contract" he had put out on an unspecified cop. (The information was said to have come to police through informants.)

Chief of Detectives Robert Colangelo, First Deputy Commissioner Richard Condon, and Chief of Department Robert Johnston, Jr. were meeting regularly to assess developments and take personal charge of the widening murder investigation.

Johnston, a personal friend of the slain officer's father, had turned out the 8:00 A.M. Friday morning shift at the 91st Avenue stationhouse, where black mourning bunting already hung over the door.

In addressing the officers who were about to go on duty, Johnston set the theme for the days of danger and intense police activity that lay ahead. "We have two priorities," he said. "One is to get the killer and convict him. The other is to protect ourselves so this never happens again. I don't want any overreaction, and I don't want any cowboying around."

Johnston urged the officers to wear bulletproof vests and ordered them to request backup under any dangerous circumstances.

So stressful was the situation that extra security measures were ordered around St. James Catholic Church for Byrne's funeral mass on Monday, February

242

29th.

One highly placed officer declared, "We're making damn sure that nothing else happens."

The New York *Daily News* featured a display ad announcing its participation in the funding of a $20,000 reward sponsored by COP SHOT—"Citizens Outraged at Police Being Shot."

Surrounded by grieving family members before the Wantagh, Long Island funeral home where his son's body lay in state, Matthew Byrne, the former police lieutenant, now a practicing lawyer in Great Neck, stood and addressed the newsmen and police personnel who had gathered there.

Said Byrne, "My son, Eddie, was executed last Friday by people who don't even deserve to be called people.

"You've all heard of the so-called drug war. Well, it became reality last Friday night-morning when my son was executed.

"This was a cold-blooded execution, of a boy who never hurt anyone by drug dealers who are telling us they've declared war on society.

"When Eddie died, a little of all of us died, because Eddie represented decent people of this world, and his death becomes a responsibility of the decent people."

Matthew Byrne called upon political officials "to put their money and their resources where their mouth is, and to do something more than paying lip service about stopping drugs."

He said, "An aroused citizenry is the only thing that will generate the kind of response we need. If we don't get immediate and drastic action, the streets will be as they are in Beirut or Bogota.

"If our son, Eddie, sitting in a police car, representing and protecting us, can be wasted by scum like that, then none of us is safe—and I don't care where you live."

When he described the three head wounds his son had suffered, Byrne's voice broke. "We can't even have the consolation of an open casket," he said.

Commissioner Ward, who had been among the dignitaries paying their respects at the funeral home, commented, "What strikes me about this thing is that the family gave me strength when I was inside. They have no bitterness and no anger. But they are so proud that their son was a policeman and they are proud that when their other son [Stephen] is done in the Marine Corps, he also hopes to be a police officer."

Meanwhile, the witness who had been a target of drug traffickers' violence and whose home Byrne had been guarding was now under the protection of a small army of cops. Two police vans, an Emergency Services truck, three squad cars, and a phalanx of heavily armed officers, some carrying machine-guns, were posted around his house on Inwood Street.

The man was universally respected by both the public and the police for the courage he had shown throughout his ordeal. Aware of the danger he still faced, the man said he was ready to die in the war against drugs.

"I'm ready to go at any time," the Guyanese immigrant declared. "I know they're looking for me, but I don't care. I stand for justice."

His attitude brought this response from one officer assigned to guard him: "You gotta hand it to him. He is responsible for putting away five guys already, and now this. Nothing seems to bother this guy. He's not running and he's not scared of anybody."

Meanwhile, some progress was being made in the case, but not enough to satisfy the investigators.

It was learned that five minutes before he was slain, Patrolman Byrne had showed no signs of concern to two officers in another radio car who had stopped by to chat.

One discouraged ranking officer commented, "We're back to ground zero, and I think we're looking at a long, tedious investigation, unless we get a magic phone call from someone who knows something very specific—like a name."

Others reported that eyewitnesses to the shooting had estimated there had been four people in the getaway car.

There was also growing conviction that the murder weapon had been a .38.

A raw late-winter wind chilled the air on Monday, February 29th, as the largest assemblage of police officers ever to attend the funeral of a slain brother-in-arms congregated before the church where the mass was to be held. Standing in ranks six deep in the streets surrounding St. James Church, more than 10,000 officers from all sections of the nation saluted smartly as Byrne's shiny black casket with silver handles was borne past them. One who attended but could not salute was Officer Stephen McDonald, the handsome young cop who had become a quadraplegic after having been shot by a young hood in Central Park. McDonald's courage through his lengthy recuperation has made him a world-wide celebrity.

The mournful strains of "When The Battle Is Over," played by a lone piper of the Emerald Society's pipe and drum corps, echoed through the crisp morning air as Byrne's coffin was carried into the church.

During the two-hour service, mourners heard the reverend father say, "Maybe Eddie has done more in his short eight months as a police officer than others might do in a whole lifetime. I pray God, our Father, that through Eddie's death, some good will come.

"His death will not be in vain, if it leads people to

245

fight the evil of drugs in our society, to stand up and be counted as men and women who see wrong, say it is wrong and strive to change it."

The priest called on the gathering to forgive those responsible for Byrne's death in the same spirit that Jesus "forgave the criminals who crucified him.

"Eddie's murderers, those who executed him, need to be pitied but also prayed for," the priest said. "For the spirit of Satan has blinded them to the holiness of life."

Gasps issued from the mourners at the clergyman's plea for forgiveness of the perps.

As the services were about to conclude, Mayor Koch stepped to the pulpit to renew a call he had made to President Reagan in an ad in the *New York Times* to cut off military aid to Panama and Mexico, said to be prime sources of much of the illicit drug traffic into the United States.

The mayor, speaking in subdued tones, compared the slaying of Byrne to the death of Franklin Delano Roosevelt, the assassination of John F. Kennedy, and the murder of Martin Luther King, Jr.

Expanding on the theme, Koch said, "Those were the three times when I felt that the very safety of the country was involved.

"If drug traffickers have become so emboldened that they can engage in the assassination of a young police officer, then our whole society is at risk, and we will have anarchy. That is why this death rivals the others. Not because he is Edward Byrne, but because of what is means to have this police officer assassinated."

Following the church services, several hundred officers, including a contingent of more than 100 from the 103rd Precinct, accompanied the cortege to St. Charles Cemetery in Farmingdale for the burial. Captain Robert Noonan, commanding officer of the precinct, presented a folded American flag to the family.

For their part, investigators assigned to the case had nothing solid to go on. And yet, their weekend sweeps of the drug-infested Queens area where Byrne was shot had resulted in over 80 arrests.

There were even setbacks to report. One concerned the growing police doubts that the impounded Cutlass had been the actual murder vehicle. Although the car matched the description of the one seen by eyewitnesses, one police official said, "There's nothing other than the physical description that would indicate that this is the car."

There was also a reluctance on the part of neighborhood people to discuss bigwigs in the drug trade who might have ordered the execution. They had been silenced by fear.

The search for the murder weapon continued with negative results.

Still the grim canvassing went on. By Tuesday, March 1st, the arrest count had reached 108 in South Jamaica. The figure covered those taken in over the weekend. This compared with usual weekend totals of 10 to 15, according to the top brass of the police department.

Deputy Inspector Francis Coyne of the department's narcotics division reported, "We've saturated the area and brought in extra people from around the boroughs. We've intensified the coverage and we're debriefing everyone who has been arrested to see if they have any information."

Once again, Commissioner Ward held a summit meeting with top aides at the 113th Precinct command post to review progress and map future strategy. Police activity now spread into the Fulton Street area of North Brooklyn in the 84th, 88th, 79th, 81st, 73rd, and 75th Precincts. Police helicopter squads found that

247

street traffic among drug dealers was substantially be-low its usual level as both sellers and customers scurried out of the sight of grim-faced cops.

The move into Brooklyn was based on the fact that there were loose alliances between Brooklyn and Queens narcotics gangs.

Police experience had shown in the past that workers in some drug organizations commuted to Queens from Brooklyn. Bodies attributed to Queens crack wars had been showing up in alleys and on rooftops in North Brooklyn.

However, the immediate goal of finding the triggerman-suspect remained beyond reach.

Once again, a top police officer appealed to the general public to cooperate in the manhunt.

Chief of Detectives Colangelo warned, "You just can't leave it to law enforcement and say, 'Let the cops do it.' Quite frankly, we can't do it alone . . .

"The schools, the churches, civic groups, community groups—they all have to put it on their agenda. It's a problem that they all have the responsibility to deal with."

In the embattled Jamaica streets, civilians were conspicuous by their absence. Uniformed cops were the only people to be seen near the murder site.

Reported one cop, "There've been no arrests here tonight because every crack dealer is already in custody."

The saturation by police caused warnings to be issued to uniformed cops by the brass. "Be aware," went the proviso, "that a great number of undercover officers have been assigned to the Queens area, and be alert and cautious when responding to avoid accidental shooting." The alert went out quickly.

One hope that things might reach a climax in the not-too-distant future came from the fact that the reward kitty had now reached the unprecedented figure of $85,000. This was the largest sum for such purposes in Big Apple history.

Colangelo said that the massive crackdown was intended as "a clear message to drug dealers: The lawless will not control the streets—whatever the cost."

He also believed that despite lack of tangible indications, progress was now being made toward a solution.

While refusing to divulge how many detectives had been assigned to the probe, Colangelo did say that the effort was receiving the total attention of himself, the police commissioner, and other top officials, as well as prosecutors, the Federal Bureau of Investigation, and the Federal Drug Enforcement Administration.

The tally of phone tips and the arrest statistics for low-level crack dealers were both soaring. By late Tuesday, some 135 drug dealers had been brought in. There had been approximately 150 hotline calls.

Media interest in Godbolt's possible involvement remained at a fever pitch. Still, Colangelo refused to be drawn into lengthy discussions concerning the man being held on Rikers Island. All he would say was, "He [Godbolt] had a motive."

It was revealed that crime scene cops had recovered four spent .38-caliber bullets—three copper and one lead. Detectives at the 91st Avenue stationhouse requested that surface, transit, and housing police report any confiscations of .38-caliber handguns so that they might be compared with ballistics fragments in the Byrne murder. On Wednesday, March 2nd, the pace quickened perceptibly at the various command posts throughout Queens. Something big was happening, and despite the continuing curtain of silence maintained by police brass, speculation was running high.

According to well-informed sources, two people had told detectives that they had been in the killer's car and had witnessed the execution. Reportedly, the two had given police the name of the triggerman who had pumped five slugs into the RMP.

NBC's Channel 4 reported late Wednesday evening that the hitman was a 22-year-old with a long police record.

The official police spokesman, Officer Peter O'Donnell, would only say, "The investigation is still continuing. We are seeking information, and we are looking at numerous suspects who may have been involved directly and indirectly."

Another high-ranking official added, "This is a very difficult, complex investigation going on here."

Still, lending weight to the rumors that the probe might be reaching its climax, nine detectives and a sergeant from the Major Case Squad joined the already beefed-up army of lawmen on Thursday.

A feeling of optimism flooded through the command post. "It looks good," one official said, adding that "a successful conclusion" to the mystery was imminent.

Thursday, March 3rd did indeed bring the search for Edward Byrne's killers to a climax. On that day, police arrested the suspected hitman and an accomplice in Queens.

Police had been working on information partially developed in Manhattan and relayed to the Queens task force. The major breakthrough came when police located the well-dressed, attractive girlfriend of the suspected hitman and rushed her to Jamaica, Queens, for questioning. She was released, detectives said, emphasizing that they did not believe she was involved in the murder.

At 4:45 P.M. on Thursday, a detachment of a dozen police cars and four vans rushed to a green and white two-family house on 209th Street. The officers surrounded the house and swiftly hauled out two men and a woman.

The men were identified as 24-year-old Scott Cobb and 19-year-old Todd Scott, both of South Jamaica, Queens. Both were described as low-level drug dealers with criminal records, and both were charged with second-degree murder.

Scott Cobb had a rap sheet going back to March 6, 1979, when he received a 1- to 3-year sentence for the robbery of an 82-year-old man at knifepoint. Investigators said that Cobb worked for Pappy Mason, an associate of Fat Cat Nichols.

Todd Scott was considered the prime suspect in the slayings of Crystal Bynum and another young woman in separate incidents. His arrest record went back to 1986.

Scott was considered, by those who knew him, to be something of "a wild man." Police alleged that Scott confessed to dancing in the street after shooting Byrne. He told police that he'd said to his accomplices, "Did you see his [Byrne's] blue eyes? Did you see his brains?"

On Friday, David McClary, who had no criminal record, surrendered to police when he heard they were looking for him.

Philip Copeland, the fourth suspect, was already in jail on another charge when he was arrested for his involvement in the Byrne murder.

Both Copeland and McClary were charged with second-degree murder. Police sources alleged that Copeland and McClary had been implicated by both Cobb and Scott.

In a news conference on Friday afternoon, Commissioner Ward gave members of the press details of the police reconstruction of the night Edward Byrne was killed.

According to police sources, Cobb, Scott, and Mc-

Clary had all given written and videotaped statements. All concurred that Cobb was the getaway driver. McClary and Scott, however, disagreed over who had actually pulled the trigger.

According to Ward, Cobb drove Scott and McClary to Inwood Street after a last-minute planning session of the assassination at the 209th Street apartment where Cobb and Scott were eventually arrested. Copeland stayed behind, near the corner of 107th Avenue, where Patrolman Byrne was posted.

Scott and McClary approached the radio car — Scott on the driver's side, McClary on the passenger's. Byrne was reading a newspaper. His service revolver rested between his legs.

McClary rapped at the window on the passenger side of the police car and motioned to Byrne to roll down his window. While Byrne was distracted, sources said, Scott opened fire at least four times with a .38-caliber pistol, hitting Byrne at least three times.

While there was enormous satisfaction over the arrest of the four suspects, those who were close to Commissioner Ward said he wouldn't be satisfied until he was able to pin the planning of the murder on kingpins on Rikers Island.

On March 7, 1988, District Attorney John Santucci's office began presenting its evidence to a Queens grand jury. Before nightfall on March 8th, the grand jury handed down indictments against Todd Scott, David McClary, Scott Cobb, and Philip Copeland, charging each with second-degree murder and criminal possession of a weapon.

On January 29, 1989, a Queens court found all four guilty of the charges. They are now serving sentences of 25 years to life for the murder of Edward Byrne.

"SWAT TEAM MISSION — FIND THE COP KILLER!"
by Peggie Mullins

The first police radio transmission in the case was made at 1:41:30 A.M. by Officer Randy Byard of the Huntington, West Virginia Police Department. The date was December 14, 1981. It went like this:

Byard: 301 to station.

Station Dispatcher: Go ahead.

Byard: Start me a back-up down this way. I got a couple of young guys looking in the window down here at a gas station. They're looking around right now.

Station: 305. Copy?

Officer Paul Harmon responds a few seconds later.

Harmon: 10-4. Let me get turned around.

Byard: 5. Take your time now. They're just looking around for now. They went around behind the building—see if they go in.

Harmon: I'll park at 19th and Jefferson.

Byard: Naw. They'll see you from there.

Harmon: I'll wait at 19th and Madison then until you give me the OK to come in.

Byard: Uh. One of 'em—uh—one of 'em just ducked—he saw me. I think.

Byard: Naw. I think he just ducked at a car that

came by on the street. They're—they're getting ready to break in, is what they're doing.

At 1:45:01 A.M., Officer Harmon spotted the individuals at the intersection of 19th Street West and Jefferson Avenue.

Harmon: I've got 'em over here at 19th and Jefferson.

Byard: There's still one over here.

Ten seconds later, Officer Byard hears a noise he can't identify.

Byard: 5. What was that?

Byard: 1 to 5.

Byard: Did he answer, Station?

Station: 305?

At 1:45:29 A.M. Byard hears a shot.

Byard: Station. I just heard a gunshot.

Station: 300B copy?

Byard: They're shooting. They're shooting. There's two of 'em. They're running. They're running west on Jefferson. I don't know where Harmon is.

Byard: He's down. Harmon's down.

Officer Ken Staten: I'm heading that way.

Officer John Davies: 2. I'm heading that way. I'm in the alley.

Byard: Send an ambulance.

Station: They're en route.

Byard: Two subjects. Looked like one had a light brown coat on. They ran west—west on Jefferson.

Station: 10-4.

Byard: Station, get an ambulance here now.

Station: They're en route.

Hogan: 300B to 301.

Byard: Go ahead.

Byard: Yes, sir. I see two subjects in a car just west of here—they're getting in a car. If they head this way, I'm gonna stop 'em.

Hogan: 10-4. Stay with the downed unit.

Byard: He's—he's hurt bad. They're backing out. They're in a Pinto—they're heading out.

Davies: Which way are they headed?

Byard: They're backing up. It's a green Buick. They're in a green Buick. They're heading north. They're heading north. North on 20th Street over toward Adams.

Davies: 302 to Station.

Station: Go ahead.

Davies: See if you can get hold of Ceredo working on this.

Byard: Station, can you copy me?

Station: 301. I copy. Go ahead.

Byard: They're headed down West 5th in a green Buick—about a '67 model—green Buick—down on West 5th. They're headed down there about 23rd or 24th Street somewhere down in that area. Get somebody down there.

Station: 10-4.

The police radio transcript ended at 1:54:26 A.M. When the ambulance arrived at the scene of the shooting, Police Officer Paul Harmon was dead from gunshot wounds.

Officers from the Huntington Police Department searched the area closely for the killers who were driving a green Buick, but somehow missed them.

Nevertheless, police from the entire area started a massive manhunt, concentrating on one of the two fugitives, the one believed to have been driving the Buick and thought to be the one who fired the lethal shot.

In an effort to locate the wanted man, the Huntington Police Department put out flyers describing the suspected killer. The handbills were circulated all across the nation.

About 3,000 posters were produced and passed out to many businesses for them to display; however, most of the flyers were sent to police departments throughout the country. The suspect was considered armed and very dangerous.

When the question was raised about the man still being in the "Tri-State Area," Police Chief Adkins told the press.

"We're not saying it's not possible he's here, but we don't really believe he is."

In the meantime, reports began to filter in over the next several days that the suspect had been seen in different areas, but some of the statements were in conflict. One reported that the suspect was seen near Athens. An Athens County deputy reported that he saw the suspect driving a red truck sometime before 11:00 P.M. on Wednesday.

Yet, the Huntington officers couldn't verify that the murder suspect was actually the one driving the truck. Then the detectives arrested another man in connection with the slaying. But they also had reason to believe they were drawing closer to the murder suspect all the time. The search was centered mostly in and around the town of Columbus.

"We've been told that the man has been seen in after-hours bars here," said one member of the SWAT team. "About ten days ago, acting on information from an informant, it looked like we were about three hours from an arrest, but it just didn't work out. We're sure he's still around."

Huntington Police Chief Ottie Adkins told the press that he believed the murder suspect was in the Columbus, Ohio area.

"We have Officer Tom Bevins working up there with the Columbus Police Department," said Chief Adkins. "We're definitely making good progress in the investigation."

The Huntington police chief also told the press that new evidence in the case had been discovered, but he declined to say just what it was. The chief stated that the whole case might be threatened if he revealed the details.

Another officer told the press that at least one other team other than his own were on the streets of the city of Columbus each day. Police were busy looking everywhere for the suspect.

"We're still out there digging," said the officer. "We're digging hard. With a guy like this, we could be next."

Detectives continued to check out records and finally identified the murder suspect. He was Bobby Dean Stacy, 30.

As the probers pushed ahead with the investigation, they suddenly received a tip—an anonymous call which gave investigators a telephone number. Detective Bevins gave it to Captain James N. Hunter, the commander of the Huntington Police Department's Detective Bureau.

In turn, Detective Hunter had the number checked out and discovered that it belonged to a man who had taken a room at a Springfield, Illinois motel.

Without any delay, detectives surrounded the motel and announced their presence over a bullhorn. After a few tense moments, Stacy came slowly out. He was barefooted and held his hands over his head.

The probers then obtained a search warrant and began checking his room. However, investigators failed to find any weapons. Nor did they locate anything in a 1970 Chevrolet automobile which the detectives found was registered to a Stacy relative.

After the capture of Stacy, the detectives told the press that the SWAT team had first surrounded the motel and had cleared it out of any patrons.

"We were prepared to use tear gas. But he did voluntarily come out of the room after a call was placed to him and we announced our presence over a bullhorn," said one of the detectives.

The probers said that Stacy had been in the Springfield area since about the middle of December or as little as a few days after he shot Officer Harmon.

"He did have relatives here. We think that's the reason he was here," said the detective.

The investigator told the press that the search for Stacy had actually been around Columbus. Also, that Stacy had made no statement when he was arrested.

Stacy was booked into the Sangamon County Jail on a charge of unlawful flight to avoid prosecution in connection with the killing of Officer Paul Harmon. At this time, bond was not set. However, it was decided that the suspect would go before a magistrate for an identity hearing.

In the meantime, Stacy's attempts to fight his extradition to West Virginia failed, and he was taken back to face his trial for the murder of Officer Harmon.

At his hearing, Judge Eugene Duban ruled that extradition warrants were good. The process was held in the 7th Judicial Circuit Court of Illinois, and the warrants were signed by Illinois Governor James Thompson and West Virginia Governor Jay Rockefeller. Stacy was then turned over to Detective Tom Bevins.

Suddenly, authorities learned about an escape attempt that Stacy had planned during his stay in the Sangamon County Jail. An inmate gave officers a tip about the planned escape.

"We had information from an inmate that there was a plan to overpower a guard. It never occurred. We watched him pretty close," said Officer Richard Groeteke of the Sangamon County Jail.

Officer Groeteke told the press that Stacy was in detention with two other inmates whom authorities felt were escape risks.

When Stacy and the officers arrived back in West Virginia, Stacy gave them no problems as he quietly entered the Cabell County Jail. According to the police, Stacy was very nervous and had a headache, but the suspect said very little to the jail police as they removed his jacket, boots, and a belt. Officers then placed him in a holding area of the jail, where he was to have his picture taken.

Finally, Stacy was brought before Cabell Circuit Judge Alfred E. Ferguson for his arraignment. He was thus charged with first-degree murder for the shooting of Police Officer Paul Harmon.

For his hearing, Stacy was in handcuffs and leg irons. He informed the court that he intended to hire his own attorney, one from Columbus, Ohio.

Meanwhile, jail officers discovered two hacksaw blades placed in the inner soles of a pair of sneakers which were mailed from Columbus. The shoes had been placed in a package and addressed to a jail inmate who was in the very cellblock where dangerous persons were held. Also, the package was on its way to the same fifth floor cell as Bobby Dean Stacy was in.

Police told the press that the name of the inmate to whom the package was mailed would be withheld. The inmate was waiting for his own trial on armed robbery. Thus, the investigation into the mailing of the two blades would have to be completed.

The blades were discovered by a regular check. They were glued to the inner soles of white canvas sneakers and placed in a package that held a fictitious Huntington return address.

It was Officer Carl F. Frick who ordered packages addressed to inmates on the fifth floor be placed in his office for checking.

"The shoes just didn't appear to be up to par," said Officer Frick. "The package showed it was mailed from Columbus," he said. "The sneakers were turned over to Huntington Police Department's Detective Bureau yesterday afternoon in an attempt on their part to locate the sender."

Investigators knew that they had their work cut out for them, because they would have to gather enough evidence against Bobby Dean Stacy to hold a case together in court. Consequently, they began to question persons who might help them.

Detectives started with the officer who was with Paul Harmon on the fatal day. Officer Randy Byard told the detectives that he heard Harmon's only recorded reference to his killers—"I've got 'em over here at 19th and Jefferson." Those words could have been the officer's last.

Byard said that one minute later he found Paul Harmon's lifeless body and saw two men running away from the area. However, he could not identify either of the two men, but one of them threw himself into a green Buick parked close by. The car then headed west.

When the detectives showed Officer Byard a photo of the car, he said that it appeared to be the same vehicle he saw leaving the murder scene.

As he continued to answer questions, Byard told detectives that the pair he saw running away were not the same two men he had seen at a gas station nearby only moments earlier.

Byard said Harmon got to West 19th Street before he answered Byard's call for help at the station.

"What I was gonna do was wait until they broke in the building and then call him in to come into the building," said Officer Byard. "Two other men must have attacked Harmon because when he said, 'I've got 'em here at 19th and Jefferson' I was still watching them at the building.

"I thought he had stopped somebody that didn't have anything to do with what I was watching for," said Byard. Investigators questioned Byard closely about his own descriptions of Harmon's attackers. Earlier, Byard stated that one man at the gas station and one of the men fleeing the murder scene wore brownish coats, as best he could remember.

When the probers asked him if he could have seen the same man twice, he told them that he had not. Detectives then left Officer Byard and prepared to interrogate other persons who might be able to give them a lead in the case.

One man told probers about an armed robbery in Lawrence County which occurred about a half hour before the murder of Harmon in Huntington.

The man stated that two robbers bearing shotguns had stolen a car before the holdup. They abandoned it later in the 900 block of West 5th Avenue.

When probers questioned the man about whether he could identify either of the robbers, he said that he couldn't. The weary investigators next sought to see if there was any connection between the holdup men and the murder of Paul Harmon.

One informant told detectives that Bobby Dean Stacy and a close friend might be part of a robbery ring.

Detectives questioned Columbus Officer John Postlethwait.

"What happened to Harmon was the aftermath of a robbery," said the officer.

"These people (who killed Harmon) were in your city for a reason."

It developed that Postlethwait had been working very closely on the case ever since Harmon was slain.

261

As he continued, Postlethwait told the investigators that there might be "five or six" people involved in the ring. He said the ring could perform armed robberies, but were not limited to that activity.

"We want to leave the door open during the investigation into Harmon's death," said Postlethwait.

"There is a possibility that more arrests will result from the investigation that may solve crimes nearly as serious as the Huntington officer's death," he added.

However, he would not give more details. When probers questioned him about more arrests in the Harmon slaying, he said, "I'd rather not comment. We've talked to several people, but whether or not I'd consider them suspects is another thing."

Officer Postlethwait assured the detectives that a pickup truck that had been reported stolen from Fort Gay, West Virginia a few hours after the Harmon slaying had been recovered on February 23rd by Columbus police in an apartment complex.

"We checked the abandoned vehicle after a resident of the complex called and reported it hadn't been moved for some time. It came back stolen," said the officer.

Postlethwait told the detectives that the truck was then examined by a police evidence unit and very clear fingerprints had been located on it. Investigators questioned him about whether Stacy and his friend might be connected with the truck, and the officer said, "They could probably be tied to the vehicle."

Captain James N. Hunter of the Huntington police told the probers that he could confirm what Postlethwait told them. Hunter said that the robbery ring was operating in Ohio, West Virginia, Kentucky, Pennsylvania, and Tennessee.

Hunter stated that in his opinion the investigation might lead to arrests that involved other shootings. He said that it was possible more than two people were involved in the slaying of Paul Harmon. However, he said there was no evidence that would place more than two people at the scene.

As the officer continued to answer questions, he told probers that he was still convinced that an attempted armed robbery of a restaurant was connected with the murder, because the attempted robbery happened only 34 minutes before Officer Harmon was slain.

"In my opinion," Hunter stated, "the robbery is definitely linked to Harmon's death. We have evidence linking two people to the scene of the shooting."

Hunter told the detectives that he believed Harmon was slain when he discovered the men on foot who thought they were about to be arrested for the attempted Ohio robbery. But at the exact moment of the Harmon killing, police did not know about the robbery attempt.

"The backup unit (Harmon) walked into these guys cold," said Hunter. "They thought they were caught. We're assuming that's why Harmon was killed."

As detectives pushed ahead with their intense probe into the slaying of Paul Harmon, they sought other persons who could give them any help at all in the case. Thus, they finally found a 10-year-old girl and her grandfather who told detectives they had seen the shooting.

The fifth-grade girl told probers that she saw Stacy fire a gun into the head of Officer Harmon while he lay in the street. The girl said that she thought the officer was being robbed, and she called her grandfather to the window to watch.

"I looked out the window. I saw a man wrestling with a cop," said the girl. "I knew he (the man over

Harmon) had something in his hand, but I wasn't sure what it was. Then I saw him stick something up to the cop's head and shoot. After three or four shots, we saw Bobby Stacy come toward our house and he came around our house to our porch," said the girl.

"When my grandfather turned on the porch light, he (Stacy) looked up and squinted," said the girl.

Detectives questioned the girl about how long Stacy was near the house.

"He was at our porch for only two or three minutes," said the girl.

She told detectives that Stacy could have been there less time than she had at first said. She told the detectives that Stacy had a "brownish-black" wig on the day he went by her house.

"The wig just scooted back on his head and a little bit of his bangs came out," said the girl. Also, she said that Stacy was wearing a checked jacket with red in it when he ran close to her house.

Detectives questioned the girl closely and asked her what kind of television programs she liked to watch, and if she liked to place herself in the show and play the part of any of the actors.

"Sometimes I watch 'Chiller,'" said the girl. "It's about killings and stuff."

"You'd like to get involved in these sorts of things, wouldn't you?"

"No," the girl answered.

"It'd be a lot of fun being in one of those movies, wouldn't it?" asked a detective.

"No," the girl again replied.

Investigators questioned the youngster about whether she was somewhat of a celebrity with her classmates because she was thus involved with the case.

"It makes you feel good, doesn't it?"

"Yes," answered the girl.

The schoolgirl told them that she watched accounts of the case in the local news media and saw Stacy's picture almost every day. She was asked if she would know Stacy from a picture even if she had never seen him before in person.

"Yes, but I knew him before they showed me any pictures," she said.

Investigators finally completed their questioning of the girl and turned their attention to Police Officer Leroy Campbell. He said that he saw a green Buick on U.S. 60 around 1:45 A.M. and 2:00 A.M. on the highway and saw a man driving a Buick west. He decided to stop.

Detectives asked the officer why he decided to stop and keep an eye on the car.

"We don't get much traffic in Kenova at that time, much less a black person," said the officer.

The policeman stated that as he went past the car, he saw a man driving it. Probers asked him if there were any other persons in the car at the time.

"There was none in my sight," said Officer Campbell.

Campbell told detectives that he wasn't certain whether he identified the man driving the car from a picture lineup before the man's arrest or afterward.

After they questioned the officer, investigators were certain that he had told them all he could. They pushed on with their probe. Working very hard, they dug up another man who might give them a lead in the case.

This possible witness told the detectives that he lived near the spot where Officer Harmon was shot down. He then identified Stacy as the man who had shot Harmon three times as the officer lay on the ground.

He told probers that he heard the sound of gunshots

and went to a window in his home. This was about 1:40 A.M. on December 14th. The man said he watched as the two men struggled at the corner of 19th Street and West Jefferson Avenue. At the time, Stacy bent over Harmon and shook him. The man said that he thought it was a robbery.

"He felt around over him a little bit, then he raised up like he was gonna get off him," said the man. "He didn't stand up. He just raised up and backed off a little, and he fired three shots right down at the body."

The man stated that Harmon seemed to be lying on his left side as the shots were fired, because he himself could see the right half of Harmon's face.

"Just as quick as he fired the shots, he raised up and came toward my house," said the man.

The man said that as Stacy passed close to his home, he turned on the porch light himself and Stacy glanced up.

"I said to him, 'What in hell have you done?'"

The possible witness gave police a demonstration on how Paul Harmon was searched by the murder suspect.

"Was he on top of him?"

"I wouldn't say that he was right on top of him, but he was hunkered down over him," said the man.

"Was he straddling him, or what?"

"No, he was—like the man was lying this way," said the man.

The man told the detectives that Stacy fired the shots at the officer from a distance of a foot or less.

When investigators were convinced that they had enough evidence against the murder suspect, they prepared to turn it all over to the State of West Virginia for prosecution. Bobby Dean Stacy was brought to trial for the murder of Paul Harmon.

A jury of eight men and four women were chosen to

hear the case and deliberate the evidence. The presiding judge was Cabell Circuit Judge Alfred E. Ferguson.

After the jury had heard all the pros and cons in the case, it deliberated for two hours and two minutes, and then found Bobby Dean Stacy guilty of the slaying of Officer Paul Harmon.

Judge Ferguson then sentenced the convicted killer to life in prison with no possibility of parole.

"THE EXECUTIONERS
OF TWO COPS!"
by E. E. Gilpatrick

Such a ceremony is an admixture of sympathy, fare-well and a reminder that the profession of law enforcement, like few others, is for keeps. Many of Chicago's finest in freshly pressed uniforms and spit-shined shoes sat in solemn silence on Tuesday morning as a funeral mass was said for Patrolman James E. Doyle, who'd been shot and killed the previous Friday night in the line of duty.

Doyle had been out of the academy and on patrol duty only a few weeks when a thief whom Doyle was placing under arrest on a Chicago Transit Authority bus pulled out a gun and began shooting. Patrolman Doyle became the 387th police officer to give his life in the line of duty since the formal organization of the Chicago Police Department in 1872.

In attendance at the services were Patrolmen Ruben Garza, Phil Graziano, Bill Fahey and Dick O'Brien. The four had met at the Gang Crimes South headquarters on South Wentworth Avenue. Garza and Graziano were experienced in working with gang members, many of whom were juveniles, in a sensitive program designed to discipline young offenders without souring them into a life of crime.

Shortly before the end of the watch on Monday, Fahey and O'Brien were detailed to moving prisoners to the Gresham station. The prisoners were gang members, and such transfers were routine stuff for Garza and Graziano. It was suggested that since all four were going to the funeral, Fahey and O'Brien could meet Garza and Graziano at Gang Crimes South, discuss and review procedures and then proceed to the funeral. On Tuesday morning Fahey and O'Brien arrived at the Wentworth Avenue location to confer with Garza and Graziano. All went splendidly and the four finished up sooner than expected. Someone suggested they leave early for the funeral and stop off for a bite of breakfast on the way. It was a pleasant breakfast, but no one talked much. Lawmen try not to think about it, but death is forever tracking them. Worse, if it happens, it's at those times when a cop least expects it. An officer can survive a SWAT team operation without a bruise in the face of machine-gun fire and bombs and end up stiff and cold because of a husband-and-wife row, trying to collar some two-bit sneak thief, or even something as routine as pulling over a car on the other side of a stop sign.

Crime cares nothing for the dead, dying or hurting. As soon as services were over, Garza and Graziano went to pick up prisoners to be taken to the Gresham station; Fahey and O'Brien went to pick up their prisoners bound for the same location. Not long after prisoner processing began, Fahey and O'Brien brought their prisoners in. Receipts signed, Fahey and O'Brien smiled, waved and headed back to the streets.

At about 2:00 P.M. on Tuesday, February 9, 1982 Fahey and O'Brien were proceeding along Morgan Street when they saw the car in front of them run the stop sign where 81st Street crosses Morgan. The officers flipped on their overhead lights and gave the siren a couple of low blasts. The stop sign runner pulled over in front of 8110 Morgan Street. Both officers got out of their patrol car, as did two men from the offending car. The officers began patting them down in a search for weapons. A scuffle broke out; one of the men began shooting, and Fahey was shot once in the head with the bullet entering close behind his left ear. O'Brien was shot three times, once in the front of his chest and twice in the back.

The two men got back into their car, drove off and, according to one account, made a U-turn to come back and seize O'Brien's service revolver. The fugitive vehicle was last seen heading south on Morgan Street.

A few seconds later, police dispatchers were startled to hear a call on the police radio: "Emergency! Emergency! Two policemen shot at 81st and Morgan!" In a matter of seconds, the intersection was filled with police and emergency vehicles. Garza and Graziano were two of the first officers on the scene. One of the fallen officers seemed to be alive but in critical condition. Both were rushed to Little Company of Mary Hospital in the Evergreen Park district of Chicago. Garza recalls, "I rode with him (Fahey) in the squadrol to the hospital." Richard J. O'Brien, age 33, was brought into the hospital by ambulance and declared dead on arrival. With the help of a respirator, Officer Fahey maintained a weak grip on life.

Before the night was out, over 200 officers would report for duty on the case to work on their own time without pay. One of the first witnesses located was the youth who'd seen the traffic violation stop but who'd paid little attention to it until it became obvious much more was going on than the simple writing of a ticket.

Other witnesses began to take notice of what was going on. A few minutes after the emergency call was made from the radio of the officers' patrol car, a call was received on the 911 emergency telephone number. The informant making this call was quickly located. The suspect auto was described as a rust-colored or burnt orange 1978 or later Chevrolet Impala. The cleanliness and shine of the auto stood out in the minds of several witnesses. Investigators were dispatched to question operators of car washes in the vicinity.

Typically, it all happened so fast no one had presence of mind enough to copy down the license number of the car. One witness thought it was: something, D14 and then something else and another number — or letter.

From collating various descriptions of the occupants of the car, the investigators believed there were two of them. One was a black man, 18 to 20 years old, about 5'9" or 10", of medium build with a light complexion, a mustache and a short Afro hairstyle. He was wearing a brown cloth jacket, a long-sleeved, brown, cotton shirt with a one-inch-wide, white stripe down the sleeve and light brown or tan corduroy pants. He was the one who had what was described as a pistol with a chrome-like finish.

The other man who several witnesses felt sure was the driver of the burnt orange Chevrolet was also black, in his early 20s, 6' to 6'1" tall, thin, had a dark complexion, a rough beard, a mustache and a short Afro haircut. He was said to be wearing a heavy cloth coat which one witness described as, "undertaker style."

As the investigators worked, Jane Byrne, mayor of Chicago, went to the Little Company of Mary Hospital to do what she could for the families of the officers and to pay her condolences to the loved ones of Officer O'Brien. She remained at the hospital for nearly three hours.

Medical examination revealed that the three slugs which had entered Officer O'Brien's chest had killed him almost immediately. The bullet which had entered Officer Fahey's skull behind his left ear had fragmented on hitting the hard bone of the skull. Several of the fragments had ricocheted off interior surfaces of his skull. As a result, there'd been extensive brain damage.

Even as the investigation progressed, politically prominent Chicago Alderman Edward Vrodolyak advised the mayor and the public that an anonymous group of businessmen had offered a $50,000 reward for anyone providing information that would lead to the arrest and conviction of the killers.

After leaving the hospital, Mayor Byrne went to a fund raising dinner at the prestigious Conrad Hilton Hotel in downtown Chicago where, in her talk, she said it was a "sad day for Chicago. I began my morning going to the funeral Mass of Officer Doyle and came here to the hospital, where again one policeman is badly wounded, and one is definitely dead."

On Wednesday morning at Gang Crimes South headquarters there was little of the usual banter and wisecracking which usually goes on over coffee and rolls. Few had anything to say. Graziano did affirm, "They were two of the best policemen we've worked with." Lieutenant William McKeon was in command that morning. Assigned Commander Ed Pleines was at home. He'd worked all night on the investigation. The phone in the commander's office rang. McKeon took the call. Stony faced, he took the message, paused and slowly replaced the phone in its cradle. "Fahey just died," he said grimly.

In the confusion following the shooting, investigators moved as quickly as possible to get preliminary statements and names and addresses of possible witnesses. After a sifting and sorting, the lawmen would then come back for more intensive interviews. In this process, three youths were taken into custody. They were reported to the Chicago police by a sergeant at a military recruiting facility only a matter of blocks from the scene of the shooting. It struck the sergeant as odd that three young men who'd just seen a shooting should suddenly want to get as far away from the city as possible, even if they had to commit several years of their lives to do so. Investigators were inclined to agree, although they were able to determine nothing specific.

One of the first witnesses discovered was contacted when he answered the knock of a police officer at his door. The witness was asked if he'd seen or heard the shooting in the street in front of his house. He said he had and was still trying to sort it out in his mind. It was the growl of the siren right out front which caught his attention. He looked out his living room window to see what at first appeared to be a routine traffic stop. Then, the scuffle broke out.

In spite of the suspects' resistance, "the police officer (Fahey) had subdued him enough to the point where he could put the handcuffs on, and then the man reached around behind the officer and came up with a shiny pistol," the witness said. "His (Fahey's) left hand was holding (the man's) wrist, and with his right hand he was still holding the handcuffs," when the shot that ultimately killed Fahey was fired, the young man stated. The man who was struggling with Fahey was the shorter of the two suspects, the one wearing the brown jacket.

In the split seconds that followed as Fahey slumped down on his face in the street, the shooter dropped to a crouch near the curb, extended both arms and fired one shot at O'Brien. O'Brien went down on the street side of the patrol car, so that momentarily the patrol car was between the shooter and the now-prostrate body of O'Brien. "(The shooter) jumped up on the trunk (of the patrol car), and with the gun in his hand, he fired two more shots toward the ground," where O'Brien had fallen. "That's when I ran and called the police," the witness said.

The investigators asked the witness what the other man was doing as this was going on. The witness said, "(The other man) stood in front of the car when (the shooter) was shooting the officer at the back of the car." The detectives asked the witness who was driving. The witness said that when the shooting stopped, the man at the front of the car jumped into the driver's seat and drove off in a screech of tires as soon as the shooter leaped into the car, slamming the door behind him.

Another witness was the youth who'd given the alarm on the police radio. He was waiting by the squad car when the first officers arrived on the scene. The witness said it was eerie—that smile. "It just stayed in my mind. When they drove by, the one guy was smiling—the guy on the passenger side. They almost ran into us. We pulled over, and that's when I got a really good view of them," the witness said.

The witness explained that he and two friends were driving around the south side when they saw a police squad car stopped behind a brown Chevrolet. Two men jumped into the brown car and sped away. It was only after the car passed them did he notice two police officers lying next to the squad car. The witness jumped out of the car he was in. "I felt the pulse of one officer. I went to the other officer, and I really didn't feel any pulse. Then, I picked up the police radio in their car."

"Help!" he cried into the radio microphone.

"Emergency—two police officers have been shot!" As he waited for police to arrive, he put a folded coat under the head of one of the wounded officers and put another coat on top of him. The officer, Fahey, was still alive. "He kept trying to get up, and I kept pushing him down. He knew he was dying. I went over to the other officer, and I knew he was dead." The witness felt sure he'd recognize the two men if he ever saw them again.

Uncharacteristically, one of the investigators muttered under his breath, "You will." The investigators thanked the witness for his help and concern.

A hypnotist was brought into the investigation in an attempt to dredge up from the subconscious minds of witnesses the exact license number of the shiny, burnt orange colored Chevrolet. The procedure seemed to work out by producing the license number: JNK 197. One hypnotized witness also recalled that the car had a CB antenna on the right rear fender. Police intelligence advised the investigators that a 1977 Chevrolet Impala bearing that license number had been stolen from the northwest side on January 26th.

Deputy Police Superintendent James E. O'Grady now ordered a block-by-block search of every street in the city. The search of 3,700 miles of Chicago streets would be conducted beat by beat in a grid pattern, first working from the north end of each beat, covering east-west streets; then, starting from the east, covering north-south streets to completion, the order stated. Military buffs would recognize this tactic as a civilian version of a sweep-and-clear operation.

The Fraternal Order of Police contributed another $10,000 to the reward fund, bringing the total to $60,000. One of the effects of so much police heat on a city, any city, is that criminal activity becomes more risky than usual. Even denizens of the underworld began to ask themselves if they wouldn't be better off if these two fugitives were in custody. At least there'd be peace on the street. This was part of the strategy—making Chicago so hot, there'd be no place to hide. As one beat sergeant observed, "Somebody is going to start talking, I think. Whoever it is, they can't keep a secret. Somebody will slip, and we'll have our man."

Said an editorial in the *Chicago Tribune:* "A good policeman is a priceless asset. The city must recognize this by doing everything possible to track down the murderer and demonstrate that attacks on its policemen will not go unpunished."

As determination mounted, another important question came to the surface. Nothing in law says there need be a motive, but for the investigator a motive can point to a possible suspect. Why had Fahey and O'Brien been killed? A traffic ticket is annoying, but rarely is it a reason to kill. Even if the officers had spotted the Chevy as stolen, a shootout seemed unlikely. Auto theft is not a capital offense. Guesses ranged from the fact that the officers recognized the two suspects as wanted criminals to the possible sighting of immediate evidence of a major crime. All the detectives had were guesses to throw into the investigatory stew pot.

On Friday morning a funeral procession more than a mile long slowly wheeled its way along Chicago streets to attend the funeral of Richard J. O'Brien at St. Denis Catholic Church. Three days previously, O'Brien had attended a funeral there for his brother officer, James E. Doyle. In his eulogy, Reverend Thomas Nangle, Chicago Police Department chaplain, said, "A police officer, any police officer, is at one and the same time both privileged and sentenced, from the moment he puts on his star, to see more of life in a year than the rest of us will see in a lifetime." In closing, Father Nangle said, "And so, we give our beloved Richard, a son, a brother, a police officer — we give him back to God whence he came, beyond injustice, beyond outrage, beyond the anger of this life."

Behind two police squad cars, Mayor Byrne, Police Superintendent Richard Brzeczek and other municipal dignitaries and senior law enforcement staff officers led the winding funeral cortege to a small cemetery on Chicago's southwest side for one last goodbye to a brave man, a brother officer, part of the family. Both lead squad cars were dirty. They'd left the manhunt just in time to make the funeral. From the cemetery, they'd return directly to the search for the killers.

It was a bad day to be a criminal in Chicago. Even small amounts of weed would probably bring an arrest where user amounts hadn't raised an eyebrow previously. The worst was the wait at the precinct house. There was a waiting line at every interrogation room. This meant cell time of probably an hour or more, maybe all night. Nerves were wearing thin on both sides of the bars. Many of Chicago's lawmen hadn't slept in days. They were running on coffee, catnaps and determination.

As specified in the grid plan, everything was checked beat by beat and block by block; every street, alley and walkway was checked, every building, every lot, every store, every business, every house, every apartment. Floor by floor, door by door, the search went on.

By Saturday morning the search had reached 114th Street on the south side. There was no letup. There were a lot of runny noses on the street. There was also a lot of amazement. There were those who'd never seen the law flex its muscles before. Street arrogance seemed to fade. Near the corner of May and 114th Street an officer spotted a rust-colored, 1977 Chevrolet Impala with a CB antenna on the right rear fender. The license plate number on the car was not JNK 197. The lawman bent down to check the nuts on the license bracket. He stood up and spoke into his radio. A patrol car and a tow truck appeared opposite the Chevy, city-contracted mechanics got out of the tow truck, raised the hood on the Chevy after checking the VIN (vehicle identification number) on the body. The motor number checked. It was the Chevy which should have been bearing license plate JNK 197. The plates on it now were stolen plates. It was the getaway car.

A carryall of police officers arrived. A police department is a military organization, although most prefer not to think of it as such, but it can, if need be, operate as an army. This day in Chicago it was. The hellish grid search was intensified. Every street, alley, walkway, open lot, house, business, trash can, pile in the alley, every floor, every door, every janitor's closet was being checked.

Unknown to the police, a career criminal was holed up in a dingy apartment in the next block. To his cohorts he was known variously as Gino or Joseph. There was a faint knock at his door and a tip that he'd better get out. There was a whole army of cops in the neighborhood. They were looking in every bag and turning over every rock; they'd found the car.

Gino made a quick phone call to ask a close friend to drive him to another place. He could lay low at a place in the 5000 block of West Jackson Boulevard. It didn't seem possible they could carry this kind of search out that far. The friend put on his jacket and cap and trotted the few doors to his friend's. The two skipped downstairs, out the back and got in a car to head out to the place on West Jackson Boulevard. As they pulled out of the alley, they saw a squad of police crossing the street to begin searching the block they were leaving.

A raiding party seemed to materialize out of what had appeared to be an amorphous throng of blue uniforms. The target was a beauty salon on West 115th Street, directly in the path of the search party which was spreading over everything in South Chicago. With direct hookups to a number of judges and a cadre of assistant state's attorneys aiding them, the lawmen had a search warrant in little more time than it took to get from 114th Street to 115th Street.

Police crashed through the back door of the beauty shop. Swiftly, and with little talk, they searched the shop from back office to hair dryers. In the search they found two police service revolvers and a shotgun. Lab personnel had been standing by for three days ready for anything. One of the service pistols, comparison firing indicated, had belonged to Officer O'Brien. Investigators could only wonder if the second one had belonged to any officer in particular. For killers to have a shotgun was not unusual.

The owner of the beauty shop called her attorney. Police questioned her till late Saturday night. She said she knew nothing of the men who'd left the guns there. A number of her customers had male friends visit them while they were getting their hair done. She didn't know who some people were. She had no idea how the guns got into her place. She thought it quite possible someone could stash them while she was giving a shampoo or dryers were running. Such noises would drown out any sound in the back.

Investigators questioned others who were in or around the beauty shop at the time it was raided. Their luck appeared to be no better than the luck of the investigators questioning the owner of the shop, but the intense activity had caused the word to spread—and the word was: "$60,000."

A city official who was in contact with an informant passed on to Mayor Byrne the tip, "If you find the guys who stuck up the camera shop, you've got the guys who killed the policemen."

Police intelligence, with a quick records check, determined that the likely robbery in question was that of a camera store on South Michigan Avenue on the previous December 3rd. Captured in the wake of that robbery had been two brothers, both habitual criminals with extensive records. Their specialties were marijuana, burglary and theft. One was Andrew Wilson, age 29, who was known to his friends as Gino or Joseph. His brother Jackie, age 21, was also known as Bubbles, Robert or Jacques. Both had been released on bond after being indicted for the camera store robbery. Andrew had quickly skipped bond, and Jackie hadn't been seen since the killings of Fahey and O'Brien. Arrest warrants were issued for both men.

Uniformed police checked homes and haunts of friends and relatives of the two career criminals; at the same time, detectives questioned friends, relatives, intimates and cellmates of the pair. Shortly after they were arrested for the camera store robbery and were being held in Cook County Jail, Andrew Wilson held a meeting of certain select prisoners. Wilson told his friend, "Hey, man, we got to get Ace out. If we don't he's gonna burn." Ace was another habitual criminal then being held on the maximum security floor of Cook County Jail. Ace's real name was Edgar Hope. He'd been indicted and was being held without bond in the killing of Officer James E. Doyle.

Closely scrutinizing the suspects' records, investigators noticed that the Wilson brothers were wanted for questioning in connection with a home invasion in Alsip, Illinois, a suburb on the south side of Chicago. Two men in postal workers' uniforms had invaded a home and said they wanted the police uniforms. It didn't make sense, for the home owners had no police uniforms. They didn't know that a man who lived two blocks over, also in a white house, and also the second house from the corner, was a retired police officer.

Going back to the original witnesses, police talked to the three youths who'd run off to the recruiting station. It had not been clear what their involvement had been and why they'd been so frightened. One broke, and said that as fellow gang members they'd been at the meeting where the Wilsons and others talked of burglarizing the home of a retired police officer to get some uniforms to be used in a plot to get Ace out of jail. The house the Wilsons had in mind was only a few blocks from the death scene. The youths had no part in the crime, but feared they might be arrested as accessories. Their only involvement was one of curiosity.

Investigators checked the house. It had been broken into, and, it appeared, items had been stolen from a closet. The retired officer was contacted in Florida. He said that as far as he knew, his last police uniform was still hanging in his closet for sentiment and ceremonies. The uniform was missing from the house. Investigators believed that officers Fahey and O'Brien had spotted the uniform or other loot in the Chevy. Andrew Wilson was a bond jumper and the plot to spring Hope was about to go down the drain. That was the motive, and it pointed directly at the Wilson brothers.

In a shabby apartment on West Jackson Boulevard the man who'd driven Gino there was about to go crazy. He needed a joint or a fix, but there was nothing on the street. He'd tried for both him and Gino.

He'd heard: "$60,000." In the early hours of Sunday morning he told Gino he had to go out for a while. On the way into the city, the driver stopped at a phone booth. There was no phone directory there, but that was OK. He knew the number he wanted: 911. Andrew Wilson was taken in the pre-dawn hours of Sunday morning.

Later Sunday morning, in a South Chicago church, a pastor was consulted by a knot of women of his congregation. They felt that the Wilsons were a bad influence on their community and only one of the brothers was in custody. The son of one of the women had told his mother where the other Wilson was, but none of the women wanted to be the one to tell the police. The pastor said he'd take care of it. He knew his son and daughter-in-law were at his home awaiting him for dinner. His son was a police officer with the Chicago Police Department.

Jackie Wilson, like his brother, was taken without incident.

Edgar Hope remained in jail until his trial in October, 1982. He was found guilty and sentenced to die in the electric chair for the murder of Officer Doyle.

In the trial of Andrew and Jackie Wilson, the defense called Mayor Jane Byrne to testify that rewards totaling $60,000 had been posted. The defense contended that prosecution witnesses cared little for truth, only money.

The Wilson brothers were both found guilty. On February 8, 1983, Andrew Wilson, the shooter, was sentenced to death in the electric chair. His brother Jackie was given a sentence of life imprisonment without parole.

"NIGHT OF HELL FOR THE NYPD!"

by Bud Ampolsk

Deputy Chief John V. Menken, executive officer of the New York City Detective Bureau, will not soon forget Tuesday night, October 18, 1988. Nor will the memories of the nine days that followed be easily erased from the 55-year-old sleuth's mind.

Chief Menken has total recall of the smallest details of the events which threw the NYPD into pandemonium and cast a pall over the entire city.

It was shortly after 7:00 P.M. Chief Menken was in a police vehicle, being driven back to police headquarters from an investigation in Staten Island. The executive officer was standing in for Chief of Detectives Robert Colangelo, who was attending a conference in Portland, Oregon.

"We heard about it on the police radio in the car," Menken says.

Alerted by the terse bulletin that a cop had been shot, Menken's driver immediately changed course. Dome light glaring an unwinking red and siren screaming, the unmarked vehicle raced towards St. Luke's Hospital at 112th Street and Amsterdam Avenue.

A Part of America Died

Somebody killed a policeman today and
A part of America died.
A piece of our country he swore to protect
Will be buried with him at his side.
The suspect who shot him will stand up in court,
With counsel demanding his rights,
While a young widowed mother must work
　　for her kids
And spend many long, lonely nights.
The beat that he walked was a battlefield, too,
Just as if he'd gone off to war.
Though the flag of our nation won't fly at half
　　mast,
To his name they will add a gold star.
Yes, somebody killed a policeman today,
It happened in your town or mine
While we slept in comfort behind our
　　locked doors,
A cop put his life on the line.
Now his ghost walks a beat on a dark city street,
And he stands at each new rookie's side.
He answered the call, and gave us his all
And a part of America died.

by Angel Sparks

The scene that greeted him at the West Side medical complex could only be described as chaotic — a mix of shouting, blinding lights of television crews, insistent high-pitched shrieks of arriving emergency vehicles, and commotion attending the appearance of Mayor Edward Koch and Police Commissioner Benjamin Ward.

For his part, Menken had little time for the panic

which has come to be associated with the mortal wounding of a police officer. "The first thing I did," he said "was to call Manhattan North operations and direct that James Power respond to the scene. And I directed that Chief Aaron Rosenthal, who is the borough detectives' commander and whose responsibility it is to do these investigations, be notified at home."

Responding to the order, Inspector Power, in charge of all Manhattan detective precincts north of 59th Street, rushed an initial force of 15 detectives to the crime scene—105th Street just west of Central Park West. They were under orders to seal off the whole area—including a small, dilapidated apartment in a building on West 105th Street, the building itself and the block where the officer had been shot.

"Usually the uniform police get there first and they will take the steps to do that," Menken commented. "It's our responsibility to keep it that way—cordon it off, secure and keep it pure until everything is recorded and documented."

It was a harrowing scene at 105th Street as scores of officers worked under the glare of gyrating flashers and mobile floodlights. Members of the crime-scene unit went about collecting evidence. Ballistics specialists conducted an inch-by-inch search for spent bullets and cartridge cases. Members of the major case squad and other uniformed cops were at work.

Said Captain Thomas P. Green, the 45-year-old lawman who coordinated the 105th Street activity from his office, "The huge influx in manpower helped insure that no piece of evidence was overlooked. In a case like this, the more people you have at the scene initially, the better off you are."

While the recovery of viable evidence went forward, other officers began fanning out through the neighborhood to canvass those civilians who might provide useful information.

On the effort to obtain accounts from witnesses, Menken observed, "You start at the center and work your way out. First you start canvassing people in the building, then you look for witnesses on the street."

Detectives' efforts are highly structured and nobody is allowed the luxury of playing a lone sleuth, Chief Menken said. "We don't have any Colombos in this department," he added. "Detective work is a team effort. All the pieces of information have to come through a central figure to make sure the case is properly put together for a court presentation."

This is what the veritable army of investigators were able to piece together in the early hours of the probe . . .

Undercover Officers Christopher Hoban, NYPD Badge Number 25547, and Michael Jermyn, both of the Manhattan North Narcotics Squad, had arrived at the house on West 105th Street at approximately 7:00 P.M. Their assignment was to have been a routine "buy-and-bust" drug operation, calling for the 26-year-old Hoban and his partner to follow a "street steerer" to a tiny second-floor apartment in the brownstone and purchase a gram of cocaine. Once the transaction was completed, the backup team, which was now in place, would move in and make the arrests.

As planned, both Hoban and Jermyn met the alleged steerers outside the five-story building. They were said to have been of particular interest to the cops because other undercover officers had scored drugs from them in the past. A second rap would warrant a felony arrest.

With the backup team on the alert, Hoban and Jermyn followed the suspected drug pusher up narrow, dimly lit steps. They had reason to believe they would find a third alleged dealer inside the 11-by-20-foot studio flat.

As they knocked at the apartment door, Hoban and Jermyn recognized that they were now in the critically perilous phase of their sting operation. For the next few moments, they would be out of sight of their backup. Anything could happen inside the flat before help could reach them.

As they entered, the officers noted that the interior of the decrepit apartment was sparsely furnished with only a chair, a sofa, a television set and a bunk bed. Working quickly—the procedure being to make a rapid buy, exit the premises and allow the backup to make the actual arrest—Hoban and Jermyn began negotiating with one of the steerers.

As the two undercover officers haggled over the price to reinforce the impression that they were cocaine users, their contact settled down on the couch. He appeared to be paying no attention to the bartering. At last a deal was struck for $50 for the gram.

Allegedly, that was when things began to turn sour. One of the men was said to have muttered some words in Spanish to the others. Neither Hoban nor Jermyn understood what was being said.

Then one of the men is said to have turned to Hoban and Jermyn and asked the three words which undercover officers dread: "Are you cops?"

The alleged trio of traffickers were apparently not satisfied with Hoban and Jermyn's denials. Another brief conference was carried out in Spanish, and then the trio allegedly demanded that the two plainclothesmen snort some coke. The cops refused.

It is alleged that two of the steerers then turned on Hoban and grabbed his shirt. They are said to have bunched it up under his armpits as they searched for a transmitter or a weapon. Because Hoban had buried his Police .38 so deeply into the waistband of his pants, the occupants of the flat missed it.

When the alleged traffickers repeated their search, this time with Jermyn as the target, the officers' luck ran out. Jermyn's revolver was visible above the waistband of his slacks. It was reported that one of the steerers tried to grab Jermyn's gun and the officer pushed him away.

In the blink of an eye, another allegedly reached behind a nearby clock and pulled out a .38 of his own. He squeezed off three shots.

Hoban responded instantly. The 26-year-old cop went for a gun he carried in a holster on his ankle. He managed to get off two shots before he himself was hit in the forehead and chest.

Jermyn's gun was knocked to the floor before he could join in the firefight.

Then the two steerers allegedly broke for the door and raced down the steps to the street with Jermyn in hot pursuit and screaming for help.

Hearing the commotion, the backup team moved with lightning speed. They ran to the building and grabbed one of the steerers as he fled west towards Columbus Avenue. They were not as lucky with the other, who ran toward Central Park West. He outraced the pursuing officers and was thought to have escaped into the Independent Subway's 103rd Street station.

Those who climbed the 44 steps to the now bloodsoaked studio flat discovered the third man dead on the couch where he had been sitting. Undercover Officer Hoban lay on the floor a few feet away from the slain cocaine dealer. Hoban's gun was under him. At this point, the officer was still alive.

Throughout the early evening hours, Chief Menken shuttled between St. Luke's Hospital, where doctors were desperately trying to save Hoban's life, the crime scene on 105th Street, and the 24th Precinct station-house, keeping in close touch with all developments.

The scene at St. Luke's had been deteriorating by the minute. Hoban's close relatives had been sped by police vehicle to the jammed corridors of the hospital, where a priest waited to give them the grim news. Christopher Hoban was brain dead and had been given the last rites of the church. It was only a matter of time.

At 9:30 P.M., time ran out for the gallant young officer. The wave-pattern reading on the oscilloscope monitoring the electrical waves of his brain went flat. The struggle to prolong his life was over.

Strong men and women, police officers, emergency room personnel and members of the working press, all wept unabashedly as they heard the word.

The night of tragedy was not ended, however. Hoban's death was, in a sense, the first act of a tragic drama.

Within three hours and three miles of the West Side murder of Christopher Hoban, an unrelated second catastrophe had taken place. A second officer was rushed to a hospital emergency room, having been shot down in cold blood. From sketchy first reports, the victim was identified as Michael Buczek, 24, of the 34th Precinct. He had been shot in the stomach and chest as he chased a suspect on Broadway near 161st Street. He was sped to Presbyterian Hospital of the Columbia Medical Center at 168th Street.

Emotionally spent from the tragedy of Christopher Hoban's brutal killing, Chief Menken even now faced the task of mounting still another all-points police action.

Shortly after 10:00 P.M., Menken, along with Commissioner Ward and Mayor Koch, was rushed due north to the hospital. The trio found a scene that was virtually an exact mirror image of what had gone on at St. Luke's. A young police officer had been mercilessly cut down by a pair of street punks. He had surprised the alleged perps in a hallway confrontation. Buczek, like Hoban, could not survive the terrible wounds he had received.

Once again, there was pandemonium and agony in hospital corridors. Once again, next of kin were hastily-called. They waited, their eyes glassy with shock, clustered near the gathering of police officers and press representatives.

For Menken, there were new orders to issue. The manhunt in the Hoban killing had resulted in suspension of service on the Independent Subway line while the tunnel was searched for a suspect. Now the pursuit was extended to the streets in the Washington Heights sector of Manhattan and Harlem. Shotgun- and rifle-toting Emergency Service Unit personnel went into action, stopping and searching cars leaving the city by way of the George Washington Bridge.

As they had earlier in the evening in the Hoban case, detectives, forensic and ballistics experts, and uniformed personnel under Chief Menken's command fanned outward from the crime scene and began the painstaking job of putting together a cohesive story of just what had happened.

From interviews with witnesses, they learned that Buczek, three-year veteran officer assigned to the 34th Precinct, and his partner had answered a dispatcher's call to assist a woman living on West 161st Street. The two officers arrived at the stricken woman's apartment to find that she was evidently suffering from an asthma attack and accompanying stomach pains.

Buczek spent the time until the arrival of an Emergency Medical Service ambulance comforting the ill woman. When the EMS vehicle pulled up to the building, Buczek and his partner, Robert Barbato, prepared to leave. They paused briefly in the vestibule to confer with the medical technicians.

While talking, they noticed two men passing the building doorway and acting in a suspicious manner. Buczek went out onto the sidewalk and ordered the men to halt.

Instead, the suspects ran around the corner to Broadway. Buczek's partner grabbed one man, who opened fire with a semi-automatic weapon. As Buczek grappled with the second alleged perp, the young officer was hit in the chest and abdomen by the gunfire. Buczek's partner dropped to his knees and managed to squeeze off four shots at the fleeing figures.

It was not known whether either of the pair had been wounded. However, one of them was heard to scream, "I just shot a cop!" as the two nightstalkers faded into the gloom.

Seeing Buczek so severely injured, Barbato lost his grip on the one culprit he had nabbed. Both partner and close friend, he gave Buczek his total attention by providing mouth-to-mouth resuscitation.

Hastily, Buczek was then placed into the very same EMS ambulance which had come to the building to administer to the asthmatic woman. A short while later, acting on tips given them by cooperating witnesses, other police officers took into custody a 27-year-old suspect, charging him with second-degree murder in the shooting death of Buczek.

Said Deputy Police Commissioner Alice T. McGillion, "We believe he was the one who did the shooting. He made a comment as he was running down the block that he just shot a cop."

A gun was reported found at the crime scene, as was a jacket. But the police could not determine immediately whether the firearm had been used during the shootout.

A graphic description of the firefight was given by workers at a food market that occupied the ground floor of the building in front of which the duel had taken place.

The workers said they had seen the two alleged perps round the corner into Broadway with Officers Buczek and Barbato in close pursuit. One of the men turned and fired at the officers, at least one of whom returned the fire. The workers said they heard at least six shots. Buczek was hit twice—once in the chest.

The two alleged killers fled south on Broadway. The still unknown partner of the arrested man had made good his escape while Barbato was busy ministering to Buczek.

From top to bottom, the entire police department was badly shaken by the loss of two young officers. Said Commissioner Ward, "I don't know of any case when two or more police officers were killed in separate incidents on the same day."

Noted one detective who had spent the long night racing up and down the West Side in squad cars as he tried to piece together the grim details of the two slayings: "I have never seen a night like this."

One uniformed officer who kept the vigil at both St. Luke's and Columbia Medical Center during the night of carnage described his feelings as "unexplainable . . . Two cops in one day—that's the worst I can remember."

While annals of the Patrolmen's Benevolent Association show that once, back on January 23, 1943, two cops were murdered in two separate incidents in the line of duty on the same day, Chief Menken wryly expressed the feelings of today's officers when he said, "That's a little before my time."

Even as the more than 28,000 members of the

NYPD, augmented by FBI agents, mounted one of the biggest manhunts in city history for Hoban's still-at-large slayer and the as-yet unnamed other culprit in the Buczek murder, there was time for fond memories and expressions of grief concerning the two fallen officers.

Relatives, as well as fellow officers, recalled Hoban as a fearless cop who had "gone undercover" because he wanted to do something about the drug epidemic.

Close family members told of how Hoban had informed them that he would be unable to see them for three days. (That had been on the Saturday before his October 8th murder.) Although Christopher Hoban had not mentioned the reason for his absence, his kin believed that the young anti-narc officer was on a special assignment.

Said his bereaved mother, "The last words out of my mouth when he left here on Saturday night were, 'Take care. I love you.' He wanted to do good. But that whole drug scene, the whole miserable scene that's out there—it killed him."

Hoban's father, a retired drug and alcohol counselor for the United States Postal Service, said that Christopher became a police officer because he wanted to help save people from drugs.

After serving three years as a uniformed patrol officer in the 88th and 77th Precincts in Brooklyn, Hoban requested an undercover assignment.

Said Inspector Philip G. Sheridan, Hoban's commanding officer at the 77th, "He was a good worker with an excellent attitude and his request for transfer was accepted."

Assigned to the Manhattan North Narcotics Squad, Hoban had taken on the raiment and appearance of a "druggie." He'd let his hair grow to shoulder-length and worn street clothes.

Some felt that the young officer's burning desire to do what he could to stamp out narcotics traffic was the result of seeing changes in his own Sunset Park neighborhood. The incursion of narcotics had driven a number of hard-working and law-abiding residents out of the area.

Although he had set up his own apartment close by his family dwelling a year earlier, he'd never really left home. His mother still cooked for him and did his laundry. She said, "We give all our children wings, along with love. Chris always knew that he could fly or come back home."

One young woman who had been Hoban's classmate in grade school recalled him this way: "If you hadn't seen Chris in a while, he'd come running up to you and give you a hug and ask what's doing. He was such a nice person. He always made you laugh."

A woman who was a close family friend recalled the first day that Hoban had walked into her store wearing his police shield. "We were all so proud of him," she said. Still, the woman could not comprehend why he had volunteered to work undercover. "He should've let them deal all the drugs they want and kill each other. Chrissy was my honey, my son's best friend."

Cops who had shared their beat with Michael Buczek admired him as the "little powerhouse."

"He was the cop all of us wanted to be," said Officer Frank Horvath. "He would have worn his uniform twenty-five hours a day if they'd have let him."

Buczek, who'd grown up in Wayne, New Jersey, joined the NYPD because there wasn't enough action in his hometown to suit him. "There wasn't even enough here (in the 34th Precinct) to suit him, even though we're one of the busiest precincts in the city," said one colleague.

Added fellow 34th Precinct Officer Drew Capui,

"Nothing scared him."

Buczek had a reputation for toughness and worked in the precinct's Sector Charlie between Broadway and Edgecombe Avenue from 161st Street to 172nd Street, an acknowledged hotbed of drug infestation. The young officer's arrest and 40 citation records were outstanding. They had caught the attention of superiors who wanted to promote him and transfer him into the plainclothes anti-crime unit. The shift would have meant more money and would have been a step toward the prized gold shield of a detective.

But Buczek turned the promotion down. "I can't work without my right hand," he'd said. The intrepid cop had been referring to his best friend and partner, Barbato.

But for all the toughness of the young officer — married just a little over a year — there was a gentleness to him, as well. This was recognized by the woman whose 911 call had taken Buczek on the last run of his life. The tears shed by the 38-year-old woman were as bitter with grief as were those of anybody who had known the officer a lifetime.

In a choked voice, she said, "His last act was helping me. He came to help me, and now he's dead. I feel that I am to blame for his death. That officer died helping me. My God!"

She told of her sudden illness, of how she had sat by her window gasping for breath, of how her 13-year-old daughter had dialed 911 seeking help. "About two minutes later, two policemen knocked at my door. Officer Buczek said, 'Hello, we were passing by and we wanted to see if you were sick.'

"He told me not to worry, that the ambulance was going to be here any minute. He said, 'Hello, baby,' to my three-year-old.

"A few minutes after the officers left, we all heard

295

gunshots from our window."

As mourning for the fallen officers spread across the city and preparations went forward for the first funeral in New York City history in which the coffins of two officers who had been murdered on the same day in separate police actions would lie side by side at final rites, one of the largest manhunts in Big Apple history was being mounted.

Crucial to that manhunt were the efforts of COP SHOT, a volunteer organization of community leaders which collected and offered rewards of $10,000 in each of the slayings for information leading to the arrest and conviction of the still-at-large prime suspects.

More than 100 officers blanketed the streets of New York, checking the known haunts of the alleged perp in the 161st Street shootout and of the Dominican Republic native who was wanted in connection with Hoban's 105th Street killing.

Flyers featuring photos of the man described as 24 years old, 6 feet tall and pock-marked, were widely circulated throughout the five boroughs. Police said the man, who had been previously arrested on August 16th on charges of possession of a loaded gun and driving without a license, had most recently been living on West 104th Street in Manhattan.

An around-the-clock watch was being kept for him at LaGuardia and Kennedy Airports on the possibility that he might attempt to flee the country and make it back to the Dominican Republic.

Aware of the mounting peril to uniformed and plainclothes police officers investigating narcotics-related crimes, Commissioner Ward issued an order that all personnel now don bulletproof vests when on patrol. (Up until the present, the wearing of such protective gear had been optional.) The directive received a mixed reception, some lawmen contending that the vests were ill-fitting and restricted bodily action.

Typical comment was that of Officer Drew Capui, the Patrolmen's Benevolent Association delegate from Buczek's own 34th Precinct. Said Capui, "Personally, I think everybody should wear a vest. I don't want anyone to lose their life for failing to wear a vest. I think everyone understands the reason why the order is out. But a month from now, everybody will forget about it."

Almost unanimous was the cry for stiffer penalties for those convicted of drug-related crimes of violence. Mayor Koch demanded that those responsible for Hoban's and Buczek's deaths be tried under the new Federal Anti-Drug law—passed by the Congress and signed by President Reagan during October—which called for the death penalty for the slaying of police officers by drug traffickers.

The sentiment of the public seemed best expressed by the Drug Enforcement Agency's New York office head, Robert Stutman. Stutman, who himself had reportedly been targeted for assassination by South American drug kingpins, declared: "I am furious. I am outraged at the killing of two more law enforcement officers in New York and over the last two years the death of five DEA agents across the nation as a direct result of the drug trade.

"It seems to me that there is a tremendous amount of rhetoric—screaming and yelling and promising changes in the laws that don't come from within the city, state, in some cases from within the federal government. The only ones dying in the war are cops and agents."

For three days, heavily-armed squads of NYPD personnel ranged the city. Toting shotguns and other high-powered ordnance, the grim-faced officers entered apartments in upper Manhattan and the West Bronx. They were buoyed by a Board of Estimate vote which would allow the department's Tactical Narcotics Team to add 600 cops and expand its operations beyond South Queens. (TNT units had originally been deployed in the Jamaica sector of Queens following the February 1988 assassination of Officer Edward Byrne, allegedly by four drug traffickers.)

In all, six search warrants were issued in the Buczek slaying. Police were said to be seeking a person with the street name "Poppy," reportedly a drug ripoff artist who had been preying on Washington Heights street dealers. Four Bronx and two Manhattan locations had been searched.

As of Friday morning October 21st, these were the developments:

— A 49-year-old suspect had been arraigned and was being held without bail on charges of second-degree murder, robbery and sale and possession of cocaine in the Hoban case. Officials alleged that he made a statement to Detective John Hachadorian in which he admitted to having been in the apartment when Hoban was shot.

Police in Miami reported that he was wanted there for attempted murder. Allegedly he had been on the lam since July 7, 1978, when he had reportedly beaten a man over the head with a pipe.

— Ballistics tests had determined that Hoban had been hit with two .38-caliber slugs which might have been fired from a .38 revolver or a .357 Magnum. Buczek was mortally wounded by a 9-millimeter bullet. The slug had passed through his body and had not been recovered. But detectives found police 9-mm. shells, a cartridge and bullet at the shooting scene. Neither murder weapon had been recovered. (It was also determined that Hoban had fired the shot which had killed one of the perps.)

It was at 9:10 A.M. Friday that officers who had

spent countless manhours in the all-out hunt for the two remaining suspects got their first big break. It came when they entered a house on Marcy Avenue in the Bronx, home of a 25-year-old suspect.

Arresting officers described the scene in the apartment as they moved in on their quarry. The suspect was in company with three men and a woman. All five of them were naked when the heavily-armed detail arrived. After day-long questioning by detectives at the 34th Precinct, the suspect was charged with first-degree murder.

According to police spokesman John Venetucci, the suspect was a native of the Dominican Republic and had been in the United States for seven years. It was not clear whether his residency here was legal or not.

One police source claimed that he had been the one who actually fired the shot which had taken Buczek's life.

It was said that the man had been arrested twice before on drug charges; the murder one charge lodged against him is the most serious of all. It concerns the killing of a cop in uniform who is clearly identifiable as a law officer. In areas of the United States where the death penalty is in force, conviction on first-degree murder charges leads to the death penalty. However, were he to be tried in New York State courts where the maximum punishment for murder is 25 years to life, he would not be in peril of execution.

As they discussed the case against the suspect, detectives alleged that an eyewitness to the 161st Street and Broadway killing of Buczek had picked his photograph from a book of mugshots.

Saturday morning, October 22nd, was raw and blustery, following an all-night downpour. It was a fit setting for the scene at Our Lady of Perpetual Help Roman Catholic Church in the Sunset Park section of

Brooklyn. It was here that the largest gathering of police officers in history, between 12,000 and 15,000, attended a requiem mass for slain brothers-in-arms and stood at rigid and silent attention as side by side, the flag-draped coffins of Buczek and Hoban were borne into the chapel by sad-faced uniformed pallbearers.

Not only did the thousands of official mourners tell the story, but the expressions of civilians who formed solid lines behind police barricades and the working cops, many of them rifle-carrying sharpshooters who stood their posts on nearby roofs in anticipation of possible terrorist activity, also gave mute evidence to the enormity of what had happened to two young and valiant men, each in his mid-twenties, who had given their lives in the performance of their duty. Buczek, with 40 citations for meritorious service, and Hoban, with two, had represented the highest traditions to which a cop could aspire.

The feelings of those gathered both inside and outside of Our Lady of Perpetual Help were summed up by the officiating priest. In his eulogy of the martyred officers, he said, "It seems fitting for Michael and Christopher to lie together in this church, because they shared so many common bonds. Christopher and Michael shared a vision that life could be better."

Throughout the days that followed the burial of Hoban and Buczek, public expressions of mourning went on. There were processions to the spot where Buczek had fallen and to the precinct headquarters of the officers. Civilians carrying memorial candles massed together in their pledges to drive the drug-traffickers from their embattled neighborhoods. It was obvious that what had happened to Buczek and Hoban galvanized anti-crime feelings to a pitch never before reached in the Big Apple.

For the task forces ranging the city in search of the

suspect, there was no respite. Despite police reticence to talk about developments, some progress had been made. A citywide search was now on for the owner of a 1983 gray Renault. It was said that drug-dealing associates of the suspect's had been seen in the car following Buczek's shooting. While the Renault owner was not considered a suspect in the murder, police wanted to question him, too.

Now New York police sought the help of Miami lawmen in tracking down the suspected murderer on the theory that he might be attempting to leave the country and make his way to the Dominican Republic.

Within days, the reports began to flood in. Indeed, the suspect was spotted in Miami. On several occasions officers were close to apprehending him, but missed him by minutes. Time became of the essence. FBI agents were notified.

On Wednesday, October 26th, New York City cops had an intercept. The suspect's friends in Miami had tried to contact associates to let them know that the alleged drug-trafficker had arrived from the Big Apple. The FBI got on his trail. It was now thought that he had already cleared Miami. The search for him shifted to San Juan, Puerto Rico.

On Thursday, October 27th, the theory paid off. As the suspect was headed for the Dominican Republic's San Juan consulate to pick up his visa, FBI agents swooped down on him in a suburban San Juan shopping-center mall where he was about to enter a restaurant frequented by Dominicans. Unarmed, he surrendered after a brief and futile attempt to outrun his pursuers. The wanted man was said to have been surprised by the fact that his 10-day flight had come to such a sudden end.

Those working on the case were equally surprised to learn that the suspect had supposedly been a police officer in the Dominican Republic from 1983 to 1987. Sources close to the situation said that he had been fired from the force after he allegedly killed a man in an off-duty shooting there. Although he was said to have been cleared of any wrongdoing in that incident, he gained a reputation for being vicious, it was said.

Sources said that he had emigrated to New York about eight months before the Hoban murder. Commented one police officer, "He was feared—literally feared—by a number of people who knew him."

According to sources, the suspect had been harbored by New York City friends for two days after the 105th Street shooting. On Thursday, October 20th, he dropped out of sight there, having traveled by train to Miami. From the Florida city, he'd flown to San Juan.

The tip that he had been seeking asylum in the Dominican Republic sent FBI agents to the Dominican San Juan consulate. There they had learned that he had indeed called upon consulate officials that very day, Wednesday, October 19th, and had been told to return on Thursday to fill out the necessary visa forms.

A fresh wound was found on the wanted man's left side following his arrest, according to FBI Assistant Director James Fox. The wound was said to have been caused either by a shot Buczek had gotten off at him before dying or in a struggle with Buczek's partner, Barbato.

On Friday, October 28th, as the suspect was shackled and handcuffed, and about to enter a federal courtroom in San Juan for extradition proceedings designed to return him to New York to face murder charges, he suffered an apparent seizure.

The prisoner began making strange noises, frothed at the mouth and vomited. He was returned to the Rio Piedras State Prison where he was being held. There he would undergo the psychiatric evaluation ordered by U.S. Magistrate Jesus Castellanos.

A team of six New York City detectives who had been dispatched to guard him on the flight back to the Big Apple would remain in San Juan pending the outcome of the medical examination.

Lawyers representing the suspect at the hearing told the court that the defendant had a history of having been struck on the head. In their opinion, he was mentally unfit to stand trial.

Meanwhile, on the very same day as his San Juan court appearance, another suspect was arrested in front of his home and charged with hindering prosecution by helping the fugitive avoid capture for three days before his Miami-San Juan junket.

Expanding on this phase of the case, Chief of Detectives Aaron Rosenthal commented, "We believe that after the shooting, the suspect drove the fugitive to a particular location where he could treat his wound. We believe he might have subsequently driven him to a number of other places."

One source reported that while he was hiding in New York after the shooting, associates had given him money and salable jewelry items to finance his alleged attempt to escape to the Dominican Republic.

As of this writing, all of the defendants in the murders of Officers Christopher Hoban and Michael Buczek are awaiting further court action on the assortment of charges against them. Under the United States Constitution, they've the right to be presumed innocent of these charges unless and until proved otherwise under due process of law.

"OFFICER DOWN!"
by Gary C. King

No cop, nor anyone else for that matter, wants to die. But when a cop, society's guardian of the law, gets up each day, puts on his uniform and gun, he or she really doesn't know for certain whether he'll make it through the day alive. Most police officers, or so this writer has been told, try not to think about the grim possibility they may be killed in the line of duty. But it remains a distinct, albeit bleak, reality, a reality which they are trained to accept. Cops do, in fact, get killed, usually when they least expect it. Such was the case for Spokane, Washington police Detective Brian Orchard, who met his unfortunate fate during a raging downtown shootout on Monday, July 18, 1983. This is the story of how it happened . . .

Nearly seven weeks earlier, two men forced their way into the home of Lyle Miller, a Wenatchee, Washington gun collector. The robbers took 180 pounds of silver, coins and rare currency, diamonds, gold and 72 firearms including rifles, shotguns and handguns, many of which were antique collectors' items. During the course of the robbery, Miller and his wife were seriously beaten, after which they were locked inside a large walk-in safe where they were left to suffocate by the robbers. Fortunately, Miller and his wife were able to escape, having been prepared for just such an occurrence, and notified the Chelan County Sheriff's Department of the incident. That was on June 1, 1983.

Weeks passed and there was no sign of the stolen goods. Police were watching all the pawn shops but, apparently, the items were just too hot to hock. But a few days prior to the downtown Spokane shootout, Miller received a telephone call from one of the robbers who wanted to sell some of the stolen items, primarily the guns, back to him for $19,000 cash. Miller told the caller he'd have to think over the offer before making a decision, and told the extortionist to call him back the next day. In the meantime Miller reported the incident to the sheriff's department, who in turn advised him to set up a meeting with the robbers for the exchange.

When the extortionist called back the next day, Miller agreed to meet him and another man in a downtown Spokane parking lot near the Holiday Inn East on Fifth Avenue and Pine Street. The exchange was to take place on July 18th, at approximately 10:30 P.M., in the hotel's rear parking area. Since the exchange was to occur in Spokane, Chelan County authorities naturally requested assistance from the Spokane Police Department.

A few minutes past 10:30 P.M. a black, older model Lincoln Continental pulled over on Pine Street near the hotel and parked. One man got out, went to Lyle Miller's car, parked nearby, and looked inside for an envelope that was supposed to contain money as payment for the return of the guns which had been stolen.

"Let's take 'em down," came the order from Detective Sergeant Tom Morris, in charge of the stakeout.

305

"Police! Stay where you are or I'll shoot," Morris yelled to the man looking inside Miller's car. At that point, Detectives Brian Orchard and Bruce Nelson pulled in behind the parked Lincoln and parked approximately 20 feet behind it. Nelson, wearing a blue baseball jacket, Levis jeans, a rugby shirt and cowboy boots, climbed out of the passenger side of Orchard's unmarked Mustang, his pistol drawn, and stood behind the open door of the car, using it as a shield. Orchard, also dressed casually, did likewise, and switched the Mustang's headlamps on to high beam, and the officers used the bright headlights as a shield against the suspect in the black Lincoln.

"Police officers!" yelled Detective Nelson, loudly and clearly. "Put your hands on the dash where we can see them." With that command, the person in the black Lincoln ducked down in the front seat. "Police officers," Nelson yelled again. "Get up where we can see you." But the person stayed down in the seat.

At that point, Detective Nelson began walking carefully toward the Lincoln and approached it from the passenger side. Again, Detective Orchard did likewise, but from the driver's side of the car. When Nelson reached the rear of the Lincoln he crouched down behind it. As he did so, he checked the trunk lid to determine whether or not it was locked. It was. Nelson then moved up the side of the car to the passenger rear window, and peered inside around the window post that serves to divide the front and rear side windows. At that point he saw someone lying on the front seat. Nelson carefully retreated to his former crouched position at the rear of the car when he heard a noise which sounded frighteningly similar to that of a gun being cocked. When he looked up he saw his partner's head on the other side of the car, moving forward.

"Brian, look out!" shouted Nelson. At that same instant a shot rang out from inside the car, and when he saw his partner, Orchard, fall to the pavement, Nelson fired a shot into one of the back tires. When he looked over and saw his partner lying in the street, he fired five more shots at the fleeing black Lincoln. During the gunfire, the suspect that Sergeant Morris was trying to apprehend fled into nearby bushes, out of sight from the lawmen.

"Orchard went down!" yelled Nelson to his backups.

"How bad?" came the reply.

"Pretty bad," said Nelson. "Call an ambulance."

"Officer down!" yelled Chelan County Sheriff's Detective Darrel Mathena, after which additional gunfire erupted, directed at the fleeing Lincoln Continental. It looked as if another tire had been hit, but the car continued on down the street. Barely a block later, however, it smashed into a telephone pole, at which time its single occupant quickly exited and fled on foot. With most of the officers at the shooting scene already in hot pursuit, tracking dogs were quickly brought to the location where they immediately picked up the scent of the suspects. However, neither the man seen looking inside Miller's car nor the man driving the Lincoln were in sight.

In the meantime, an ambulance arrived at the scene of the shooting, and paramedics quickly began administering first aid to the fallen officer. He was then loaded into the waiting ambulance and rushed off to the emergency room of Sacred Heart Medical Center. Upon his arrival at the hospital, emergency room personnel quickly noted that brain tissue was visible around the wound, which was located on the right side of the detective's head. The wound was described as a large hole.

"Blood was literally just pouring out of this wound and onto the floor," said an emergency room physician.

Because of the severity of the wound, "it would be hard for me to imagine any kind of purposeful motor function immediately after the injury." Brian Orchard continued, however, to breathe without the aid of a respirator, and maintained a strong pulse for some time after his arrival at the hospital. The prognosis, however, looked bad for the detective in spite of the strong vital signs that were recorded upon his arrival.

While detectives, sheriff's deputies and reserve officers were busy attempting to track down the suspects, other lawmen were busy rounding up witnesses. One of the witnesses who saw the entire incident was Lyle Miller, who was watching from a hotel room with Chelan County Sheriff's detectives. Miller, it should be recalled, was the victim from whom the valuable guns were stolen, along with other valuable items, during the June 1st robbery of his home in Wenatchee.

"As this individual approached the car (the black Lincoln Continental), I heard a loud report," Miller told the investigating officers, statements which were affirmed by the Chelan County detectives in the room with him. "The man (Detective Brian Orchard) just fell like a stone. He didn't attempt to break his fall. He just crumpled to the ground." Miller and the others in the room said the first shot came from inside the Lincoln.

Linda Hall, a beautician who works in the neighborhood where the shooting occurred, told the investigators that she saw two men on July 15th, three days before the shooting, who spent most of the day loitering in the vicinity of the hotel parking lot. She told the cops she thought the pair had been let out of a dark colored Lincoln Continental, which continued to return to the area again and again that day while the two men were in the parking lot. The two men, she said, had with them a black briefcase which they placed

308

underneath some bushes, as if they were trying to see if the briefcase could be seen from the street or parking lot. She said they went through the same routine several times, using various bushes in the area. She said the dark Lincoln eventually parked nearby, but when it drove away she said she "didn't see the two men anymore."

"The person I saw driving the car had dark hair and wore glasses," said Ms. Hall. "He was a third individual. He was driving around at the same time as the two men were walking around."

John Wickstrand, another witness who occupied a second-floor hotel room facing the action below, told police he first heard noises which prompted him to look outside.

"I heard sounds like people running, a scuffling noise," said Wickstrand. "Then someone said, 'I'm a police officer,' or 'I'm the police,' then there were more sounds of scuffling." Wickstrand then said he saw flashes of gunfire near where Detective Orchard was shot, at which time he fell to the floor to avoid the possibility of being struck by a stray bullet. Wickstrand said the gunfire lasted for approximately 20 seconds, after which he heard a voice say, "Call an ambulance! Brian's hit! Brian's down." "Frankly, I saw a portion of his head disappear in a pink cloud . . . as he crumpled to the ground" when the first shot rang out, said Wickstrand.

Two additional witnesses, occupants of a nearby apartment, told police that they had heard loud shouting outside prior to the barrage of gunfire. The witnesses said they had heard the word "police," after which a flash of what looked like gunfire came from inside the black Lincoln. Because of the statements from the various witnesses, it was evident that the Lincoln's occupant opened fire first.

Approximately an hour after the shooting occurred, tracking dogs led officers to the location of one of the suspects. He was hiding in some bushes and, upon hearing the commands of several police officers, whose weapons were steadily trained on the bushes, the man came walking slowly out, his hands raised high. He was quickly taken into custody, after which police identified him as 34-year-old Donald E. Beach.

Beach, it turned out, had a long criminal record dating back as far as 1970. When he was 21, Beach was sentenced to Washington State Penitentiary on a conviction of grand larceny. Paroled two years later, he remained clean for a while, getting into only minor scrapes with the law. In 1979, however, he was arrested in Wyoming on charges of burglary, was convicted and sent back to prison. He was paroled again, after serving only two years.

Meanwhile, tracking dogs picked up the scent of the second suspect and led police to a nearby apartment house. However, a search of the building did not yield a suspect. From that point the tracking dogs lost the scent, and the investigating police officers really didn't know which way to go.

It would have been helpful if the lawmen knew the name of the second suspect. Then they could have set up stakeouts around the homes of all his known friends and relatives. They had only a sketchy description of the man, a tall, slender white male with long hair, and the only officer who even came close to getting a good look at him was Brian Orchard, lying unconscious in a hospital bed and unable to help identify his assailant. And since Beach wouldn't talk, the cops had to work that much harder in their attempts to identify the second man.

Following three hours of surgery, Detective Orchard was placed on a breathing machine. However, in spite of the efforts to save his life, he died approximately 33 hours after the downtown shooting incident. Spokane Police Chief Robert Panther announced the sad news about the divorced father of three, and stated that it was the first time in 54 years that a Spokane police officer had died in the line of duty.

Panther told the stunned city that Orchard had joined the force in April, 1968, was promoted to officer first class in December 1971 and eventually joined the detective division in 1979, and had worked undercover in the narcotics and vice department, said Panther. He was a 15-year veteran of the police department.

While recovering from the shock of losing one of their own, other Spokane lawmen assigned to track down the second suspect got their first break when a male subject who fit the description of the man who fled the scene of the shooting was last seen driving west out of Spokane in a bronze four-door Plymouth Fury with Montana license plates. After running the car's license plates through the state motor vehicles computer, investigators learned that the driver was Lonnie James Link, 24, who'd had many run-ins with the law in Montana and Washington, including several crime network investigations. Through perseverance and determination, the Spokane investigators eventually tied Link to the other suspect, Donald Beach. But where had Link fled to? Seattle? Portland? Back to Montana? California? To narrow the possibilities, the Spokane lawmen did an extensive background on Link to uncover possible contacts in other cities, other states.

Meanwhile, more than 1,300 people, mostly law enforcement officers around the Northwest, gathered at Our Lady of Lourdes Roman Catholic Cathedral in Spokane to pay tribute to the slain policeman.

"It betrays a saddened heart and a broken spirit,"

said the priest of the silent homage. "It was an angry, senseless act of irresponsibility that took this life. It was an act which stunned us with its nearly unbelievable outrage. The fabric of the heart is torn by such heedless acts of violence," said the priest to the listening lawmen, among them the 240-man Spokane police force whose badges were draped in black as a gesture of mourning for their slain fellow officer, most of whom vowed not to rest until both of Orchard's killers were apprehended and brought to justice.

It didn't take long for the second arrest. Investigators quickly traced Link to Portland, Oregon, where he was believed to be holed up at the home of a friend. Surveillance was carefully set up around the Southeast Portland home, and officers patiently waited for Link to make his move.

At approximately 8:30 on a Thursday evening, Link, disguised by bleaching and cutting his hair, left the house on foot, obviously unaware of the police stakeout. Police quietly followed him to a nearby store, where he made some purchases. When he emerged from the store at approximately 8:45 P.M., police units moved in and arrested him without incident. According to Sergeant John Giani of the Portland police homicide detail, Link was held without bail on a Spokane warrant charging him with first-degree aggravated murder in connection with the shooting death of Detective Brian Orchard, the same charges that had been leveled against suspect Donald Beach.

During interviews with Portland police detectives, which were tape-recorded, Lonnie Link said that he came to Spokane in March, 1983 after being placed on parole for a burglary conviction in Missoula, Montana. Link told the detectives that he and Beach were "bagmen," hired by a third party to sell the stolen guns back to their original owner. When asked who the third party was, Link refused to tell them. Link said that he and Beach had been working for "big-timers," people he said he was afraid to expose. Link did say, however, that he and Beach were planning to keep the money for themselves after making the exchange in downtown Spokane.

"You were planning to rip off the guy who hired you?" asked a detective.

"Yeah," Link replied. Asked when he met Donald Beach, Link replied that he became acquainted with him shortly after his arrival in Spokane.

"How was it that you met him?"

"It's a long story," Link replied. "I really don't want to say." At that point a detective asked him how he felt about the shooting in Spokane, about everything that had happened.

"I can't say how I feel," he replied. "I'm so f-----g sorry for (the cop)," Link said. "I wish it was me instead of him. I wish there was a way I could turn it all back."

When the Portland detectives were finished with their initial interview with Link, they returned to the Southeast Portland home where Link had been staying at the time of his arrest, where they interviewed the occupant, Julie Hoag. Afterward, the detectives questioned Link a second time after telling him that Julie Hoag had given them a different version of the shooting incident. They told him that Hoag had said that Link had told her that he knew that Orchard and the other man were police (Link has maintained since his arrest that he had no idea Orchard and Nelson were cops). The detectives also told Link that Spokane policemen said there was no doubt that Link fired the first shot.

"They will testify to that," said the Portland detective.

"I know that's what they'll testify to," Link replied. "That's why I didn't want to get caught by the Spokane police. I honestly thought they were going to kill me." Link was also asked during the Portland police interviews why he had gotten involved with the plot to sell back the stolen guns to their original owner.

"To be honest with you," he replied, "when I came out of prison I was dead set in my mind that I was going to make it good. My big problem was my parole officer. When I was doing good, he restricted me on things that didn't mean nothing. He didn't want me to drink. I'd want to come home and have a few beers and take my girlfriend out . . . So I just got a sh---y attitude toward him, and I quit my job. I quit to get back at him and show him he didn't have control of my life, which he did. You didn't know how bad I wanted to change things so many times. But I needed some help. And there wasn't anyone to help me."

In August, 1983, Lonnie James Link was brought back to Spokane, Washington. Shackled in handcuffs and chains, and heavily guarded, Link pleaded innocent to the charge of aggravated murder. Earlier, Donald Beach pleaded innocent to identical charges. Donald Brockett, Spokane County prosecutor, announced that he would seek the death penalty for both defendants, who were ordered to stand trial separately.

After countless delays, including changes in defense counsel, illnesses of defense counsel, the filing of legal briefs and motions to dismiss the charges, changes in judges and difficulties in selecting a jury, Lonnie Link's trial finally began in Spokane County Superior Court in mid-September, 1984, more than a year after the shooting death of Detective Brian Orchard. The case was heard before Superior Court Judge John J. Ripple.

Link's defense was simple: He claimed he didn't know that Brian Orchard and Bruce Nelson were police officers and, fearing for his life, he fired at them only after being fired upon. The prosecution contended, on the other hand, that Link (and Beach) knew Orchard and Nelson were police officers and that Orchard and Nelson had identified themselves as police officers. It was then, the prosecution contended, that Link fired his weapon first, hitting Orchard in the head.

During the early phases of the trial, Spokane Police Detective Al Hales displayed diagrams and sketches to the jury that depicted the paths and the locations of bullets which hit the black Lincoln Continental Link and Beach were driving when Link allegedly fired on Detective Orchard. He also showed the jury photographs of wooden cases which contained literally dozens of stolen guns that were recovered by police from the trunk of the Lincoln. He also showed the jury photos of a .38-caliber handgun that had been left on the front seat of the Lincoln when Link fled after the car had crashed.

Link maintained throughout the trial that he had been listening to the radio in the car and had been unable to hear the approaching policemen identify themselves as such. Hales countered that contention, however, when he testified that he examined the Lincoln while it was in police storage and found that the radio was indeed on, but the sound had been turned completely down. Hales also said he found that the rear window on the driver's side was down, which would have enabled the voices of the approaching policemen to appear audible to the occupant inside the car.

Sergeant Tom Morris, in charge of the stakeout the night Orchard was shot, testified early in the trial, as did Detective Gary Gow and Detective Bruce Nelson. Morris told the jury that moments before the shooting he told the other detectives, "OK, let's take 'em down." A man later identified as Donald Beach had been, at that time, looking for an envelope in Lyle Miller's car, but had quickly fled into nearby bushes when the shooting began. Morris testified that he fired two shots at Beach before he disappeared from sight.

Detective Gary Gow explained to the jury how he and another officer had been patrolling the area in an unmarked car when the incident began. Gow said that when he saw the black Lincoln turn the corner at Pine Street and Fourth Avenue he opened fire on it, emptying his pistol in the process.

"There was a head between the seats and I was shooting in the back window at that bushy hair," said Gow.

"You mean you were shooting to kill?" asked defense attorney Mark Vovos.

"Yes, sir," replied Gow.

Orchard's partner, Detective Nelson, testified that he identified himself as a police officer twice before the gunfire erupted, and gave a somewhat chilling account of the events that led to the shooting of his partner.

"The person ducked down in the front seat," after the identification was loudly yelled, said Nelson. "Again, I said, 'Police officers. Get up where we can see you.'" After giving the commands, to which there were no replies and no movements from inside the Lincoln, Nelson said he and Orchard carefully approached the car, he on the passenger side and Orchard on the driver's side.

"I crouched down and placed my hand on the trunk lid of the car to make sure it was latched," Nelson continued. "Then I moved up to the window post by the back side window. I peeked into the car, and could see someone laying in the front seat. At that point I was concerned about concealing myself from the person in the car, and from anyone else who might be in the area." For those reasons, Nelson said, no further identifications were made.

"I heard a noise," said Nelson as he explained to the jury how he remained crouched beside the Lincoln Continental. "It sounded like someone cocking a gun. I looked up and I could see Brian's head, standing on the opposite side of the car a few steps forward from me." Nelson said that's when he shouted the warning to his partner, as the car began to move slowly forward. "I heard a shot from inside the car. I took a half step back, and shot a hole in the back tire. But the car continued down the hill, slowly at first, but then it picked up speed . . . I looked over and I saw Brian lying face down in the street. Then I fired five more shots into the back of the car."

Detective Don Johnson said that he and Detective Gow had been on foot searching for Beach after he escaped into bushes when the black Lincoln turned the corner to come up Pine Street. Johnson said that he and Gow each fired six shots into the Lincoln, emptying their weapons.

"I could tell somebody was down back there," Johnson said to Deputy Prosecutor Clark Colwell. "I didn't know at the time whether it was Detective Orchard or Detective Nelson." Johnson said he fired all six shots into the left front tire of the Lincoln as it approached him. "I was trying to disable the vehicle so it couldn't speed away." When the car hit the pole, said Johnson, "the door came open and a man jumped out and started running . . . It was dark out, and the guy could have gone anywhere."

Toward the end of the six-week trial, Lonnie James Link took the witness stand to testify in his own defense. In a deep, soft but often shaky voice, Link told the jury that he didn't know that the men who approached him as he sat in the Lincoln in downtown Spokane on the evening of July 18, 1983 were policemen. He said he fired his own gun only after being fired upon, and that he hadn't been aiming at anyone in particular. It should be noted that for Link to be convicted of aggravated first-degree murder, it was necessary that the prosecution prove that Orchard's killing was premeditated.

"I was scared to death," said Link under questioning by his attorney, Mark Vovos. "I just wanted to get out of there. I was afraid I would be killed."

"Did you hear anyone identify themselves?" asked Vovos.

"No, sir, I did not," replied Link.

"Did you see a badge?" asked Vovos.

"No, sir, I did not."

"Did you aim the gun at anyone?"

"No, sir, I did not," said Link, who also explained to the jury that he acted in self-defense after being fired upon. He claimed he thought Orchard was trying to kill him.

"I was sitting in the car and I heard a couple of shots—well, I didn't know what they were at the time—a couple of loud bangs," he said, right after which he noticed two men, one on each side of the Lincoln. "The person on the driver's side was pointing a big revolver at me using different language telling me to get out of the car. He was telling me to get out of the car . . . I was way down almost on the floor of the car. I didn't aim the gun at anyone," he said.

"If you were worried about your life, Mr. Link, how is firing randomly in the air going to help you?" asked

Prosecutor Donald Brockett.

"I don't know," Link replied, saying that he fired the shots just to make noise so that the men would stay away from him.

"You shot him to get out," charged Prosecutor Brockett.

At one point in the trial the prosecution presented a witness, John Ballard, a cellmate of Link's, awaiting trial on theft charges, who testified regarding a statement Link purportedly made to him in jail in February, 1984. "If the pig had not gotten so close, he would not be dead," Ballard quoted Link as having said during the conversation.

"We have evidence of preparation," said Deputy Prosecutor Colwell in arguing against a motion filed by defense attorney Vovos to suppress a statement by a witness that indicated premeditation on the part of the suspects. "They (the suspects) acquired guns," he continued. "The guns were loaded. The defendant's accomplice (Donald Beach) had a gun. There was the statement, 'We'll have to hold court in the street,' if police interrupted them." Judge Ripple ruled in favor of the prosecution, stating that it was his opinion there was enough evidence indicating premeditation, and the statement, 'We'll have to hold court in the street,' purportedly made by Link's accomplice, was allowed to stand.

Before closing arguments were heard, Judge Ripple instructed the jury they could find Link guilty of aggravated first-degree murder, second-degree murder, second-degree felony murder or they could acquit him.

"I think it's time, ladies and gentlemen, just like the TV game show, that the real Lonnie Link stand up," said Deputy Prosecutor Colwell. Colwell accused Link of lying on the witness stand, and said that Link's claim that police fired the first shot wasn't supported by the evidence. Colwell also told the jury that Link provided "great description" of the officers approaching his car, including how they had been dressed, but contradicted himself by later saying that he only got a glimpse of them prior to the onset of gunfire.

"He would have you believe they shot first and shot right at him," continued Colwell. "He would ask you to believe the officers were the aggressors. If the officers were the aggressors and they were trying to shoot him, do you think he would be here today? No, they would have blown him away. But he is here today and an officer isn't . . . He, at that point in time when he killed Brian Orchard, thought he could get away because he didn't want to go back to prison and that bad old parole officer," said Colwell.

Also participating in closing arguments was Prosecutor Brockett, who began by showing the jury photographs of the bloodstained street where Brian Orchard had fallen from his fatally inflicted wound. Brockett pointed out for the benefit of the jury that Link had maintained that he didn't hear Detective Nelson identify himself and Orchard as police officers, but admitted that he heard the officer yell a command to him to stop the car after it began moving forward. "Why would you try to obey the command of authority when you deny that the person is in the position of authority?" Brockett asked.

"This is the place in Spokane County, Washington," continued Brockett, pointing at the photographs of the crime scene, "where the life of Brian Orchard, a policeman in this community, was taken. Now I didn't say lost. I said taken . . . (the premeditated intent is shown by the click of the gun), the time that passed, the fact that Mr. Link waited until Orchard got close (before he fired at the detective)," said Brockett.

"Understand where I'm at," said defense attorney Vovos. "I'm an advocate. I've taken a position for my client. He's not the best person in the world and not the worst. Because you possess stolen property or you deal in guns, it doesn't make you a murderer." Instead, said Vovos, Link likely heard Sergeant Morris, stationed down the street, fire shots at Donald Beach as Beach fled into bushes, actions which, Vovos and Link contended, set off a gun battle in which Link was shot at first. Fearing for his life, he fired wildly in an attempt to frighten off the men approaching his car. The defendant's contention that he was shot at first naturally raised the possibility that he shot in self-defense, a matter for the jury to decide.

"By the time they (Orchard and Nelson) got to the Lincoln," said Vovos, "Morris had shot at this man, Mr. Beach, in the bushes.

"Common sense tells us," he continued, "that no premeditated killer of a policeman is going to leave his gun, talk twice to police, remain unarmed, call his mother and brother to (talk about turning) himself in . . . and come back to Spokane (before fleeing to Portland). Either he's insane, he's a fool or he's truly scared and innocent of what he's charged with."

Following nearly 40 hours of deliberations, the Spokane County jury returned a verdict of guilty of aggravated murder against Lonnie James Link after deciding that Link did know Brian Orchard was a policeman when he shot him the night of July 18, 1983 in an attempt to conceal his own identity from the police.

"Outstanding," said a member of Orchard's family. "We have nothing but utmost respect for the jury and for Judge Ripple. Judge Ripple ran a tight ship. We got the verdict that is deserving . . . I've always felt that God's running the show."

Under the law, the same jury was now faced with deciding Link's fate, either death by lethal injection or by hanging, or life in prison without the possibility of parole.

"Obviously there was someone else involved," said another relative of Brian Orchard's while waiting for the sentencing verdict. "And neither one of these two (Link and Beach) will name him. If they are in fear of their lives, there must be some pretty aggravating circumstances involved . . . I hope he (Link) never sees the outside of those prison walls . . . I believe society has the right and the responsibility to protect itself in this way. I believe that if it weren't for the literally thousands of lawyers out there who go to any fantastic ends to keep the criminal element on the street and out of court, that criminals would not view capture and prosecution and punishment as merely an occupational hazard. The pendulum of justice has got to return to center . . . Regardless of what the court system does to Lonnie Link, it won't bring Brian back. That's what we have to live with now," said the relative.

The Spokane County jury sentenced Lonnie Link to life without the possibility of parole. Before sentence was formally passed, Judge Ripple asked Link if he had anything he wanted to say.

"I would just like to say again that I'm terribly sorry that all this tragedy had to occur," said Link. "Even though I was found guilty by a jury, I want you to know that it wasn't a premeditated act. I want the Orchard family to know that if there was any way I could change what happened, I would do that. I mean that with all my heart and soul." The judge then passed sentence.

"To know every day of your life," said one of Orchard's relatives, "when you get up inside that prison that you're never getting out of there — I don't know. I think death might have been better than that (sentence)."

On Thursday, November 15, 1984, Donald Edward Beach pleaded guilty to the lesser charge of felony second-degree murder in a plea-bargaining arrangement worked out with the prosecutor's office.

"While I was diving into the bushes," said Beach, "he (Sgt. Morris) fired some shots at me, and then everything broke loose up by the Lincoln while I was in the bushes . . . I did have a gun with me. I didn't use it; I didn't plan to use it; I did not go there with any premeditation. I'm just sorry that it happened, but I'll accept my responsibility."

"Had we gone to trial," said Beach's attorney, Roger Peven, "we would have conceded he's guilty of second-degree murder. He (Beach) is happy the way it turned out."

"The state is satisfied that justice will be satisfied," said Prosecutor Brockett.

Beach was sentenced to life in prison, but could be paroled in 13 years and five months, according to standards set by the State Parole Board.

EDITOR'S NOTE:
Lyle Miller, John Wickstrand, Linda Hall, Julie Hoag and John Ballard are not the real names of the persons so named in the foregoing story. Fictitious names have been used because there is no reason for public interest in the identities of these persons.

"DID A SHOPLIFTER
AMBUSH THE BELOVED COP?"

by Joseph Koenig

ATLANTA, GA.
JUNE 6, 1986

In the early 1970s, when he was still new to the
force, Atlanta Police Officer Philip Bruce Mathis
curbed a car driven by a pretty young woman at the
intersection of Piedmont and Peachtree. Unlike many
of the motorists with whom he came into contact, the
supected speeder—newly arrived in the Georgia capital from the small town of Moultrie—did not put up
an argument when flagged down by the dashing, dark-
haired policeman. In fact, she seemed to enjoy their
brief interview.

When it ended, Bruce Mathis asked her, in addition
to her license and registration, for her phone number.
A lifetime resident of North Atlanta, the Dykes High
School graduate felt that in addition to ticketing her, it
was also his civic responsibility to show the newcomer
around his hometown. And, after a courtship that
lasted four years, the handsome couple was wed.

For Bruce Mathis, struggling to raise a young family on an Atlanta patrolman's $22,000 salary, police work was something apart from just another job. It was a special calling that was not to be set aside at the end of a normal working day, a day which extended well into most nights. For, in addition to his regular tour of police duty, he was also employed as a security guard at a department store in Lenox Square, and had been throughout all the 15 years he was an Atlanta policeman.

"He was always there to protect people, always smiling," Atlanta Police Chief Morris Redding would recall after the fateful events of April, 1985. "That's why they loved him."

The warm Thursday morning of April 25th began no differently than most other days for Bruce Mathis. Up at 5:30, he shaved and showered and got dressed and then rushed to the Zone 2 precinct house on Atlanta's Ponce de Leon Avenue. Barely 10 minutes after the 6:30 roll call, he pulled into the street in car 54.

"He liked to stay on the street and not hang around the precinct," said a fellow officer. "He would zip in here, grab his stuff and be gone."

The first two alarms of the day turned out to be false ones for Officer Mathis and the next was the report of an attempted burglary at an apartment complex on Roswell Road. At 9:40, Mathis visited another apartment complex on South Pharr Court, a high-rise development that was home to some 400 elderly people.

"He'd been stopping by once or twice a week ever since last year," one resident would recall, "when a couple of armed robbers held up someone in the parking lot."

"He was good about maintaining a high visibility for the old folks," said the building's administrator. "He impressed me as being the sort of person that all public

325

servants should be. He didn't seem preoccupied with the role that he played as far as throwing his weight around as the local arm of the law."

Around mid-morning, Mathis drove to the scene of a serious traffic accident at the corner of Northside and Arden. A fellow officer was already at the scene tending to the injuries of a five-year-old boy whose head had been cut when a station wagon flipped over.

"Bruce came over and put his hand on my shoulder and asked how the boy was," the other officer would recall. "Then he asked what he could do."

Then Mathis made himself useful by directing traffic around the accident scene while other officers cleared away the wreckage.

The next stop of the day was a quick meeting with his wife and five-year-old daughter in the parking lot of the Northside Parkway School where the girl had just completed a 10:30 class.

"He had just worked the wreck," his wife would say later, "and he told (their daughter) about the little boy and told her to buckle her seat belt and be careful."

In the afternoon there wasn't much for the veteran patrolman to do. He spent some time checking out the report of a hazardous roadside vehicle and then responded to another false alarm. By 3:30, he was back at his Sandy Springs house for an hour with his wife and little girl and a chance to rest up before the start of his second job.

Around 5 P.M., Bruce Mathis drove up to the giant department store on Lenox Square. He told his plain-clothes partner on the store's security force that he would be keeping his eyes open for a man who had been stealing clothes in a series of hit-and-run crimes. Just one week earlier, the man had run into the store, grabbed an armful of windbreakers and ran out again into a waiting car.

Mathis, his partner would remember, seemed to be in unusually good spirits that evening.

"He talked about the Atlanta Braves and how the game started at 8:40 P.M., against Houston. We discussed being in the TV department for the start of the game."

But around 8:05, more than half an hour before the first pitch, Bruce Mathis was in a third-floor stockroom adjacent to the television showroom when he surprised someone who didn't belong there.

"I was in the (security) office and I didn't dispatch him," Mathis' partner would recall. "He yelled into the radio, but anything he yelled was unintelligible. I yelled, 'Repeat, repeat,' but I didn't get anything back."

It was an appliance salesman on the third floor who phoned the security office, just minutes later, to report that Bruce Mathis had been gunned down near the open doorway leading to the television showroom. When his partner arrived on the scene, it was apparent at once that there was nothing that could be done for the 38-year-old officer. Mathis had been shot at least twice in the upper body.

Summoned by Mathis' partner, Atlanta police rushed to the department store en masse. While some of the policemen crowded around the still form of their brother officer, others cordoned off the building.

"We don't know why Mathis went to the storeroom at this particular time," one officer said. "And we don't know how long he was there. What's obvious is that someone shot him down before he could even unholster his gun."

Among the first witnesses located by the officers were employees in the nearby luggage and electronics departments who said that they had heard voices coming from the storeroom and then a number of gunshots, perhaps as many as five. Then Bruce Mathis had staggered out of the storeroom and collapsed on the floor.

Other witnesses reported seeing a man flee through another storeroom and then race down an escalator to the street. They described him as a tall, slender black man, about six feet, two inches tall, with a long, thin mustache, and a medium, Afro haircut. He was clad in a lightweight blue jacket with a white collar, dungarees and black shoes.

Atlanta police, stunned by the death of a fellow officer, wasted little time in pressing what they would term a "comprehensive" search for Bruce Mathis' slayer. It centered, in those early hours, on the area around the giant department store where the shooting took place. Dozens of officers set up roadblocks along neighborhood intersections to halt and inspect traffic. Finding nothing, they tore down the roadblocks and returned to the department store for a floor-by-floor hunt. Officers also visited other stores in the Lenox Square Mall, but without result.

"The problem," one investigator explained, "is that the department store is so incredibly big and has so many rooms and places to hide that we can't even say for sure that the gunman still isn't in here."

Meanwhile, news of the slaying of Bruce Mathis cast a pall over the entire Atlanta police department that night.

"He was one of the nicest guys I ever knew," one grieving officer said. "He was quiet and unpretentious. He grew up with the department."

An executive of the Fraternal Order of Police who had shared a patrol car with Bruce Mathis 10 years earlier said that the slain officer was "good-natured," but very careful.

"He was always cracking jokes about one thing or

another. He was friendly to everyone. He was a veteran, highly professional. It doesn't make sense that he would get himself into a situation like this. He was very cautious."

Bruce Mathis had been a veteran of the Army National Guard. As a Sergeant First Class with the Headquarters and Service company of the 151st Military Intelligence Battalion assigned to Dobbins Air Force Base, he had been in charge of the unit's food service operations.

"He had started his Guard career as a cook," an officer with the battalion remembered, "but recently had been cleared for promotion to warrant officer. He was an outstanding soldier, one of the best mess stewards I've seen in a long time. He was in charge of getting the rations, preparing them if he had to. He ran the whole mess section."

On Friday, April 26th, Dr. Saleh Zaki, the associate Fulton County medical examiner, informed homicide investigators that Bruce Mathis had been shot in the back, the groin and the left side, all three bullets passing through the body. It was the shot to the back, which ruptured the lung and aorta, that had killed him.

Although the medical examiner was unable to determine the distance between Mathis and his slayer during the fatal incident, he was able to say that the shots were not contact wounds.

That same day, after a grim night spent combing the department store and environs for witnesses to the shooting, detectives were attempting to identify a man spotted leaving the huge store around the time of the incident. Armed with heavy books of mugshots, some investigators spoke with a number of witnesses, while others responded to phone calls from aroused citizens who believed they recognized the suspect in a freshly released police composite drawing.

Late that day, Major B.L. Neikirk, chief of the homicide bureau, said that two of the callers had offered police the same name for the suspect. Of more than half a dozen witnesses interrogated by his men, Neikirk said, several had reported seeing a man moving quickly from the storeroom on the third floor and then taking an escalator down.

"But there was a lot of confusion at the time, and the witnesses aren't sure he was involved," Neikirk was quick to note.

"It's strange, the way it happened," Neikirk went on to say, "that the officer would be shot so many times in a storage area when there appeared no reason for it to happen. There was no scuffle involved, and the officer didn't even have a chance to pull his weapon."

Neikirk theorized that the killer might be wanted for other crimes, or else was someone who felt that he could not risk capture. As a result, the probers returned to the store on Friday to question executives about the possibility that a disgruntled employee, or anyone with a criminal record, had been giving the store a hard time.

On Sunday afternoon, April 28th, no fewer than 500 uniformed police officers from the Atlanta area and all over Georgia flocked to the Sandy Springs United Methodist Church to join some 750 other mourners for funeral services for Bruce Mathis. Burial followed at nearby Arlington Memorial Park, where a bugler played taps, a seven-gun salute was fired, and four police helicopters hovered overhead in the missing man formation.

The following evening, as frustrated Atlanta police continued to receive calls from the public, Detective Carl Price looked away from his phone to tell a newsman, "I'm waiting for the mysterious call to come in, for the caller who says he knows the guy and wants to put him behind bars as soon as he can. We keep hoping, but that only happens on TV."

Along with Detectives Jerry Pendergrass and Lou Moore, Price was also finding the time to go through stacks of criminal records in the hopes of lining up a promising suspect. Price pointed out that after countless hours of sorting, they had come up with 34 possible suspects. Of greater interest, though, were two other men—bystanders—college students who claimed to have heard the shots on Thursday night and to have seen a man walking slowly away from Officer Mathis' body.

On Friday night, the detectives said, both witnesses had spent five hours with a police artist putting together the composite drawing of the suspect. However, on Monday night, when one of the young men asked to look over mugshots of the suspects selected by the detectives, the results—according to Pendergrass—were "not good, not bad."

Another detective said, "The way it happened, we think the killer had been hanging around the TV department when he slipped into a luggage storeroom and removed some very large bags in which he could hide a television. He figured he could make an easy escape down the service elevator. Probably, he had stolen items from the store the same way, and things probably were going his way again, until Bruce came along.

"We really aren't sure what happened next," the investigator went on. "The two witnesses who heard the gunshots said they ran to a TV salesman who told them that the sound they heard was only the elevator. They weren't buying any of that, though, and they went to another salesman and got him to look around. He was the one who discovered Mathis' legs on the floor and put in a signal 63 call for help."

"We do have some physical evidence," another prober put in. "Four bullets were recovered at the scene, and three have traces of blood on them. We found the fourth one this morning, in the storage room door. It's a .38, but it's in such bad shape there's really not too much else we can say about it. And we're still looking for the gun that fired it. We're also saving all the fingerprints we found at the scene. Problem is, there must be thousands of them."

On Thursday, May 2nd, exactly one week after the shooting, Atlanta police announced that they had arrested a suspect for the murder of Bruce Mathis. R. Mark Harris, a 37-year-old Southwest Atlanta man with a lengthy criminal history of drug and theft offenses, highlighted by a 1975 theft from the department store where the killing took place, had been charged with murder and ordered held without bail in the Atlanta City Jail.

Atlanta police said that Harris was picked up near the intersection of Auburn Avenue and Hilliard Street. Homicide Chief Neikirk said that his sleuths had been aware of Harris—who had been paroled from his latest prison stay on July 1, 1984, and completed his parole supervision on October 19th—for the past few days.

"We had some evidence come to the surface that gave us enough probable cause to secure a warrant for this individual," he said.

Another source close to the case said that the information consisted of a number of tips from informants.

But the two most important witnesses, the college students believed to have eyeballed Bruce Mathis' slayer, were not so sure that Harris was the man they saw a week earlier. The two were among three witnesses who, on Friday afternoon, May 3rd, were unable to identify Harris or any of five other men in a police lineup.

"It's back to square one," said Detective Price after learning of the witnesses' inability to pick out a suspect.

"Obviously," said Major Neikirk, "his not being picked out by the witnesses doesn't help anything at this point of the investigation. I'm still searching for the killer, still taking information, still following tips.

"We had no other choice but to go ahead and serve the warrant. (The arrest) does not close it out on this investigation, or this individual."

Neikirk said that Harris claimed he had an alibi. It was something the detectives would have to check out.

Homicide investigators would reveal that Harris had been charged with the murder after a witness had selected his photo from among 26 pictures shown by detectives. When no witnesses were found who could link the ex-con to the slaying at the department store, however, the charges against him were dropped.

On Tuesday, May 7th, as disappointed Atlanta probers vowed to redouble their efforts in the case, the local chapter of the International Brotherhood of Police Officers announced that it would add $5,000 to a $15,000 reward already offered for information leading to the arrest and conviction of Bruce Mathis' slayer.

For nearly three long months, detectives struggled to come up with a badly sought clue in the case. But it wasn't until the last week of July that they learned of an inmate in the Fulton County Jail who bore a striking resemblance to the composite drawing of the suspect seen fleeing the department store.

"We're reluctant to say this person is a suspect," Homicide Lieutenant Cleveland Whitehead told reporters. "We certainly don't anticipate charging him at this time. But he does resemble our composite."

Reportedly, the inmate had been placed in a lineup

on Monday afternoon, July 29th, for the benefit of at least one of the witnesses who had seen a man fleeing the store after the shooting. Police said that the 31-year-old man had been taken into custody on July 22nd for violation of probation resulting from a 1983 drug arrest.

"He's one of several people we're looking at," noted Lieutenant Whitehead. "We will continue our investigation and, if we need to have a future lineup, we will."

In time, however, it became apparent to homicide probers that the man was not the one they were looking for, and interest in him as a suspect in the murder of Officer Mathis ended.

The next break in the case came in the first week of September, when Atlanta police revealed that one of two men facing charges of shoplifting from the department store had been questioned closely in connection with the murder. In a motions hearing for the 38-year-old suspect, who was slated to be tried on shoplifting charges resulting from a June 3rd incident, Detective Price told a Fulton Superior Court judge that the man admitted to being inside the storeroom area of the store on the night Mathis was shot.

Price, who was backed up in his testimony by Detective John Turner, told the court that the suspect had been arrested on May 2nd after an informant said that he was in the store at the time of the shooting. In a statement to police, the suspect reportedly had identified himself as a "creeper," a man who made his living by stealing from Atlanta department stores.

Price said the man would enter a store neatly dressed in a shirt and tie and pass himself off as either an employee or shopper to gain entrance to the stockroom areas where he would steal merchandise of "quality and quantity."

"He says when he's on a roll he has an $800–$1,000-

a-day drug habit," Price said.

Following the May 2nd arrest, Det. Price went on, police recovered a pair of bolt cutters from the man's gray Mercury Capri. The lock on the door to the storeroom where Officer Mathis had been shot, Price noted, was cut with similar cutters.

When he was asked if he knew anything about the shooting, the suspect reportedly had said that he did not know who had done it. He went on to say that he had entered the store about 8:35 that evening, took an elevator to the second floor, but left after seeing Detective Price, who was there investigating the shooting.

Despite the high hopes Atlanta police had for the suspect, he soon was eliminated from consideration in the Mathis murder case. Barely a few days later, however, another suspect would emerge.

His name was Charles J. Edwards, and he was taken into custody on Tuesday evening, September 11th, at a Campbellton Road nightspot. The possessor of a lengthy arrest record showing entries in Georgia, California, Alabama and Washington, Edwards had escaped from the Carroll County, Georgia, Correctional Institute on January 10th, after walking away from a work detail. At the time, he was serving a three-year term handed down in 1984 on Fulton County charges of theft and burglary.

The day after Edward's arrest, Atlanta police said that an alias name of the suspect had surfaced in connection with the murder of Bruce Mathis late in April, but had not been given much attention because of an abundance of what investigators had believed to be more promising leads.

"We had this guy's name real early in the investigation," Major Neikirk told reporters. "We didn't turn anything on him and we had hundreds and hundreds of leads."

335

Although no charges were lodged against him in connection with the Mathis case, Neikirk said, he was a "good suspect."

"We're now going in the direction of Edwards, and it looks very good. Until somebody is charged, it's an open investigation."

Other sources close to the case said that probers had been led to Edwards when an informant had surfaced several weeks earlier. Edwards, they said, had spent a good deal of the previous two decades locked up on charges relating to larceny, theft and burglary, in addition to occasional drug possession counts.

It was Tuesday, October 1st, when a Fulton County grand jury indicted 38-year-old Charles James Edwards on charges of murder in the commission of a felony stemming from the death of Officer Bruce Mathis. Over the next several months, however, investigators learned that Edwards was actually one of a number of aliases used by the man they now identified as Richard Fleming Vinson.

At Richard Vinson's murder trial, which got underway in Fulton County Superior Court in the first week of June, 1986, Assistant District Attorney Harvey Moskowitz, in his opening statement, told the jury how Bruce Mathis was slain.

"Ladies and gentlemen," he said. "He was ambushed. He was killed. He was shot in the back.

"He walked in, was surprised, got shot and then tried to leave that room when he was shot again." A third shot, the "assassin's shot," was fired from not more than 18 inches away from the officer.

Defense counsel countered by telling the jury that the police had arrested the wrong man.

"I expect the evidence to show that throughout his ordeal (the defendant) has denied any involvement in the murder. The only evidence against Rick Vinson is circumstantial."

Among the prosecution's lead-off witnesses was a man who had attended high school with the defendant and was with him on the night of the slaying at a Southwest Atlanta nightclub. When they heard a radio broadcast about a shoplifting incident, the witness recalled, Vinson allegedly responded that, "If they ever catch me in one of those stores, or malls, or anything like that . . . whoever it was would have to lie down and let me get away, or I'll just have to blow them away."

Also testifying for the prosecution was a woman who said that she drove Vinson and a companion to Lenox Square on the night of the slaying so that the defendant could take care of a "layaway" item. While she shopped downstairs with the other man, the witness added, Vinson went off on his own, returning via the escalator several minutes later.

Still another prosecution witness told the court that on the day of the killing, Vinson had attempted to sell him a .38-caliber revolver. The witness said that when he attempted to purchase the weapon, Vinson changed his mind. The witness added that he remembered the date was April 25th, because not long after talking with Vinson he had heard about a police officer being shot.

On Thursday, June 5th, a police technician told the court that Richard Vinson's fingerprints had been found on a box containing electronic equipment in the storeroom where Bruce Mathis was shot.

That same day, testifying for the defense, a former Atlanta resident who was the state's chief eyewitness told the court that Richard Fleming Vinson was not the man he had identified in a physical lineup. Nor was he the man the witness had seen going down an escalator in the department store in the minutes after the slaying.

In his closing argument, defense counsel reminded the jury that a key prosecution witness had denied that Vinson was the man he had seen step over Bruce Mathis' body at the time of the slaying.

"His answer was, 'No, that's not him.' Clearly, this man has not been identified as the perpetrator of the crime," the attorney said.

The attorney also contended that the fingerprint cited as a key prosecution exhibit had been matched with his client's fingerprint only on the third try, and that the print could have been left at some time other than the evening of the shooting.

"The absent evidence speaks loud and clear," the attorney said. "You don't just make somebody pay. You make the person responsible pay."

Assistant District Attorney Moskowitz insisted that Vinson could be placed at the crime scene because the woman who drove him there that night had told the court of the evening's events.

On Friday, June 6th, after some four and a half hours of debate, the jury of eight women and four men announced that it had found Richard Fleming Vinson guilty of the murder of Bruce Mathis.

The tall, wiry defendant responded to the verdict by rising to his feet and shouting, "I don't want to be sentenced. I ain't done a damn thing. I ain't killed nobody."

After the defendant had been restrained and handcuffed by Fulton County deputies, Superior Court Judge Isaac Jenrette sentenced him to a term of life imprisonment.

Fulton County District Attorney Lewis Slaton, noting that the only physical evidence linking Vinson to the slaying was the lone fingerprint, told newsmen:

"We always would like to have more evidence."

Yet, he said, he was not surprised by the verdict, given the "fingerprint, a composite and given testimony . . . placing him in the mall at the time of the crime."

EDITOR'S NOTE:
R. Mark Harris is not the real name of the person so named in the foregoing story. A fictitious name has been used because there is no reason for public interest in the identity of this person.

"ALL UNITS. OFFICER DOWN. NEEDS ASSISTANCE!"

by Tom Basinski

PHOENIX, ARIZONA
JULY 7, 1986

Bill Williams and his wife were entertaining Fred Renfro and his wife in the Williams' apartment in Phoenix, Arizona, on Wednesday night, January 8, 1986.

The four people had been playing Trivial Pursuit and eating snacks. They had run out of beer shortly before 11:00 P.M.

While Williams' wife began preparations for making a pizza, Bill and Fred decided to walk over to a liquor store two blocks away at 11th Street and Indian School Road. They left about 11:20.

Williams and Renfro took a short cut down the alley behind the store. In some cities it is wise to stay out of alleys after dark, but this part of Phoenix is not one of those areas.

To be sure, Phoenix has its share of crime, but all cities do.

As the men approached the rear of the liquor store they saw a pair of headlights. As they got closer they recognized the familiar white car with the horizontal blue stripe and emergency light bar of the Phoenix

Police Department.

The overhead emergency lights were not on. As the two walked closer they could hear that the engine of the police car was running. The spotlight by the driver's door was on, but pointing toward the ground and the back of the store.

As Williams and Renfro walked even closer they spotted a form lying on the ground next to the open patrol car door. Williams nudged Renfro and said, "I guess that guy's had enough to drink for one night."

Renfro laughed and added a comment of his own, wondering where the cop was who had stopped the drunk.

When they were just a few feet away, they froze simultaneously. The lighting in the alley was poor, and neither the headlights nor the spotlight had properly illuminated the form on the ground.

The two friends were now able to see that the person on the ground was wearing the dark blue serge of the Phoenix Police Department.

Williams said, "My God. It's a cop. What's going on?"

"Call for help on his radio. I'll get to a phone," Renfro said.

Williams approached the officer and asked, "Hey man, you okay?"

The officer did not budge. There was blood near his head and Williams feared the worst. Williams tried to extricate the officer's walkie-talkie from his gun belt. In his haste and panic, Williams could not do it.

He stepped over the officer's body and pulled the radio microphone from the dashboard holder. Williams looked at the apparatus, which was about the size of an electric razor, pushed the red button and said, "My name is Bill Williams and you have an injured officer in the alley at 11th Street and Indian School Road.

Can anybody hear me?"

The dispatcher was a cool five-year veteran. She was accustomed to hearing people say all sorts of frantic, frenzied things when she had telephone duty. She was a pro, and handled everything with speed and accuracy. Nothing much ever bothered her.

Yet, this radio transmission caused a shudder to run through her. Goose bumps formed on her arms, and for a millisecond she could not breathe.

The dispatcher hit the "alert" button on the console in front of her and said, "All units, officer down, needs assistance, in the alley, 11th and Indian School Road. A citizen is calling in from the officer's unit. All available units respond."

The dispatcher instructed Mr. Williams to stand by and wait for the officers. In the meantime, Fred Renfro had dialed 911 from the pay phone in front of the store and told another dispatcher the same story.

In a matter of seconds, four patrol cars had arrived, and an ambulance was on the way.

The first officer at the scene recognized the downed officer as Bob Fike. First aid measures were immediately put into operation.

The ambulance was on the scene at 11:34 P.M., six minutes after Williams had first broadcast his message. The attendants put Officer Fike in the ambulance and raced to Good Samaritan Medical Center. On the way, the paramedics worked feverishly to revive Fike who had a small hole under his left eye.

Fike was pronounced dead at 11:53 P.M. The paramedics knew Officer Fike from the many times he called for them to help injured victims. The emergency room staff also knew Fike from the compassionate and courteous way he had interviewed crime and accident victims and even criminal suspects in their facility.

The emergency personnel felt chilled and drained seeing their friend lifeless on the gurney and knowing that all of the expensive equipment and miracle injections they had at their disposal could not help him.

The head nurse picked up the phone and called the county medical examiner to come for the body. It was an awful phone call.

Meanwhile, for the staff of the communications division at the police department, the mourning had to wait. There was work to do, notifications to be made.

The first order was for the homicide team to roll out. Next, Chief Ruben Ortega and all the high level commanders had to be notified. The captain of the Squaw Peak substation, from which Fike had worked, also responded from his suburban Phoenix home.

Detective Larry Martinsen, a 20-year veteran with seven years of homicide investigation experience, was picked to head up the investigation. Martinsen, who had the on-call responsibility for the week, climbed from bed, washed his face, picked up his shaving kit and briefcase, which was already packed, and drove directly to the scene.

When Martinsen arrived he saw that the patrol officers had the crime scene cordoned off with bright yellow plastic tape that said, "Police Line Do Not Cross."

The news media had begun assembling even as Martinsen drove up. Sergeant Brad Thiss, the official spokesman from the chief's office, would deal with them.

Williams and Renfro were seated in the back of two separate patrol cars. As witnesses, they were being protected from the media. Martinsen told the officers to take the witnesses to police headquarters, let them call their wives, get them some coffee and have a homicide detective get a complete statement from them.

Martinsen affixed his badge to his suitcoat breast

pocket and ducked under the yellow tape. A new patrol officer who Martinsen did not recognize came up and obtained Martinsen's name and identification number and noted the time that Martinsen had entered the crime scene.

Martinsen did not resent the time it took to identify himself to the young beat officer. This procedure would protect the integrity of the crime scene when the case went to court, if it ever did.

Martinsen took the first patrol officer aside and was briefed as to what he had found upon his arrival.

The officer was Robert Fike's friend. Martinsen studied him as the officer gave a professional concise description.

The driver's door of the patrol car had been standing open. The spotlight was shining toward the rear of the store. An eyeglass case was on the ground.

Officer Fike's holster was empty and his service revolver was missing. Fike's flashlight was on and was a few feet from the officer's body, which was about 10 feet from the patrol car.

That was it. The emergency light bar on the police car was not on, meaning that a traffic stop had probably not been made. Martinsen wondered why Fike had been back there.

The crime was photographed by a lab crew. A pair of new bolt cutters had been found near the back of the store. Martinsen did not know if the bolt cutters meant anything.

The cutters were photographed and logged into evidence, and a work request was filled out to have them processed for latent fingerprints. Fike's patrol car was towed to police headquarters where a lab crew would go over it for latent prints and other signs of physical evidence.

By dawn, Martinsen felt that things appeared to be

pretty well organized, at least from an investigative standpoint. The crime scene was done, and done well. If the killer had left any evidence inside the roped-off area, it would be linked to him, or her, if a suspect ever surfaced.

Martinsen had some feelings plaguing him that he tried to push off to the side and deal with later. All veteran homicide sleuths try to give little or no thought to their victims. A victim may be a good person who is a pillar of the community, or a sleazeball, who society is better off without.

The good detective never ventures into the area of judgment or involvement with a victim. A victim's body is a piece of evidence. At all costs, a homicide detective must stay away from emotional interest or attachment.

Yet, in this case, Martinsen was dealing with the death of a fellow officer. Martinsen himself had worked a beat for a lot of years. Bob Fike was 43 years old. He had a wife and young children who expected him home at the end of the shift.

Police administrators have well-chosen words to the press when a police officer gets killed. They usually say, "We place no more value on the life of an officer than we do on the average citizen. Sometimes we do employ extraordinary measures when searching for a cop killer because of the symbolism to society.

"If a person holds no regard for the life of a uniformed officer, that person will hold less regard for the life of an average citizen."

Most veteran cops will hear that line and spit out a curse. They believe when someone kills a cop in uniform, he must be captured. That's all there is to it.

"We can't have some creep sitting around bragging to his buddies how he killed one of us," said one lawman.

Martinsen kept his personal feelings in check and went about the task of formulating a plan of attack.

The autopsy of Officer Fike would be held in the early afternoon of Thursday, January 9th.

Meanwhile, the clerk at the liquor store was interviewed about her customers just before the shooting. The clerk said she did not hear anything resembling a gunshot.

The store had a videocassette surveillance camera that ran for 24 hours and was used to identify people robbing the store. Martinsen studied the tape over and over, thinking that maybe the killer was in the store and had bought something.

After the purchase, maybe the person went out back, was confronted by Officer Fike for one reason or another and ended up killing him. Martinsen did not see anything on the tapes that seemed to be of any help.

Nearby residents were also interviewed. A few had heard a "pop," sound but nothing more. The area residents thought the noise was a firecracker or kids playing a prank.

Martinsen and his team began working one more obvious lead. In Phoenix, the patrol cars are equipped with their own computers. With this piece of equipment it is possible for an officer to query a license number to find out to whom the vehicle is registered and whether or not it is stolen.

Officer Fike's mobile computer terminal was checked and it revealed an entry at 10:55 P.M., approximately five minutes before he was killed.

The computer entry was for a 1979 Ford Fairlane. Officer Fike had checked it for registration and to see if it had been stolen. It had not been stolen. Martinsen and another detective tracked down the owner of the Fairlane at his apartment shortly before 11:00 A.M. on

Thursday.

A young man answered the door in an old football jersey, Levis, and running shoes. He was 25 years old, worked for a computer repair firm and had received one traffic ticket two years before for running a red light in nearby Scottsdale. He had never been arrested. It was his day off.

The man explained that he had been at a bar with two of his friends from work. They had met at the bar about 8:30 and stayed until midnight.

The bar was only two blocks away from the liquor store. Martinsen took the young man's picture. His two friends from work were interviewed later, along with the cocktail waitress who had their station in the bar. The young man and his companions had not left the bar, she said. They were not considered as suspects.

Martinsen theorized that Fike drove through the parking lot of the bar and something about the Fairlane caught his eye. Fike ran a check on the vehicle and drove on when it checked out okay.

That afternoon, it was time to attend officer Fike's autopsy. This is always an unpleasant task no matter who the victim is. Yet, to walk into an examining room and see the body of a fully-uniformed patrol officer, complete with badge and gun belt, is unreal and gives a dizzying sensation to a fellow officer.

Det. Martinsen would not talk about it later.

The autopsy revealed a single gunshot wound under Fike's left eye. There were powder burns on the skin indicating that the gun was fired from close range. Officer Fike's uniform showed some scraping marks on the knees. Other than that, his body did not show that he had been involved in a fight, or had been harmed in any other way.

The medical examiner said Fike had died instantly.

When the bullet that was removed from the officer's body was analyzed, it was determined to be a .38-caliber. Fike had carried a standard .38-caliber police revolver.

Phoenix police would not confirm anything to the press, but the evidence showed that Officer Fike was shot with his own gun. This meant that the assailant was armed before being in contact with Fike. Now, the killer had two guns.

Martinsen and the other detectives met in Chief Ruben Ortega's office Friday night for a progress report and strategy session. Martinsen had used his shaving kit twice. He had not yet gone home for a rest.

Martinsen explained to the chief that all of the usual "checklist" things had been done. The obvious had already been thoroughly investigated and nothing of value had turned up.

Officer Mike Petchel, president of the 1000-member Phoenix police union said, "Whoever committed this is going to talk to someone. That's probably what will give us a break in the case.

"Somebody must have seen this murderer—a car, someone running away, someone leaving. It may be the more innocuous clue that will lead us to the killer. That's why it's important that people call in with any information."

Twelve detectives were assigned to the case. Chief Ortega said that if a break did not come soon he would ask for a special squad of investigators.

The funeral was held Saturday, January 11th, and the sleuths were nowhere near making an arrest. Nearly 900 law enforcement officers and friends solemnly paid their respects.

For a brief time, the residents of Phoenix reflected on the impact of police in their city.

The chaplain for the Squaw Peak precinct said, "It

was Bob and the others like him who have brought a measure of stability to us not found anywhere else in the world. Bob was among those who stand between me and my family and disorder."

Officer Joe Koren had shared a cup of coffee with Bob Fike about an hour before he died. "He dedicated his life to making Phoenix a better place for all of us. And then he gave us his greatest gift, his life."

Detective Martinsen paid his respects to the fallen patrolman, but knew he had to maintain a distance in order to run a competent investigation. Martinsen knew Fike before his death, but only in passing.

Martinsen went to the personnel division and pulled Officer Fike's records. It was a task Martinsen disliked intensely, but he knew he had to do it.

All signs pointed toward Fike being the victim of a random incident. Martinsen guessed that Fike came across something or someone, and had grounds to arrest that someone. The person did not want to go to jail, so he pulled a gun and killed Fike.

Martinsen was relieved and happy to find out that Officer Fike was not only a model police officer, he was a model husband and father. This, of course, made his death harder to take. But at least Martinsen knew there was no vengeance involved.

Martinsen also felt confident his homicide team would solve the case and that when a suspect was arrested, no sordid story of police corruption would surface.

The following Monday Chief Ortega had another meeting with Martinsen and his crew. They reviewed the fact that there was little or no physical evidence found at the crime scene.

There were no bloody footprints or shoeprints. In order to prove any guilty actions of a suspect, it would be necessary to have an eyewitness, or hope that the suspect told someone who would have the common decency to come forward with the information.

Larry Martinsen had interviewed a lot of killers in his homicide investigation career. He knew that most killings are done by ordinary people. There are very few professional killers.

Chief Ortega was not happy to hear about the lack of physical evidence. Police chiefs do not normally get involved in the day-to-day handling of cases and physical evidence. Most chiefs have to be concerned about budgets, race and sex hiring quotas, equipment purchases, and meting out departmental discipline.

Ortega had not been a street cop for a lot of years, but he did know that the case did not look good.

Meanwhile, a private organization known as Silent Witness offered a reward of $5,000 for information leading to the arrest of Fike's killer. This non-profit foundation was composed of citizens who help the police solve difficult cases by means of cash rewards.

In a way, it is a sad commentary on modern man that a fee need be paid to do what any decent person should do anyway. But, as one homicide cop said, "We ain't proud. We'll take help wherever we can get it."

The weeks went by with no significant break in the case. People called in and gave names of people who were likely to have committed the murder, but there was never any proof.

Some of the people named were already in prison. Some had alibis. Some had no alibi, but denied any knowledge of the crime. Without proof, the cops completed the interviews, wrote their reports, and went on to investigate the next tip.

On January 23rd, Silent Witness upped the reward offer to $15,000. This increased sum came from money donated by a private citizen who wanted to remain anonymous.

350

One thousand dollars had been donated by neighboring Mesa Public Safety Foundation and $1,000 more from the Associated Highway Patrolmen of Arizona.

Some unspecified amounts came from the Phoenix Law Enforcement Association, the Phoenix Police Union and the Management Association of Police Employees which represented the Phoenix police sergeants and lieutenants.

Silent Witness had never offered more than $1,000 for information on an unsolved crime. Sgt. Brad Thiss, the information officer for the department, said, "If there is somebody out there who has the information and is waiting to see how high the pot will grow, we're serving notice that this is it."

There is an old saying that "money talks." Shortly after the increased reward was advertised, Detective Martinsen received a phone call from a woman who had been near the liquor store on the night of Officer Fike's death.

The woman could only provide a fragment of information, but it was something. She said that as she walked past the alley she could see a police car with its headlights on. There did not appear to be any people around.

As the woman continued walking she saw a late model red Pontiac Fiero drive away rapidly from the police car. The Pontiac had only one occupant, a white male with long hair.

Martinsen had the witness come to the office of the homicide division to get a complete, formal statement from her. He also wanted her to look at some pictures of automobiles to be certain that she was referring to a Pontiac Fiero, and not some other kind of car. She was positive of the car.

At the end of the interview, Martinsen delicately

asked her if she had been following the investigation in the newspaper. The woman sat across from him, chewing gum with an open mouth. She cracked the gum every few seconds.

Yes, the woman had been following the investigation. Martinsen asked her if she was aware how frustrated the police were since they had uncovered nothing. The woman shrugged and said, "I figured you guys wasn't doing nothing because you didn't have no leads."

Martinsen asked her why she had waited over two weeks before coming forward with the information. She shrugged again, chewed her gum, looked at the fingernails on her left hand and turned her body away from Martinsen.

"I dunno. This kinda stuff makes me nervous. Gives me the creeps, you know? I didn't want to get involved." She turned toward him. "If you get the guy, do I get the reward?"

Martinsen explained that Silent Witness was not connected to the police department. Besides, they were a long way from an arrest. The Phoenix metropolitan area had over a million people. Those million people owned a lot of red Pontiac Fieros.

The woman seemed almost disappointed that she could not have the check on the spot. Martinsen said that Silent Witness had never cheated anyone yet.

Another detective came in the room after the woman left and found Martinsen staring into his coffee cup. Martinsen told him about the woman. The detective said, "There are some prize people out there, aren't there?"

The next day another phone call was received. This one urged sleuths to check the police records for an armed robbery at a 24-hour bank depository about two hours before Officer Fike's death.

The caller said, "The two guys who did that are Matt Milburn and Ron Cashman. They held up that lady. One of them killed your cop. Check it out. I'll call you back in two hours." Click. The line was dead.

Martinsen queried the computer for any street robberies on the night of Fike's death.

Sure enough, on January 8th, at 9:30, a woman employee of a shoe store was making a night deposit at a branch bank in the 4200 block of Thunderbird Road. Two men held her up. One had a gun. They took $201 in cash and some checks. They drove away from the area in a small, red car that was new and looked sporty.

Martinsen checked records for Milburn and Cashman. Both were well-known to the street officers. They were small-time thieves and druggies with no significant history of violence.

The caller phoned again two hours later and said, "I'll call you when you've got them on the robbery. Milburn did your cop friend. He told me he did." Click.

Martinsen disliked the caller intensely. Every time he wanted to ask a question the man hung up on him. Yet, the mysterious voice gave the best information so far.

Martinsen found recent pictures of Milburn and Cashman. He also checked his file on the case and found that Milburn had been named initially by an anonymous caller who only said, "Check out Matt Milburn." The sleuths had. Milburn was cooperative and had an alibi. The alibi was not an iron-clad one. There was nothing more to go on.

Martinsen made up two photo lineups containing six pictures each. He showed the lineups to the woman who had been robbed.

She studied the first one for a full two minutes before she pointed to one of the pictures and said, "I'm pretty sure this is one of them." It was Cashman.

She looked at the second lineup for about 10 seconds before pointing to Milburn. "He had the gun and drove the red car. You won't let him hurt me, will you?"

Martinsen now had solid evidence to solve a robbery. He was working a homicide, however, and needed to link the two incidents.

A stakeout was set up and Cashman was nabbed without incident. Milburn proved to be quite elusive, though. Attempts were made to locate him at the residences of two sets of relatives and his former place of work. When the probers were unsuccessful there, they knew Milburn had the word that he was hot.

The police kept looking and put out feelers to their various informants that Milburn was wanted.

On Wednesday, February 26th, officers heard that Milburn was at a certain address in Phoenix. They surrounded the apartment and waited. Four two-man teams took up strategic positions at the front and rear points of entry.

Around 7:30 A.M., a tall, gaunt figure with shoulder length hair emerged from the front of the apartment. He looked around furtively, up and down the street.

The lead detective saw him from behind the tinted glass of an unmarked surveillance van. The sleuth picked up the colored polaroid photo and gave it one more look to be sure.

The detective keyed the button on his handi-talkie and said, "All surveillance units. He just came out on the east side. Long hair, green T-shirt, jeans. Take him now!"

The surveillance van was about 50 yards from Milburn. It lurched forward and headed toward him. Tires squealed up and down the street as officers converged on Milburn.

For a moment, Milburn froze when he heard the accelerating engines and squealing tires. He ran north to the corner of the apartment building until he saw his path was cut off by two beefy detectives wearing plaid shirts, jeans with western belt buckles and Phoenix police baseball caps.

Milburn turned and ran back south until he saw two skinny, bearded guys in ragged clothes running at him from around the back of the building. At first Milburn thought the two were strung-out junkies until he saw the badges on their belts.

Milburn turned sharply to his right and ran two steps until he was face to face with the largest person he had ever seen in his life. The detective had a mustache and was as well dressed as the undercover officers chasing him were shabbily dressed.

The tall officer had a deep voice, and was very calm. "Sit down, son. It's all over."

Milburn sat down and was handcuffed. He was taken to the homicide office where he was allowed to use the bathroom and was given a cup of coffee.

Meanwhile, Martinsen and another officer interviewed Cashman. The interview was a typical cat-and-mouse game. First, Cashman denied everything. Then, when he was sure that they had him on the street robbery, he admitted to it.

Cashman, however, denied killing Officer Fike. He said that after the robbery, Milburn dropped him off. Later, Milburn told him he had killed the cop.

Cashman said, "Can you get me a deal? I didn't kill no cop."

Martinsen would make no promises. He let Cashman think about everything while he interviewed Matt Milburn.

Milburn sat in the interview room, skinny, unbathed, and sulking. He refused to be interviewed and asked for an attorney. Later, however, Milburn agreed to be interviewed by a newspaper reporter. He denied the street robbery and the murder. "I didn't do it. I don't know why somebody's trying to frame me."

Milburn told the reporter he believed someone was trying to get him convicted in order to collect the reward money. "I am sure that's the reason," he said. "I don't know who in the hell did it — probably it was one of my friends who's not really a friend.

"I know nothing about the bank robbery. Whoever told them I committed that murder is probably the one who did the robbery."

Milburn said he was at home with his wife on the night Fike was killed. Later in the interview, however, Milburn said he may have been with other relatives.

Milburn told reporters he would undergo a polygraph examination to prove his innocence.

"Hell, yeah, I'd take it. I have got nothing to hide," he said. "I wouldn't kill a cop. I ain't going to try to take credit for a dumb thing I didn't do. What do you think?"

Milburn was asked why he ran from the police. "I took off because I didn't want them messing with me."

Martinsen began checking more on Milburn and found out that he was a near-genius with a 133 IQ. One of the detectives said, "Wow, that's almost as high as the Chief's."

Milburn was a high-school dropout. He had been confined to juvenile detention centers in Phoenix and Tucson.

In August of 1982, Milburn pleaded guilty to two burglaries in Phoenix and Glendale and was sentenced to 3.75 years in prison. Milburn served time in prisons in Tucson, Perrysville, and Florence and was released January 25, 1985.

Martinsen gathered up everything he had and took it to the Maricopa County District Attorney's Office. The case was assigned to Deputy Prosecutor K.C. Skull who had a reputation for being tough and thorough.

Skull could see right off that Cashman's statements about Milburn doing the murder were self-serving and designed to steer guilt away from him. Skull knew this case would be difficult. But he never panicked. Milburn had access to a red Pontiac Fiero, and that was what was seen leaving from behind the liquor store.

Also, the witness from Silent Witness agreed to come forward and repeat that Milburn had told him he had killed the officer. The person was a relative of Milburn's.

Prosecutor Skull communicated with Milburn's attorney, David Appleton. The attorney was reminded that the potential for a death penalty existed and that Appleton should tell Milburn exactly what was in store for him if they went to trial.

Juries do not like to see uniformed police officers assassinated. Skull's last admonition was for Appleton and Milburn to think about a guilty plea. Skull told Defense Attorney Appleton to inform his client that he was had.

After relaying this ominous message, Deputy Prosecutor Skull waited to see what happened. While he waited, he also prepared to go to trial.

It would be a difficult case. Defense Attorney Appleton would show that Cashman was testifying against Milburn to save his own skin, and to get immunity.

Appleton would also show that the Silent Witness was testifying not to further the truth, but to line his pockets with $15,000.

There were no witnesses with any decent motives.

Even the woman who saw Milburn's red Pontiac flee from the scene took her sweet time about reporting what she had seen.

Juries did not like these kinds of witnesses. Juries liked people who had jobs and were responsible. Juries liked women who wore housedresses and baked cookies, not ones who hung around bars at midnight.

Skull knew it would be tough, but he knew he had to work with what he had. Also, he knew he had the right man.

Preparations for the case were moving along. There had been no contact between Skull and Appleton.

Then, just days before the preliminary hearing was to begin, word reached Skull that Milburn was ready to plead guilty. Skull's first instinct was to ask, "Plead guilty to what? Disturbing the peace?" Skull had been down that road with defense attorneys before.

Skull and his superiors took a hard line on any potential bargains. They knew they had a tough case to prove, but thought they would win.

On May 9, 1984, Matthew Milburn pleaded guilty to robbery and murder. The death penalty was not sought. Appleton told Judge E.G. Noyes of Maricopa County Superior Court that Officer Fike surprised Milburn as he was sitting in his car behind the liquor store.

Skull later clarified that statement by pointing out that Milburn was sitting in his car injecting cocaine. Officer Fike ordered Milburn from the car. Milburn did not know if he was in trouble for the robbery he had done, or for the cocaine he was using.

Once outside the car, Milburn tried to run from the officer. Fike tackled him and the struggle was on.

Milburn pointed his own gun at Fike and said, "How does it feel to be on the other end? You better say your prayers." Then he shot the officer in the face.

358

On July 7, 1986, Judge Noyes sentenced Milburn to life in prison. The term consisted of eight years for armed robbery and a consecutive life term for the first-degree murder of Officer Fike. Milburn has no possibility of parole for 30 years and three months.

Judge Noyes told Milburn he was lucky to receive the chance to plead guilty. The judge said he thought Milburn could have been sentenced to death if a jury had found him guilty.

It was also learned that, after the robbery, Milburn dropped off Cashman. Then Milburn went to a west Phoenix nightclub where he bought cocaine. Then he bought syringes at an all-night drug store one block from the death scene. The rest is history.

Sentiment from the police was varied. Some felt Matt Milburn should be executed. Others felt a minimum guaranteed sentence of 30 years was acceptable.

Larry Martinsen, weary from the strain, said, "There are no winners in this. There's no reason for anybody to be happy."

While Officer Fike's family is trying to learn to live without him, Matthew Sterling Milburn is serving his sentence in the Arizona prison system.

EDITOR'S NOTE:
Bill Williams, Fred Renfro and Ron Cashman are not the real names of the persons so named in the foregoing story. Fictitious names have been used because there is no reason for public interest in the identities of these persons.

"FLUSH OUT THE COP KILLERS!"

by Jack Heise

SPRING CREEK, N.C.
OCTOBER 5, 1985

Very likely there wasn't a happier young woman in the entire state of North Carolina than the 17-year-old on Saturday afternoon, September 14, 1985, as she drove along Highway 63 from Bryson City to Ashville on a shopping trip.

Her boyfriend had popped the question.

Some felt that 17 might be young to take on the responsibility of marriage, but there was no question about her boyfriend.

Robert L. Coggins was a 27-year-old rookie state highway patrolman. He had been raised in Bryson City and was known to most of its 1,500 residents. He not only cut a handsome figure in his trooper's uniform, but folks said he was just a fine young man and would make an excellent husband.

The girl's thoughts as she drove along were a jumble of things concerning her upcoming wedding. There were the wedding dress, bridesmaids, the reception and, of course, where they were going to live.

She spotted the patrol car, with its blue light flashing, parked on the road shoulder just outside the hamlet of Hot Springs. She knew it would be Bob because he patrolled that area.

She slowed, but did not stop. Bob had warned her not to stop when he had anyone stopped, as it would interfere with his duties. He was a cop who went by the book.

She tapped the ring of her car horn as she approached the patrol officer who had stopped a bronze and white pickup truck. It was Bob. He waved at her and she waved at him, and her thoughts went back to the wedding.

A short time later, a Madison County medic came along the same stretch of highway. He too saw the flashing blue light of the patrol car parked on the road shoulder. The pickup truck was no longer anywhere to be seen.

The medic slowed down and noted that the trooper appeared to be slumped over the steering wheel. Thinking that he might be ill and in need of attention, the motorist stopped.

There was nothing he could do for Trooper Coggins, however. Two bullet wounds in his head had taken his life instantly.

The medic used his car radio to contact the Highway Patrol dispatcher and reported that the trooper had been slain.

The dispatcher had been waiting for a call from Coggins, who had radioed in that he was stopping a bronze and white pickup truck with an Arkansas license tag.

At the time, Coggins had said that he recalled such a vehicle with Arkansas plates had been on the "hot sheet" for stolen vehicles. He asked the dispatcher to make a computer check, to see if it was the wanted pickup.

The dispatcher made the check and it came back affirmative. The pickup had been reported stolen in Franklin County, Arkansas, two weeks earlier. The dispatcher had attempted to give the information to Coggins, but there hadn't been a response.

The dispatcher sent out a broadcast for all cars in the vicinity to go to the scene, four miles south of Hot Springs.

Next, he put out an alert to all police agencies in the northwest area of the state and the adjoining states of Tennessee, Georgia and Alabama, requesting that roadblocks be set up on all highways. The killers had only a few minutes' headstart, and would likely be fleeing to put as much distance between them and the murder as possible.

The first officers on the scene noted that Coggins had been shot while seated in his car. He apparently had still been going by the book, which would be to wait until the dispatcher confirmed whether or not the pickup he had stopped was stolen. He would then wait for a backup unit before taking into custody the two young men he had seen in the pickup.

There were two spent .22-caliber shell casings on the road alongside the patrol car, and the killers had taken Coggins' .357 Magnum from his holster.

The slain trooper's body was left in the car until a team of lab technicians arrived to photograph the scene and check the area for possible physical evidence.

In the meantime, a call was put in to Franklin County, Arkansas, for additional information concerning the pickup Coggins had stopped.

Sheriff Bob Pritchard took the call, and said that the men in the vehicle were most likely two escaped convicts, Jimmy Rios, 23, and William Bray, 21.

Rios had been in the county jail on a charge of theft

and forgery; Bray had been jailed on a charge of reckless driving, after fleeing from a police officer, and for having a concealed weapon and a controlled substance on him.

The pair, along with three other inmates, had escaped from the jail after slugging the jailer over the head with a piece of pipe. Two of the prisoners had been captured, but the other three were still at large.

Pritchard said that Rios and Bray were a couple of mean, tough customers. He had learned, following their escape, that they had spent four days hiding in the Ozark Mountains, spending most of their time perched up in trees.

Pritchard said he was almost certain that it had been Rios and Bray in the pickup. Tracking dogs had picked up their scent and followed it to a farm where the vehicle had been taken.

"We haven't heard from them since that time," Pritchard said. "But I'm surprised that they've kept that truck this long. We've had an alert out on it covering the whole country."

Hours passed without the killers or the pickup spotted at any of the roadblocks. It seemed almost impossible that they had gotten out of the area. Interstate 19 is the only main highway through the Great Smokey Mountains. There are a few other state highways in the area, but they had also been blocked within a short time of the murder.

Investigators at the scene where Coggins had been shot were puzzled as to how the killers had managed to ambush the trooper. The shell casings indicated that they had been fired from a rifle. Apparently Coggins had been distracted by one of the men as he waited for a report from the dispatcher, and the other man had been able to sneak up on him with the gun.

Lawmen found the pickup at seven o'clock in the

evening. It had been abandoned on Highway 63, near the tiny town of Spring Creek in Madison County, in the foothills of Doggett Mountain, 15 miles from where the slaying had taken place.

The killers, apparently, had been aware that Coggins had called in for a make on the pickup, and that the murder would soon be discovered. They had abandoned the truck to keep from being stopped at a roadblock.

The immediate question was whether they had stolen another vehicle and had managed to get through the roadblocks or had fled on foot and were holed up somewhere, possibly with hostages.

The roadblocks continued throughout the night, and the officers manning them were given descriptions of Rios and Bray.

By morning, the small town of Spring Creek was swarming with officers. Colonel Jack Cardwell had arrived with every available highway patrol trooper, many of whom were off-duty, to join the deputies of Madison County Sheriff E.Y. Ponders. The FBI sent in agents to search for the fugitives from justice on the escape charge from Arkansas. Neighboring county and city police joined the others in the search.

A command post, to coordinate the efforts of the various agencies, was set up in the Spring Creek Volunteer Fire Department building.

Meanwhile, fingerprints lifted from the stolen truck positively identified Jimmy Rios and William Bray as having been in it.

By mid-morning, with no report of anyone missing in the area or of any vehicles being stolen, it was presumed that the killers had taken off on foot into the rugged Doggett Mountain area.

The news media was asked to issue an alert to all residents of the area. They were told to keep their doors and windows locked, and to report immediately if they saw strangers.

Motorists were warned, "If you see anything, don't stop. If someone jumps out in front of you, run over him. These men have killed a state trooper and have nothing to lose. They are armed and extremely dangerous."

Ab Taylor, a 31-year veteran with the U.S. Border Patrol, was training a class of 13 students in the area. He learned of the murder and brought his students to Spring Creek. They had all been instructed in tracking: to search for footprints, disturbed areas in creek beds, bent twigs, bruised vegetation, and to determine how fast a quarry might be going.

Bloodhounds from the state penal institution were brought in by Deputy Steve Graves of the Burke County Sheriff's Office.

By nightfall Sunday, there were 200 officers in Spring Creek, and 100 more still maintaining roadblocks around the area under investigation.

Sheriff Ponders told the news media that he and other officers were certain that the killers were somewhere in the forest and thick underbrush of Doggett Mountain. He said that the area was completely surrounded, but rooting the killers out would be difficult and slow.

"There's plenty of wild apples and water for them to survive on," Ponders said. "And we can't be just running pell mell through the woods. We know they've got a rifle and Coggins' weapon, and they may have more guns. They're got nothing to lose by further killings."

On Monday morning, officers were assigned to ride the school bus bringing children into Spring Creek.

The 15 members of the volunteer fire department gave their time to cooking breakfast and making sandwiches for the search teams.

Four state police helicopters with spotters came in to make treetop-high sweeps of the area. A special chopper, the only one of its kind on the east coast, was flown in from Fairfax County, Virginia. It was equipped with an infrared heat-seeking device that can sense a change of one percent and differentiate the warm object from its surroundings.

The choppers, however, had a difficult time. Sunlight, reflected from the leaves on the trees and the thick underbrush, obscured their view of cleared areas.

Late in the afternoon, the track dogs picked up a scent. Thus, the officers knew that the killers were still in the mountain area. They were moving in a zig-zag pattern, ducking into underbrush when they heard helicopter motors approaching overhead.

The dogs followed the scent up to a rocky area and lost it. The search was called off at dark.

Joe Dean, of the North Carolina Department of Crime Control and Public Safety, informed the news media that Coggins was the third trooper killed during the year. All had been ambushed while making routine stops of cars.

The first to be slain was Giles A. Harmon, a 26-year-old trooper, who had stopped a car near Waynesville. A 25-year-old man from Lexington, Kentucky, had been apprehended and was charged with the murder.

The second to die was Raymond E. Worley, 44, of Conway. He had stopped two vans for a routine check on Highway 95 and had been shot to death. A 30-year-old man from Washington, D.C., had been charged with the murder, and three other men were charged with being accessories to the crime.

Dean said that at least part of the blame for the deaths of the three members of the 1,137 troopers on the force could be placed on lack of funds, which resulted in the use of solo patrols.

"You put one man out there, and he sees a speeding vehicle or some other infraction of the law," Dean said. "When he makes the stop, he doesn't know if it is some local citizen, or someone fleeing from a robbery or another murder.

"With two men in a car, he stands a chance. Alone, he is vulnerable. But until we can receive more funds and hire more troopers, we have to operate the way we are to cover the territory we have to protect."

More volunteer officers joined those at Spring Creek on Tuesday. Many were using their days off and vacation time. And a group from the United States Forest Service arrived to help.

Tuesday morning, a 76-year-old widow and her niece came to the command post in Spring Creek. The elderly woman said that she lived alone in a small house with a tin roof on the side of Doggett Mountain overlooking Highway 209.

She said she had stayed alone in the house on Sunday and had observed all the police officers carrying weapons as they searched through the woods.

"Late Monday, I started getting fearful," the woman said. "Something inside me kept telling me to leave, and I kept rebelling against it because I'm used to living alone. But it got to me as it started to get dark, so I called my niece and told her, 'Come get me.' It must have been around eight o'clock."

The elderly woman and her niece returned to the house at seven o'clock in the morning. She said she immediately checked her gun rack in the house.

"I've always felt if the guns were all there, things were all right," she explained. "Well, right off I saw one gun gone. It was a rifle that had belonged to my daddy.

"Then we went into the bedroom and, sure enough, I saw my quilt pack broken into. Right then, I said to my niece, 'Let's not mess around in here any longer,' and we came straight here."

Officers returned with the women to the house. They found that someone had entered it by breaking a window.

Relating it later, the elderly woman told reporters, "They got my nightcase full of clothes and dumped the clothes out on the floor. Then, they went into the kitchen and filled it up with most of my canned goods.

"They drunk a half-gallon of milk I had and a half-gallon of orange juice. They must have been thirsty, but they didn't find no liquor because I don't keep no liquor.

"I had some Salisbury steak made up and they ate all that. Then they got my frying pan out and fried up a whole dozen of eggs. And do you know they left the pan dirty."

The widow concluded by saying, "The way I've got it figured, they were out there watching my house. If I'd stayed on all night, I don't doubt that they'd have come in on me. I guess the time I've spent in church praying has given me its reward."

Locating the spot where the fugitives apparently had spent the night was a break. Deputy Graves and his dog Brandy led the way for a group of well-armed pursuers as they left the house.

Graves let his dog follow the scent 30 feet in front of the group. "He'll let us know when the scent gets hot," Graves told the officers. "He knows his business, and if we just hang back a bit, it will keep anybody from running up on them and maybe getting shot."

The strategy had been laid out at the command post for the officers who were not in the pursuing group to form a line completely around the area and keep them contained on Doggett Mountain.

"They've got their bellies full of grub and a suitcase filled with canned food," Deputy Frank Ogle said. "Unless we can root them out, they could stay holed-up out here for quite a time."

The lawmen reasoned that was what the fugitives had in mind. They'd stay in the wild mountain region until some of the heat cooled, and would then try to make a break for it, possibly by taking someone with a car as a hostage and breaking through a roadblock.

Brandy followed the scent, but the fugitives were doing their best to cover their trail. They crawled through thick underbrush, waded up small streams and kept in the cover of trees.

It was slow going, since it was known that the pair had a rifle and ammunition. If the searchers got too close, they could be picked off by the desperados.

The day was spent going from one rough section to another on the steep mountain. The fugitives were traveling fast.

Brandy was still on the scent at dark but gave no indication that he had come close to the quarry. The search was called off for the night. They would start again at daybreak.

Officers accompanied the children home on the school bus. Residents were warned to stay inside their homes, and to contact the command post by telephone in the event they had to leave. Officers would be sent out to accompany them. They were also asked to keep in touch with each other by telephone, to be certain that the fugitives had not broken in somewhere and were holding hostages.

The tight road blockades continued during the night. Every vehicle was stopped, with the cars, drivers and passengers checked out.

"I don't know how long it may take us to find them,"

Sheriff Ponders told news reporters. "But, however long it takes, we'll be here in force until we do get them."

He pointed out that as long as the fugitives were hiding somewhere on the mountain, sooner or later the parties pursuing them would catch up with them. The only fear was that they would get to someplace civilized, take a vehicle and attempt to smash their way out.

The search began again in the morning. Brandy picked up the scent from the spot where the search had been called off the previous evening.

Helicopters hovered over the officers following the trail of the fugitives. The search party kept in contact with the command post. Several times during the morning, it was thought Rios and Bray had been spotted, but they were gone before the officers could reach them.

At noon, Brandy picked up the scent where the fugitives had slid down a steep rocky bank to a wooded section below.

"They're headed for the road," Graves told the officers with him. "If we can keep them from doubling back, we'll force them out into the open."

The location was given to the command post. Groups of officers were sent out to form a line along the road where the fugitives were headed. Everyone was aware that a showdown was coming soon. Lawmen held their weapons in nervous hands. The question was whether Rios and Bray would surrender or try to shoot their way out.

A little after two o'clock, a spotter in a helicopter reported he had seen movement in some heavy brush. He told the officers following Deputy Graves and Brandy, "I'd say you are about fifteen minutes behind them. They're traveling fast and headed for the road."

Shortly before four o'clock in the afternoon, Brandy stopped at a heavy thicket in a hollow and let out several sharp barks. Graves called his dog back.

"They're in there," Graves told the officers. "That's the way Brandy has been trained to let you know when the scent is hot."

Trooper R.E. Grant used a radio to contact the command post. He gave the location as being in the Charlotte Branch area, with the thicket in a hollow behind a ridge that paralleled Highway 209. There was a stream running through it, and the fugitives apparently thought they could lose the dog by wading down the stream.

The command post radioed back that there were five officers on the road under the command of SBI Agent J.W. Bryant. They would take up their positions on the ridge.

A helicopter crew hovered overhead, giving the exact location to all the officers. When both groups were in position, an officer with the group that had been pursuing the fugitives called out, "We know you are in there! Come out with your hands on your heads!"

There was no response.

"You are surrounded," the officer shouted.

"I am going to count to ten. If you haven't come out, we'll open fire on you."

The officer began shouting out the numbers. At the count of five, two figures popped up out of the underbrush with their hands on their heads. They were Jimmy Rios and William Bray.

The suspects were handcuffed and taken to a car. Agent Bryant said later, "It looked like they'd been run to death. They didn't say anything when we got to them."

The guns, food and blankets the fugitives had been carrying were found in the thicket where the men had come out to surrender.

Word reached the command post in Spring Creek before the officers and suspects arrived. A group of people gathered on the road and began to cheer as the handcuffed suspects were taken into the volunteer fire department building.

Rios and Bray were taken to the Madison County Jail in Marshall, where they were booked on charges of first-degree murder.

Finally, the manhunt was over. The little hamlet of Spring Creek returned to its quiet way.

One of the residents commented, "It's the biggest thing that ever happened in the 50 years I've been living around here. I'm downright sorry about that young trooper who got killed, but it sure was exciting for awhile. It was like being on the set of one of those big city cops-and-robbers shows that they put on television."

Meanwhile funeral services were held for Robert Coggins in Bryson City. Hundreds of police officers in uniforms joined the local residents in paying their last respects to the slain trooper in the red brick First Baptist Church.

In his eulogy for the slain trooper, the reverend said, "Bless all our men who work in law enforcement and who are ready to give their life that we may have protection from those who would take our freedom of life from us."

Among the notable mourners were North Carolina Governor James G. Martin and State Attorney General Lacy H. Thornburg. Coggins' 17-year-old fiancee wept throughout the services.

The metal casket, draped in the red, white and blue state flag, was carried out by six state troopers, and a procession was formed to take it to a mountaintop cemetery, accessible only by a one-lane road, above the town.

At the time the funeral services were being held, Rios and Bray were taken before the Madison County District Court for a preliminary hearing on the charges of murder that had been placed against them.

The prosecutor informed the court that the state allegedly had evidence that the .22-caliber rifle found at the spot where the defendants had surrendered had been identified by ballistic experts as the weapon that killed Coggins. The prosecutor stated that he would seek the death penalty for the defendants.

Court-appointed attorneys for Rios and Bray entered an automatic plea of innocence to the charges.

The court ordered that both Rios and Bray be held without privilege of bond, pending further legal proceedings.

Jimmy Rios and William Bray must be presumed innocent of all the charges against them unless proven otherwise in a court of law.

"OREGON TRACKDOWN OF A LADY COP KILLER!"

by Gary C. King

FLORENCE, OREGON
OCTOBER 22, 1982

In view of the increasing crime rate in Oregon, Governor Vic Atiyeh recently launched a new anti-crime campaign, which included proposals to bring back the death penalty and to eliminate insanity as a defense plea, possibly due, at least in part, to the verdict delivered in the John Hinkley, Jr. case involving the attempted assassination of President Reagan.

An additional part of Atiyeh's war against crime required that funds for the Oregon State Police Criminal Investigation Unit be doubled, a move that would add $8 million to the division's budget. And instead of constructing more office buildings, Atiyeh said he'd introduce a proposal that would add more cell space at Oregon State Penitentiary. He also introduced a plan to form a governor's special commission against violent crime, whose job would be to study the overall problem of crime in the state.

"If we do not control crime," said Atiyeh at a recent news conference, "it will control us. A holding action against violent crime is not enough," he continued, calling on all Oregon residents to participate in an effort to help ease crime in the state, "not as vigilantes but as decent, law-abiding citizens."

However, in spite of the governor's good intentions, another violent crime would be committed, namely the crime of murder.

On Tuesday evening, June 15, 1982, Springfield, Oregon, police dispatcher Laura Ann Jack failed to return home after a single day's visit to the Oregon coast. At first it was thought that she was merely late in returning, possibly stopping off for dinner before driving on home. But as the evening wore on with no word from the 26-year-old policewoman—or even a phone call—her husband naturally began to worry.

Since Laura was known for her punctuality and alertness, both necessary characteristics for a police dispatcher, it is readily understandable why her unusual tardiness concerned her husband, who is also a Springfield police officer. But as time passed by with still no word from Laura, the husband's worry soon turned to agonizing despair.

Had Laura become ill? he wondered. If that were the case, why hadn't she called to inform him? Had she been involved in an automobile accident on her way to the coast (or on her way home)? That seemed a more likely possibility, particularly since she hadn't called. But if she had been in an accident, particularly a serious accident that would have required medical attention, why hadn't police authorities notified him? After all, she carried police identification, and surely the state police would be able to get in contact with Springfield police, who in turn would naturally notify her husband. But the worried husband had no answers to these nagging questions. All he could do at this point was wonder and worry, until he could wait no longer. When it became evident that Laura was not going to return that night, her husband notified his own department, as well as the state police, of the mysterious circumstances surrounding his wife's trip to the beach.

Although foul play was seriously suspected when Mrs. Jack failed to return home by the next morning, there was little doubt left when state police troopers found her abandoned car that Wednesday morning along U.S. 101 near the town of Reedsport, approximately 20 miles south of Florence, which was Mrs. Jack's destination. After contacting their dispatcher, the cops were instructed to remain at the scene until the Oregon State Police crime lab personnel arrived to process the vehicle for clues.

When crime lab technicians arrived at the car's location they looked it over for any obvious clues and signs of foul play. Finding nothing significant, however, they had it towed to their garage where they would go over it with a fine tooth comb, so to speak.

In the meantime, the cops organized a search for the missing woman in the vicinity where her car had been found, looking for any physical evidence that might be present as well. Their efforts, however, merely ended in frustration.

Meanwhile, at the crime lab garage, technicians first dusted the car for latent prints. Finding identifiable impressions, the scientists had to speculate they probably belonged to Mrs. Jack or her husband but couldn't be sure until the latent prints were verified. The technicians also vacuumed the interior, finding several hairs and bits of clothing fibers, both of which proved nothing, as those items are found inside any car in the world. Such items can prove useful, however, if foul play is confirmed and a suspect is apprehended, and it was with this thought in mind that the trained personnel carefully sealed and labeled the items for possible later use.

In spite of the intense frustration the cops were experiencing—particularly since the missing woman was *one of their own*—they remained optimistic and hopeful Laura would turn up alive. Early the next morning, at daybreak, they launched another massive search effort, covering old ground as well as new, which included air surveillance. But their efforts seemed hopeless. The woman just wasn't anywhere to be found, or so it seemed.

According to police reports, authorities received a call the next day, Thursday, June 17, 1982, while search efforts were continuing for Laura Ann Jack. The call was to inform them that a body had been discovered in a fresh water pool at Ocean Beach Wayside, 14 miles north of Florence. When the state troopers arrived at the wayside, they quickly discovered the body was that of a woman, and they guessed her age to be mid-to-late twenties. Carefully observing the pallid, hollow-eyed corpse, the cops soon suspected foul play after noting the bruises and abrasions about her neck. Taking note that the woman was dead and that no help could be rendered, the cops returned to their patrol car and radioed their findings to their dispatcher.

The scene of a murder—or any other type of crime scene for that matter—is itself evidence, as any trained policeman or detective well knows. For that reason it is vitally important that the scene be protected to assure successful clearance of a particular case, because improper protection can, and usually does, result in the loss or contamination of part or all of the physical evidence present, which would ultimately render the evidence useless. Therefore, the first officer to arrive at the scene of a crime immediately and automatically realizes that it is his or her responsibility to secure and protect the crime scene from unauthorized persons such as curiosity seekers and anxious members of the press.

The state troopers who were first to arrive at the aforementioned wayside immediately set about determining the dimensions of the suspected crime scene. Although there are no definite rules which can be applied to defining the dimensions of a homicide scene, the officers knew from experience that the best physical evidence is normally found at or near the site of the immediate area surrounding the body. However, in this case, the troopers were not sure if the victim was killed at the present location, or if she had been killed at a different location and dumped in the ocean to wash ashore. To make that determination, they would have to await the results of an autopsy to see if salt water was present in the victim's lungs. In the meantime, however, the troopers roped off a considerably large area of the beach and set up police barriers with signs which read: THIS AREA IS CLOSED TO THE PUBLIC DUE TO AN INVESTIGATION BEING CONDUCTED THEREIN.

Shortly after the homicide probers from Lane County arrived at the crime site, the victim was identified as that of 26-year-old Laura Ann Jack, the missing police dispatcher from Springfield, some 60 miles to the east. It really came as no surprise to the detectives because of the fact that two days earlier Mrs. Jack's husband had reported his wife missing when she had failed to return home. Although upset because the victim was a fellow police officer, the detectives remained objective and as calm as possible.

The officials followed proper procedures at the crime site, not allowing the body of the victim to be moved from the area until the experts from the state crime labs and the medical examiner's office arrived. As part of their immediate protection measures, the detectives ordered uniformed officers to control and keep spectators from entering the areas they expected to have high potential for yielding physical evidence. Investigators also had officers cover certain areas near the body to protect the scene from wind and the ever-present possibility of rain.

Additionally, the detectives and officers knew they had to prevent and avoid any unnecessary walking about, as well as avoiding moving items on or near the body. They also knew they had to avoid touching any item which was likely to yield latent fingerprints.

As additional emergency vehicles began to arrive, so did curious passersby. It wasn't long until a small crowd had gathered, much as one would at the scene of an automobile accident. But police barriers were soon put up in the wayside parking lot to keep the intruding motorists out.

It wasn't long before a man from the Lane County Medical Examiner's Office arrived on the scene, as did vans carrying photographers and specialists from the Oregon State Police crime labs. They quickly began unloading the tools of their trade, which included cameras, tripods, floodlights, evidence bags, and other miscellaneous equipment necessary for the completion of their specialized tasks.

But before the criminalists were allowed to begin performing their various duties, the scene had to be photographed. And as an added precaution, a police artist made a sketch of the woman's body in relation to the surrounding area just in case the photos turned out damaged or defective.

When the Lane County medical examiner scrutinized the victim's body, he noted the many variables which affect the rate of putrefaction. Although he knew it was extremely difficult to estimate the victim's time of death from the state of putrefaction alone, he also knew that several factors could aid him in arriving at an estimated time of death. For example, a body discovered submerged underwater, such as that of the victim, displays certain specific changes which occur under certain conditions which can help investigators immensely. Noting that the water was slightly warm, the medical examiner observed that the skin of the victim's fingers and toes was nearly white and wrinkled. He could also see that the condition had spread to the hands and soles of her feet, a clear indication that Mrs. Jack had been dead at least 24 to 48 hours. Of course the fact that the victim had only been missing for two days before being found dead played the major part in determining an estimated time of death in this case. But the changes from being submerged in water strengthened the validity of the estimate.

Accidental drowning was quickly ruled out as the medical examiner carefully observed the badly bloated face of the dead woman, swollen because of a number of possibilities, including damage incurred while being transported by water (possibly hitting rocks or driftwood), intake of water, and strangulation. Or possibly a combination of all three.

As the medical examiner observed the abrasions, which covered a good portion of the neck and face, his curiosity began to focus more on the area of her neck instead of her face. The neck was badly swollen and distorted, as if extraordinary pressure had been applied, as in a strangling, and there was severe hemorrhaging in the eyes, which is common in strangulation victims.

Because the victim had a crushed trachea in addition to swelling, bruises and neck abrasions, it didn't take long for the medical examiner to conclude that Mrs. Jack had been strangled. But as a matter of routine in a homicide investigation of this nature, the body would have to be sent to either Eugene or Portland, where it could be examined by the state medical examiner. After recording the victim's body temperature and noting general observations made at the scene, the coroner turned the body over to detectives after informing them that he couldn't add anything more to the scenario.

As they went about their tasks, the detectives began taking detailed notes of their observations. They noted the position of the victim's body on the beach, the fact that there were no open wounds or bloodstains, and the fact that no weapon was present, not even a rope or a cord. As the investigators searched for evidence, they kept in mind that they must be able to identify each piece they collected, even months after they collected it. They also had to be able to describe the exact location of the items at the time they were obtained, and they had to be able to prove that such evidence was continuously in proper custody from the moment it was collected to the time it would be presented in court, if at all.

The homicide detectives knew that in any type of criminal investigation, especially a homicide, they had only one opportunity to search the crime scene properly. They also paid special attention to the relative position of items they found, noting that such attention can be as important to a detective as an item of evidence itself.

Statements were taken from witnesses at the scene, witnesses who had been detained by the first officers to arrive so that detectives would be able to conduct interviews with them. Not expecting to learn anything useful from the witnesses, the detectives were surprised when two of them said that they saw a man, approximately ... years old, following the victim as she was walking on the beach. Their description of the man was sketchy at best, and police refused to release any details concerning the description other than the man's approximate age.

Other investigators chose to examine an area nearby but away from the critical area being searched. They designated that area a trash collection site, a move which would enable them to keep track of all items found at the scene while at the same time separating evidence from useless material. Once organized, the investigators noted all the obvious evidence to be collected, then decided what order they would collect such items. At the same time they determined what should be searched for that wasn't obvious, and decided as well how to split up the area for a successful and organized search.

Using the sector method of search, in which probers are assigned lanes of designated width, the investigators covered the entire area for clues. They searched behind and under small pieces of driftwood, in clumps of grass and seaweed, and spread out to examine areas not previously covered in pursuit of any clue that might help them solve the case.

Unfortunately, clues were scarce, and detectives learned little more than the fact that they had a dead woman on their hands killed by a person or persons unknown for no apparent reason. But the cops knew that a motive *must* exist, and they would use every means at their disposal to discover that motive.

Was Laura Jack's death the result of a stranger-against-stranger homicide? the cops wondered. Their instinct told them no, but at this point they had no evidence to indicate otherwise. And according to police statistics, nearly half of all murders committed are done so by strangers to their victims.

The cops knew that when a relationship of some kind is present between the criminal and the victim a case is much easier to solve. But when none is present, as they were assuming in this case, a lot of hard work and luck is involved in obtaining an arrest and a conviction.

From the condition of the corpse, such as the abrasions about the face and body, the homicide investigators soon theorized that the victim had been killed at a different location from where her body was found and that her body had subsequently been dumped in the ocean only to wash up on the beach at the wayside. Just how far away from the present location the woman was killed the cops couldn't say or even speculate. But it appeared to them that the woman's killer had planned to make her death look like a drowning accident, a plan that had been so sloppily executed that even the greenest of cops could see through it.

The detectives knew they had to be able to account for every item they touched for future elimination of clothing fibers, hair, or even fingerprints. They also had to remember every place they had walked so they could later distinguish their own footprints from those of a possible suspect.

Searching for clues, crime lab sleuths sifted the sand on the beach near the woman's body for such aforementioned items of evidence such as hair or bits of clothing fiber. But such items were nowhere to be found and realizing that little else could be done at this point in the investigation, the victim's body was zipped up inside a black body bag and removed from the beach to a waiting van.

As one day followed another, detectives were becoming less and less optimistic about the case. No one, except two witnesses who saw a man following Mrs. Jack on the beach, had seen or heard anything unusual on the day the victim was strangled. If anyone else had noticed anything suspicious, they were not talking.

And when the cops searched the victim's car earlier, they noted there was no sign of a struggle or forced entry, nothing that had suggested foul play until Laura Jack's body was found on the beach. Everything considered, the sleuths had not been able to turn up much more about the mysterious killing than the investigating officers who had found Mrs. Jack's body at the beach wayside.

The only plausible theory detectives could come up with was that Mrs. Jack had driven to the coast for the day — as her husband had stated earlier — and that she had decided to go for a walk on the beach after the nearly two hour drive from Springfield. The cops theorized she was followed by a man on the beach who either attempted to rape or rob her, or both. Although there were no signs of sexual contact, the cops had to consider the possibility that the thought of rape had entered the criminal's mind sometime during the assault. But they leaned more toward the robbery theory considering that Mrs. Jack's car had obviously been stolen and driven several miles south of where her body had been found.

The cops ruled out as a probability that Mrs. Jack had been strangled at the location her body was found because of two major reasons: 1) The distance was too great for her body to travel in the ocean current before washing up at the wayside where it was found; and 2) There were the two witnesses who saw the still unidentified man following Mrs. Jack on the beach near the wayside.

By the next day detectives had not yet uncovered a solid motive in the murder of Laura Jack, only theories. No further clues turned up in the case, and with no new leads the case was now beginning to appear hopeless, made to seem more so because the cops had no suspect as yet to zero in on. They only had the sketchy description of their mystery man.

After going over their notes again in an attempt to unravel the mysterious case, homicide sleuths decided to have another talk with their two witnesses. Concentrating on any kind of description they could get from them, the detectives called in a police artist to put together a composite drawing of the man seen following Mrs. Jack on the day of her death.

After several hours of tedious work, not only on the part of the artist, but on the part of the witnesses as well, a reasonable composite drawing of the suspect was completed and was satisfactory to the witnesses. By the next day, copies of the drawing had been circulated as far as Astoria to the north and Gold Beach to the south. The picture also appeared in newspapers in nearly every town on the coast, as well as in newspapers in the Willamette Valley to the east.

Within hours after the photo's release, police authorities in many towns and cities received phone calls from people claiming to have seen the man in question. Unfortunately, however, the cops knew that most of the calls were from cranks trying to get attention, and they equally knew that distinguishing reliable calls from the crank calls would require time and patience. As time passed, police failed to turn up anything solid.

Baffling as the case already was for the cops, they were stumped even further by the fact that Laura Jack had no known enemies. And since they couldn't connect anyone she knew, even remotely, to her death, the police had to resign themselves to accept the probability that the victim's murder was a "stranger-against-stranger" homicide making their investigation more difficult than it already was.

After studying the evidence so far obtained, the detectives began compiling reports, knowing full well that they needed the presence of a relationship of some sort between the criminal and the victim, a problem made all the more difficult because they didn't even have a prime suspect to zero in on yet. For all they knew, the man seen following Mrs. Jack on the beach could have been nothing more than a harmless beachcomber.

In spite of the frustrating aspects of the case, they felt hopeful that something more useful would eventually turn up if they persevered long enough. But after completing their tests and going through all the items found at the crime scene on or near the victim, not to mention the questioning of witnesses who were on the beach at the time the victim's body was found, the cops felt they would end the month of June, 1982, with little more useful information than they had uncovered on day one.

On Wednesday, June 30th, however, the Lane County detectives received the break they had long been waiting for. As it turned out, someone called and reported that the man they were looking for in connection with Laura Jack's death was 38-year-old John Wychick, Jr., who was reportedly last seen in the Barview, Oregon area, located between Coos Bay and Charleston on the coast, the previous Monday evening.

When the cops checked their records, they discovered that Wychick was a resident of Charleston, as well as a possible fugitive from the East Coast. One source stated that he may have been an escapee from Attica State Prison in New York, although those reports could not be immediately confirmed. In the meantime, local cops obtained a warrant and searched Wychick's last known residence on the evening of June 30th.

When the cops arrived at the residence, the 38-year-old cannery worker was nowhere to be found. After an intensive search of the dwelling, the cops left, remaining tight-lipped about what they found.

The next day, however, July 1st, a warrant was issued against Wychick, charging him with the slaying of Laura Ann Jack. Still not revealing whether or not they had any solid evidence against the suspect, the cops did say they discovered Wychick was wanted in Reading, Pennsylvania, on charges of rape, aggravated assault and reckless endangerment. They also discovered that he sometimes went under the alias of Frederick Paynter Burrows.

Police searched the Coos Bay area the next two days for Wychick, but without success. Authorities feared he caught on to the fact they were looking for him and fled the area.

Days passed with no new leads. It wasn't until July 7th that police received a tip. Campers had spotted Wychick several times walking in a secluded area along the lower Rogue River in southern Oregon. According to officials, travelers and campers entering the area were given warnings, as well as descriptions of the murder suspect.

A manhunt, coordinated by Oregon State Police Major Tom Phillips of the Salem office, was immediately initiated in that area of the Rogue River, with state troopers from as far away as Medford and Grants Pass joining in the manhunt. All in all, more than 100 law enforcement personnel were called in to search the rugged wilderness area.

"I think Wychick's too intelligent to stay in the area," said one law enforcement official who wished to remain anonymous. "I think he's gone. His name's been in the papers and on television, and it's almost a household word locally. With that much publicity and knowing how the community feels about him, I think he's got more sense than to hang around here and try to lay low."

"We're still investigating any and all leads, and that includes locally," said another searcher. "Hell, he could double back. He could be anywhere by now. Your guess is as good as mine."

Fearing that Wychick would lay low during the daytime and move at night, the cops felt sure that he would use the darkness as a cloak of cover. Another point against the cops was the fact that Wychick had lived in the area for more than two years, giving him ample time to learn the area and become resourceful.

Unsure of his direction of travel, authorities called off the search for Wychick later that afternoon. However, campers in the area were asked to report any missing equipment that might be stolen during the night while they were sleeping and were also asked to report anyone suspicious wandering around the woods. Police were now beginning to fear that Wychick may have headed for the mountainous regions of southern Oregon, which was indeed rugged terrain. If he was in the dense mountain forests, authorities would have a tough time catching him.

However, as fate would have it, a Forest Service employee spotted Wychick on July 7th, walking along an old, infrequently used logging road about seven miles up the Pistol River. However, when Wychick saw the man, he reportedly fled into the woods.

"He had been reported by a Forest Service employee who had one of our fliers with his description and photo that we've passed out all over the country," said manhunt coordinator Major Tom Phillips of the Oregon State Police.

When news of the sighting reached authorities, "mantrackers," a special police unit trained in tracing human footprints, picked up Wychick's trail. His shoe prints were followed along the logging road on which he was spotted, occasionally going into the woods, then back onto the road. Several square miles were cordoned off as an aid to the mantrackers, and a Lane County Sheriff's Office helicopter was sent to help in the search.

Special weapons and tactics teams (SWAT) were dispatched from the Eugene-Springfield area, and all roads surrounding the search area were blocked off. However, Wychick managed to continue to elude his pursuers, and by that evening, was still at large. As a precaution, many of the 100 police officers taking part in the search set up camp in the forest that night to prevent Wychick from leaving the area in the dark.

The next day, Sergeants Robert Hurita of the Oregon State Police and Jerry Lea of the Curry County Sheriff's Office were driving slowly along the seldom-used logging road that runs by the Pistol River toward their temporary command post when they saw Wychick walking toward them. But Wychick saw them as well, and fled into the brush. Because the area is so dense, he was out of sight as soon as he left the road.

Hurita immediately stopped the car. He and Lea rushed into the brush at the point where Wychick had left the road. The brush was so thick that it was difficult for anyone to remain standing and impossible to move with any great speed. Hurita and Lea could see the fugitive just ahead, however, and watched him stumble. Wychick got up and was able to go about another 20 yards or so. Hurita yelled for him to halt and give himself up. Obviously tired and exhausted from being constantly pursued, Wychick stopped and allowed the two policemen to take him into custody without any further resistance. The three-week search for the murder suspect had ended.

"I'm happy he's caught," remarked one of the officers at the scene. "The community's concern is my concern. A lot of credit has to go to the officers of the different departments that cooperated in this extensive manhunt. Their work was outstanding."

John Wychick Jr. was held without bail following his arraignment in Lane County District Court the next afternoon on a charge of murder and theft. He did not enter a plea at that time. On October 22, 1982, Wychick pleaded innocent to the charges leveled against him. A trial date was not immediately set.

However, on Friday, December 3rd, 1982, Wychick surprised authorities when he pleaded guilty in a trial by "Stipulated facts." It should be pointed out that in his agreement to a trial by stipulated facts, Wychick merely agreed that the state had enough evidence to convict him if the case went to trial. In such an agreement, the defendant retains the right to appeal the verdict.

In the meantime, Wychick was transported to Reading, Pennsylvania, where he was scheduled to plead guilty to the previously pending charges of rape and aggravated assault. In return for the plea, the count of reckless endangerment would be dropped.

Following his sentencing in Pennsylvania, Wychick will be returned to Oregon to hear Lane County Circuit Judge Gordon Cottrell pronounce him guilty of aggravated murder and theft. The charges were merged for purposes of sentencing, ensuring that Wychick will receive a minimum term of 20 years in prison for the strangling of Laura Ann Jack.

"TROOPER WAS GUNNED DOWN BY MAD TERRORISTS!"

by Gary Miller

On December 21, 1981, a New Jersey State Trooper was shot to death in the line of duty. Neither the victim nor the manhunt which followed his slaying could be termed ordinary.

The victim's name was Trooper Philip Lamonaco. Mention that name to any lawman in New Jersey and the reaction is the same: awe and a deep sense of respect—as well as an overriding passion to see his murderers brought to justice.

Trooper Lamonaco was, and is, legend.

If it weren't for the fact that his arrest record was fully documented, one might believe Lamonaco's phenomenal record of arrests and narcotics busts could only have been accomplished by an entire police force, working overtime.

Once, during a reporter's interview, he made a simple yet unnecessary request: "Don't make me look too corny. Make me look tough."

Tough? Maybe—but as any state trooper who knew him would say, tough was too simple a word to describe him. He was both "Super Trooper" and a modest, gentle family man. And, on the highway, there was simply no one else out there like him.

Among his too numerous arrests to mention, there were several that stand out. During his patrol on Route 80, he stopped a vehicle for failing to keep right. When the car had pulled over, however, Lamonaco detected a strong odor of marijuana. A search warrant was obtained, and the vehicle was thoroughly searched. It netted New Jersey State Police a drug bust consisting of approximately 1,700 pounds of marijuana.

Lamonaco was also instrumental in another huge narcotics case involving 500 pounds of marijuana recovered from an auto.

Working on the theory of odds (the more cars you stop, the more criminals you are likely to arrest), Trooper Lamonaco recovered approximately $2.5 million worth of stolen property and at least 200 illegal guns on Route 80 alone.

He had become so feared by those trafficking in illegal narcotics that a well-known national drug magazine warned its readers to avoid Route 80 if they were carrying drugs. Chances were Lamonaco would get them.

Even after gaining recognition for his outstanding achievements by being named Trooper of the Year in 1979, he would not let up. Asked to explain, Lamonaco said simply, "It's what I'm good at."

Offered a desk job, he turned it down: "Desk jobs are all right for some people," he said, "but I'm not one of them. The criminal element is out there, on the road, not in an office. Someone has to go after them. I've just gotta be on the road. That's all there is to it," he concluded.

What was this extraordinary lawman's personal background? Most of his life was spent in New Jersey, where he attended Roselle Park High School. After graduating, he served his country in the U.S. Marine Corps.

The legendary trooper recalled the first time he thought of being a state trooper: "One day, I saw an application to the State Police academy, and I've never wanted to do anything else since."

Although he was well known throughout New Jersey and had received a great deal of media attention in his work, Lamonaco's privacy was important to him. He lived with his wife and three children in a remote area of Warren County, New Jersey, and rarely socialized with neighbors.

Residents in the area, however, described him as a good-natured person. Whenever a neighbor had gone away on vacation, Lamonaco's natural instinct to protect made him keep an eye out on their property. But that quality which made Philip Lamonaco unique and legendary, would be short-lived.

The time was approximately 4:15 on December 21st when Trooper Lamonaco was patrolling Route 80 eastbound in the Knowlton Township section of New Jersey. Another trooper, Kurt Trauger, had just stopped a vehicle, and Lamonaco pulled to the side of the road as a back up. Everything went smoothly, and soon, Trooper Trauger continued his patrol along eastbound Route 80 while Lamonaco swung around to the westbound side.

The time was now approximately 4:30 P.M. when Lamonaco noticed a vehicle with Connecticut license plates. At some point, the New Jersey State Trooper pulled this vehicle over to the side of the road.

Exactly what transpired between Lamonaco and his eventual killers may never be known with complete accuracy, but detectives have a pretty good idea.

The trooper approached the driver of the car and told him to exit the vehicle. The passenger, who sat on the opposite side in the front, remained seated. Lamonaco then asked to see the driver's credentials.

At this point, the passenger on the opposite side of the car exited the vehicle and opened fire on Trooper Lamonaco with a nine-mm. automatic.

Eight bullets, one after another, smashed against Lamonaco's chest. He was wearing a bulletproof vest, but the impact of the slugs caused him to turn, and, as he was turning, a bullet circumvented the vest and caught him under his armpit.

The slug entered his heart, killing him almost instantly. The beloved trooper lay lifeless, sprawled on the side of the road. His killers, meanwhile, jumped back in their vehicle and drove off, and headed for the Delaware Water Gap, which leads into Pennsylvania.

Only moments later, a trucker screeched to a halt as he noticed the trooper lying on the shoulder of the road. He got out of his vehicle and checked on the victim. Then he scrambled to the patrol car and reported the down officer over the police radio.

In a short while, the crime site was teeming with homicide detectives, ambulance personnel and scores of state troopers throughout the area.

Phones at State Police headquarters were ringing incessantly as witnesses began calling in. Some had been passing by when the shooting occurred, while others saw the vehicle speeding away towards the Delaware Water Gap. Still others had seen the auto turning off Route 80 before it reached the water gap.

Once identification of the deceased was established, police departments throughout the state of New Jersey were contacted, and troopers who were on duty and even those who were off duty began volunteering to search for the killers of their idol.

All told, as many as 300 New Jersey State Troopers were out on the field that night. Some covered the

Pennsylvania front. Others manned toll booths on either side of Route 80, while still others searched for the vehicle at each turn off before the Delaware Water Gap.

Then, approximately two hours after the shooting, New Jersey State detectives found an abandoned Connecticut registered vehicle that seemed to be stuck on the side of the road only three miles from where the shooting had occurred.

Lawmen converged on the scene and compared the license plate number with the number described by witnesses. It matched.

A forensic team was soon on hand and removed several latents from the interior and exterior of the auto.

Once this was accomplished, detectives pored over several documents that had been left in the car. There was a Connecticut driver's license in the glove compartment in the name of Barry Eastberry.

Sgt. Richard Ryan from the New Jersey State Police contacted Connecticut authorities asking for information on this Barry Eastberry.

This request started an entirely new investigative ball rolling when Connecticut authorities—as well as the New Haven, Connecticut, branch of the FBI—unearthed the fact that Barry Eastberry was none other than Thomas Manning.

New Jersey police immediately sent the fingerprints removed from the getaway vehicle to the State Police crime lab, where it was conclusively proven that the prints were in fact those of Thomas Manning.

Manning was a known member of a terrorist organization, and the FBI had already compiled a case file on him, covering his personal history. This included detailed knowledge of his known associates, relatives and close friends.

The New Jersey State detectives headed by Captain

John Leck and Sergeant Richard Ryan began putting together an accurate picture of their suspect. In many ways, Manning's profile would be considered exemplary. He was a high school graduate and served honorably in the navy during the Vietnam War. Manning also appeared to be a happily married man with three children, and he was faithful to his wife, a boast few married couples can make nowadays.

Manning also made certain his children received the best education, sending them to a highly respected Montessori school.

But he had somehow gotten himself involved with the prison reform group, SCAR. The group was begun with good intentions, but police in Maine were able to connect a number of bank robberies and bombings to members of this group.

New Jersey detectives followed up all leads to track down Thomas Manning. They contacted Maine, Massachusetts and Pennsylvania authorities requesting any information on Manning or his associates. They had earlier reasoned from several bags of merchandise in the abandoned getaway vehicle that Manning and his passenger had gone shopping in New Jersey and were returning to Pennsylvania.

When Pennsylvania officials informed the New Jersey sleuths about a resident with a name similar to Manning's alias, Jersey probers immediately travelled to Pennsylvania, obtained a search warrant, and, together with the authorities there, converged on this suspect's home. It was located in a rural section, consisting of dirt trails and thick forested areas. It was the kind of place where calling on a neighbor means getting in your car and taking a five-minute drive over rough terrain.

In preparation for their stakeout, detectives questioned several neighbors. Although they reported that they knew little of the people down the road, they did identify the picture of Manning but said they hadn't seen him for several days now.

Soon after speaking with Manning's neighbors, the lawmen surrounded the wood-frame house. A detective, using a megaphone to project his voice, informed whoever was within to walk slowly out with their arms raised above their heads. The officer repeated his command several times without effect.

The lack of response, coupled with what detectives learned from questioning neighbors, convinced them to rush the house.

Inside, they found numerous incriminating articles, indicating the suspects were in possession of a quantity of semi-automatic weapons, rifles, shotguns, handguns and bomb components and large quantities of ammo. Also discovered were papers identifying another person named Richard Charles Williams. One article, seemingly out-of-place in this weapon arsenal, yet fitting in with Manning's familial profile, was a fully decorated Christmas tree.

A forensic unit was on the scene gathering together articles and prints for processing. Meanwhile, detectives checked with the FBI for information on Richard Williams. It was established that Williams was a criminal associate of Manning's since the late 1970s.

The New Jersey sleuths compared the prints on file for Richard Williams with those latents removed from the getaway vehicle in the Lamonaco homicide, and they matched. They then compared the file prints with those recovered at Manning's home in Pennsylvania, and they also matched.

Other fingerprints recovered at Manning's home were identified as those of Manning's wife and another associate, Raymond Luc Levasseur.

Although Levasseur was not a suspect in the Lamonaco homicide, the FBI knew him well. He was on the FBI's Ten Most Wanted list. Levasseur was also known to be Manning's best friend. The FBI had already compiled a huge dossier on Levasseur, and, as in the case of Manning, his background was exemplary. He was "an all-American boy," Captain John Leck recalled. He was also popular with women, and he, too, served his country during the Vietnam War, leaving with an honorable discharge.

It was after returning home from service that Levasseur showed a marked change in his behavior. He was arrested in Tennessee for a narcotics crime. He was then transferred to Maine, where he apparently met up with Manning and joined SCAR. He then became involved with a terrorist organization called the Jonathan Jackson-Sam Melville group, which was involved in numerous bombings, including an Eastern Airlines jet as well as a courthouse in the Boston area, where at least 22 people were injured.

Not long after being released from prison, Raymond Levasseur was arrested again, this time for attempting to hold up an armored car in Rhode Island. Local police there were informed of a suspicious-looking car in the area, and when they checked, they recovered an arsenal of automatic weapons and explosives in the car with Levasseur.

Levasseur was able to post bail, but instead of facing trial, he became a fugitive.

Through the FBI's profile of these terrorists, the New Jersey sleuths realized that if one of them lived in an area, it was almost certain the other lived nearby so that if there was any trouble, any one of them could be called on for help.

The items recovered in Manning's home not only indicated Levasseur's presence there, but also contained in bold clear lettering an address where he could be reached. This item had to be a vital clue in tracking down Lamonaco's alleged killers. From the disarray of Manning's house, detectives were certain they had left in a hurry.

They knew the suspect couldn't have gotten too far. And the most likely place for them to go would be to Levasseur's residence. Of course, these terrorists weren't stupid. They must have known they left behind evidence leading sleuths straight to Levasseur's home, so if they did head out there, they probably wouldn't stay long.

A contingent of lawmen was formed consisting of detectives in radio cars as well as several police choppers and fixed-wing planes. They weren't taking any chances. All units were on hand when the law officers swooped down on Levasseur's house which was approximately 30 miles away from Manning's in Germansville, Pennsylvania.

Here, however, the place was completely cleaned out. The suspects didn't waste their time. Although the probers pored over the place with a fine tooth comb, they recovered nothing of any significance to further their investigation.

Forensic experts checked for tire tracks and, although they found some trails, they didn't get far with this approach.

There was also the day-in-day-out questioning of neighbors, gas station attendants, and anyone who might have recognized the fugitives, but nothing came of it.

New Jersey sleuths also stayed in constant touch with the FBI, New England authorities, and officials in Maine for any new leads. The trail, however, grew cold.

It was at this point that Colonel Clinton L. Pagano, Superintendent of the New Jersey State Police, set up a command post with one solitary objective—to track down and bring to justice Lamonaco's killers. It was a sign of New Jersey's staunch commitment to law and order, and in many ways, apart from the Lamonaco probe, it has proven an effective tool in the fight against crime.

The command post, spreading its web throughout the states, has aided in the capture of many criminals. Associates of Thomas Manning and Richard Williams have been ensnared in its net as well as other criminals having nothing to do with the New Jersey outlaws.

According to Captain Leck, "At least fifty other people have been arrested as a result of this dragnet, not even connected with the Lamonaco investigation. It just so happened that they might have looked like one of our subjects, and the people of the town thought they looked suspicious, contacted our command post, and when we investigated it, we found they were involved in other criminal activities. We've affected arrests for robbery, assault and battery, narcotics and murder."

In one instance, Leck recalled a $700,000 drug bust: "The New York State Police received a tip that there was a family up there that looked like our people. The FBI, New York State police and our people checked it out and made the bust."

The hunt for Manning, Williams, and Levasseur hasn't been cheap. In addition to maintaining a full-time 15-man contingent at the command post in New Jersey, two New Jersey troopers are permanently stationed in New England.

There are also the 500,000 fliers that have been sent to every state in the union, as well as to hundreds of publications, gas stations and other public facilities.

There is also the expense involved in tracking down the more than 8,000 phone calls coming in to the command post regarding possible sightings of the fugitives. All told, an estimated one million dollars has already been spent on this manhunt. Officials say it is perhaps the most consuming task facing New Jersey lawmen since the 1932 Lindbergh probe in which the child of world famous aviator Charles Lindbergh was killed in an attempted kidnap for ransom.

Aiding New Jersey authorities in the hunt is a 16-member task force of FBI and New England lawmen.

The New Jersey command post has received full cooperation in their efforts from local authorities throughout the states as well as from the Bureau of Alcohol, Tobacco and Firearms.

Through their intense, leave-no-stone-unturned effort, the New Jersey task force has made significant headway in their probe. For instance, they learned where several of the firearms used by Manning and Williams were purchased. They have also learned a great deal about the methods these terrorists use to obtain false identification.

Knowledge of their methods of obtaining false ID had already led to a close encounter with Raymond Levasseur in Vermont. Levasseur was trying to obtain false identification in an office building in Brattleboro, but a policeman, knowledgeable about the identifying characteristics of the reputed terrorists, proceeded to arrest the suspect. Levasseur, however, was able to disarm the officer and make a clean getaway.

Their efforts have also resulted in close encounters with other suspected associates of Manning and Williams. In North Attleboro, Massachusetts, several known members of the Jonathan Jackson-Sam Melville group were involved in a shootout with state police.

The subjects had stopped their vehicle on Route 95 in North Attleboro at a rest area. They had been getting a lot of heat lately since the New Jersey police had been trying to locate them, so they decided to leave Massachusetts. A trooper pulled up beside the vehicle, and noticed a distinct resemblance between the passenger and photographs distributed by the New Jersey State Police.

He walked over to the passenger side of the car and requested credentials. He also noticed something peculiar about the rider. The man was wearing only a jacket, yet he seemed to have something bulky underneath it.

The officer asked him to exit the vehicle, proceeded to pat him down and discovered a nine-mm. automatic as well as a bulletproof vest. The trooper then handcuffed the suspect and radioed for a back-up team.

But the driver of the vehicle bailed out on the opposite side of the car and opened fire on the trooper while attempting to flee into the woods.

The trooper returned fire, but apparently missed, and the suspect managed to escape. The other individual was arrested.

In another incident, New Jersey probers have helped in the capture of another FBI fugitive involved in narcotics. In this case, the owner of a gas station in Kentucky who'd received a flier from New Jersey, contacted Sergeant Richard Ryan about a suspicious-looking person who resembled one of the photos of the suspects wanted for questioning.

Investigation revealed the suspect was wanted by Indiana authorities. Ryan contacted them and requested them to follow up on the information. "They continued the lead down into Kentucky where they apprehended the individual," Ryan recalled.

When it was finally over, an Indiana official just couldn't understand it. "How are you in New Jersey telling me where my fugitive is in Kentucky?" he asked.

"It's a long story," Ryan replied and left it at that.

As for the trackdown of Lamonaco's suspected killers, it has been tough going. Sgt. Ryan and Captain Leck believe they will get to them with the aid of civilian-witnesses who have been made knowledgeable about the suspects' behavior and physical characteristics.

They had earlier hoped that by tracing Manning's children, the schools they went to and so forth, they'd develop a crucial lead, but, so far, nothing has been forthcoming in that respect.

They did trace Manning's son to a Montessori school, where a teacher informed them about what he had merely thought of as the boy's highly active imagination. The child had spoken of shooting "pigs" and robbing banks. A lot of children will say these kinds of things, the teacher told the detectives. It was like cops and robbers. Only, in this case, the boy wasn't playing games.

In order to make school officials more aware of the case, the command post has sent thousands of fliers to many public and private schools.

There is always the possibility that Manning's children are no longer attending school, but officials believe it is highly unlikely, since it would cause a great deal of suspicion among neighbors, something these terrorists are at pains to avoid.

New Jersey detectives believe the fugitives are probably hiding out in some rural area, where they can practice using their artillery without fear.

There are many other possible hiding places, however. As for Raymond Luc Levasseur, one theory is that he may have escaped the country and could possibly be residing in the French provinces of Canada

403

since he is fluent in French. With his help, Manning could also make a go of it in Canada.

Williams is another story. He is more of a city man, having spent a good part of his life in the Boston area. In fact, detectives wouldn't be surprised if they caught up with Williams in one of the big cities. It's happened before.

In January of 1984, the New Jersey detectives, working together with the FBI, captured an accomplice of Manning's in Fort Worth, Texas, where both were wanted for a 1975 bank robbery.

As for what civilians should look for when they spot someone resembling the suspects: An identifying feature of Raymond Levasseur is a missing ear lobe; Manning's arms are emblazoned with numerous tattoos. His basic method of changing his appearance, which is surprisingly effective, is to wear a pair of eyeglasses. Williams can be distinguished by a missing little finger on his right hand.

The most significant problem with identifying these suspects, however, is simply that they look just like everybody else, explained Captain Leck and Sergeant Ryan.

The search for Lamonaco's alleged killers has certainly not been a bed of roses for investigators. But by covering all the bases, they are confident something will break.

In December of 1983, after hearing witness testimony and based on evidence recovered, a New Jersey grand jury returned indictments against Thomas Manning and Richard Williams for the murder of Trooper Philip Lamonaco. Williams was named in the indictment as the triggerman.

A reward poster including photographs of the suspects and their family is displayed in this issue of *INSIDE DETECTIVE*. Anyone with any information about Manning or Williams is urged to contact the New Jersey command post at the following address: New Jersey State Police, Rt. 94, Blairstown, New Jersey 07825. Attention: The Lamonaco Command Post. The phone number is: (201) 496-4174.

Thomas Manning and Richard Williams must be presumed innocent of all charges lodged against them unless proven otherwise in a court of law through due process. Raymond Luc Levasseur is being sought for questioning by New Jersey police.

"MAYDAY! MAYDAY!
TWO CHiPS DOWN!"

by Bruce Gibney

"I didn't know they had killed anyone, I was just trying to get off the freeway," the excited woman told the
detective. "I spotted them after they swerved that big
Buick right in front of me and damn near hit me. I
looked inside and saw their faces. They had wild, excited looks, happy looks, like the way people look after
a football team scores a touchdown. Or someone hits a
home run."

The men inside the car had not been to an L.A.
Rams game or participated in some sporting event.
They had been very busy all afternoon playing a vicious grown-up version of cops and robbers. The game
changed to a more deadly form of entertainment after
they sped down the freeway and spotted the two men
in uniform.

The freeway on which this insane and blood-
drenched game was played out runs between Los
Angeles and San Bernardino, California. It is a four
laner separated by a wide median and at any time of
the day or night the traffic flow is heavy with vehicles
enroute to or from Las Vegas, Nevada, Palm Springs
and on to Arizona and San Diego.

Even a minor fender-bender can stack up traffic solid for a mile within a few minutes.

State Highway Patrol Officers John R. Martinez and James Szabo had just gone on duty and were patrolling the eastbound lanes on their motorcycles at 2:55 P.M., October 1, 1981 when they spotted some lumber that had fallen from a truck in the westbound lanes.

Vehicles were swerving to avoid the debris in the road. To the experienced eyes of the patrolmen, it was a wreck in the making.

Martinez motioned to Szabo to go on ahead, cross over the median and slow the traffic while he went back to clear the roadway.

Szabo gunned his bike and went a couple of hundred yards, then crossed over the median and waved a warning flag as he zig-zagged his bike to clear the traffic off the lanes ahead where Martinez was removing the pieces of lumber. Within moments, the traffic behind Szabo began to stack up as the drivers maneuvered to shift lanes.

Suddenly, a Buick sedan bulled its way through the traffic, swerving back and forth and causing drivers to veer away.

Szabo saw the reckless driver in the Buick and was waiting when the car approached. He pulled up alongside it on the driver's side and used his thumb to motion the vehicle to the lane he had cleared and then on to the median. There was no question that the driver deserved a ticket.

The Buick slowed and as Szabo moved in closer to shout an order for it to stop, the driver thrust a hand out the window with a gun in it.

Flames belched twice from the barrel.

Szabo fell from his moving bike and sprawled on the pavement. The Buick swerved back into the traffic

407

lanes to escape.

Up ahead Martinez was busy clearing the lumber from the road when he heard the two shots and whirled in time to see his partner fall to the pavement.

There was no time to reach for his gun or duck for cover. The Buick was already upon him. The driver stuck the gun out the window and fired two more shots.

Martinez staggered backward and fell. He managed to crawl to where his bike was parked and used his radio mike to call out weakly, "Mayday! Mayday! I've been shot!"

The radio dispatcher at headquarters in Los Angeles asked repeatedly for the officer's location so help could be dispatched. But there was no response. The bleeding Martinez was unconscious with the microphone still in his hand.

The unprovoked shooting of the two CHP officers had been witnessed by Mike Callahan, an LAPD officer who was on his way to work. He used the radio on Szabo's motorcycle to inform the dispatcher what had happened, giving the location and a request for an ambulance and an aid unit to be sent from the city of Alhambra.

Both officers were alive but in critical condition when they reached the Alhambra Community Hospital. Szabo had been shot in the neck and the abdomen. A bulletproof vest he was wearing had slowed the slug that tore into his stomach. Martinez hadn't been wearing a vest. The slugs ripped into his chest and abdomen.

Within minutes after Callahan reported the shooting to headquarters, CHP officers in the area along with deputies from the Los Angeles County sheriff's office and police from the city of Alhambra were on the scene. A dozen shocked witnesses had curbed their vehicles and gave them an account of what they had seen.

The statements leading up to the shootings were virtually identical. "The Buick was all over the road," one witness said. "And when the officer motioned the driver over, the guy just pulled his gun and started blasting."

There were two men in the car. Witnesses described them as being "Latino-types" in their 30's. The driver had dark, curly hair sticking out from under a blue watchman's cap and a mustache. The other had a shaved head, wore a short beard and mustache, and had a teardrop tattoo by his eye, apparently indicating he had been a member of a Mexican-American prison gang.

Witnesses agreed on the description of the car. It was a late 1960 or early 1970 model Buick Riviera with black over green paint and a black top. One witness obtained a partial license plate. It was 1BJZ followed by three numbers.

Information on the license was called into the Motor Vehicle Registration Division in Sacramento with a request for the names and addresses of all vehicle owners, particularly for an older Buick Riviera, with the starting sequences 1BJZ.

Police were stumped for a motive. It was possible that the gunman was deranged and had decided to vent his anger at the first symbol of authority—two law enforcement officers doing their job.

A more tangible motive surfaced just hours into the investigation. "This is only speculation on my part, but it may be they were wanted and thought they were being arrested," said Orin Camendish, an assistant CHP commander.

Minutes before the shootings two gunmen matching

the description of the suspects, had burst into a store in Las Tunas and emptied the cash register of $5,000.

A store witness said one of the gunmen had a large caliber handgun, either a .38 or a .357 Magnum. Bullet fragments taken from the bodies of the wounded patrolmen were believed to have come from a .357 Magnum.

Witnesses helped police artists work up a composite photo of the gunmen. These were later aired on the TV news programs and printed in the newspapers.

Callers immediately flooded CHP headquarters in Los Angeles and the LA sheriff's office. One man who matched the drawings was a disgruntled small-time felon who lived in San Diego. He had complained to several persons that he was going to "blow away" the next lawmen who harassed him. Detectives acting on a tip, arrested him as he left a massage parlor on National Avenue in San Diego. He was grilled about the shootings but was dropped as a suspect when detectives were satisfied that he had been in San Diego at the time of the shootings.

Meanwhile, doctors worked frantically to save the lives of the CHP officers. Szabo was listed in stable condition at the Alhambra Community Hospital with wounds in his neck and back. He had regained consciousness but had been unable to tell investigators anything that they had not already received from other witnesses. "I really didn't get much of a look at the guy who shot me," he said. "I was busy at the time trying to keep the traffic flowing and clear the lanes ahead of Martinez."

Martinez had been admitted with bullet wounds in his chest and abdomen. A spokesman said the bullets lacerated the liver, kidneys, intestines and diaphragm. Though listed in critical condition, doctors held out hope that Martinez would recover. He underwent six hours of surgery Thursday evening, and returned to the operating room for a second operation. He required numerous blood transfusions and the CHP called for donations of his blood type, O-Positive. Dozens of persons lined up at the county blood bank to donate blood. Then, on Friday morning, Martinez succumbed to his wounds. The eight year CHP veteran and father of a five-year-old daughter and one-year-old son died without regaining consciousness.

Sheriff Peter Pitchess with Dale Fargo, chief of the Southern Division of CHP and Alhambra Chief of Police Joseph T. Mally, called a news conference to announce the death of Martinez and the arrangements being made for his funeral.

Reporters were informed that Governor Jerry Brown had authorized a $10,000 reward for information leading to the arrest and conviction of the killers of Martinez. Six thousand members of the CHP added another $15,000 to the fund.

Lieutenant Al Etzel, in charge of the investigation for the sheriff's office, said his men were almost certain that the bandits who robbed the store in Las Tunas had shot the patrolmen. "We figure that they thought they had been caught in a road blockade," Etzel said. "What additional crimes they may have been involved in, we don't know at this time. We're asking any who may recall having seen the car, either before or after the crimes, or who might recall the man with the shaved head and teardrop tattooed below his right eye, to contact us. We'll keep the information confidential and the person with the information may be eligible for the reward money."

By Saturday contributions by private citizens and law enforcement agencies had increased the reward to

411

$27,000. Dozens of witnesses had called in with tips of the CHP shootings. Some callers were just golddigging; others simply wanted to help. "Something like this happening makes everyone sick," one remarked. "Those cops were just trying to clear the freeway to make it safe. There was just no reason to go shoot them."

What appeared to be the first solid lead came on Saturday evening. A Buick Riviera, painted black over green, was spotted parked in front of an older apartment building in the Hollywood area. The license didn't correspond to the one spotted at the crime scene, but a check with the Department of Vehicle Registration revealed that it had been reported stolen in San Francisco.

Plainclothes officers were sent to keep a watch on the car and take into custody anyone who attempted to move it, while plans were being made for the next step.

Informants in the gritty neighborhood located within walking distance of the Paramount Studios said the car had been parked by the apartment since Friday but did not know who it belonged to.

Police waited until 9:45 p.m. Then, convinced no one was coming, they decided to move in. SWAT officers went door to door evacuating the building. Dozens of newsmen were at the scene but were embargoed from broadcasting anything about the operation until after 10 p.m. There wasn't much for them to do except go around and interview the residents who had been driven from their apartments by the SWAT officers.

The next morning the media crowded the downtown L.A. sheriff's station like hungry dogs let loose in a butcher shop. They came expecting to hear the two gunmen had been apprehended, or at least identified.

They were bitterly disappointed.

"We questioned eight people but they had nothing to do with the shootings," Deputy John Radeleff, the sheriff's media spokesman, said. The car stolen from San Francisco "is similar to the one we are looking for, but that's all. It is not the getaway car used in the shootings."

Radeleff said detectives were working on a number of hot leads but refused to comment on them. "When we have something for publication, we'll let you know."

Investigators meanwhile had been able to connect a dozen robberies in Orange and Los Angeles counties to the two suspects. One of the pair was also believed responsible for the bizarre kidnapping of CHP Officer James David Hansen. On July 3rd, Hansen was in routine patrol on Long Beach Freeway when he spotted a cream colored Chevy speeding in the southbound lanes. Hansen tried to pull the driver over and ultimately chased him to a parking lot on Washington Boulevard in the City of Commerce. The suspect then jumped out of his car, pulled a semi-automatic pistol from his waistband and marched the officer to the rear of the parking lot where Hansen was made to lie down behind a large, high voltage, electrical box. Hansen's feet were tied with his belt, his hands were cuffed, his gun was tossed into the bushes and his traffic citation book was stolen.

Before making his escape, the gunman muttered something about having to get to San Francisco for a drug deal. The getaway car was described by witnesses as a red and white Chevrolet. Authorities said they believe the car was also used during two armed robberies in Long Beach, and at least one other in Santa Ana.

As detectives expended every possible effort to locate the suspects, funeral services were held in Ontario for Officer Martinez.

An overflow crowd, with 1,300 uniformed officers, some coming from as far away as Massachusetts and Illinois, attended the memorial services. James Szabo insisted upon leaving the hospital and was present in his uniform and in a wheelchair. An honor guard of CHP officers, wearing their tan uniforms with green jackets and blue and gold helmets, escorted the pall-bearers, who were Martinez's three brothers and three brothers-in-law.

An eulogy over the bronze casket, draped with an American flag, was delivered by a priest from St. George's parish. Governor Brown spoke briefly, calling the crime a "coldblooded, ruthless act" and stated he had ordered all flags in the state flown at half-mast in memory of Martinez.

The widow, holding her daughter's hand, placed a small bouquet of roses on the coffin. A cavalcade of 300 motorcycles and patrol cars escorted the funeral procession to the Bellevue Cemetery.

Calls continued to flood switchboards at the Alhambra police department and the L.A. sheriff's office. Each was logged, then checked out and catalogued by one of the five detectives working full time on the case.

It was tough going. Then, on October 15th, two weeks after the shootings, it all came together when an anonymous tipster told authorities about a late model Buick that was parked on a residential street in Alhambra.

"It has been here five days," the tipster said. "I think it might be the one you guys want. The body is all dinged up but the paint job is brand new."

Investigators scraped away a bit of the black paint and found green underneath. Positive identification was made when witnesses picked photos of the car as the one they saw when the two officers were shot.

* * *

The car was impounded and searched. On the floor of the back seat detectives found a crumpled sales receipt for several cans of dark spray paint.

The receipt was traced to a local hardware store where a clerk recalled selling the paint to a customer. "The guy comes in here all the time," the clerk said. "He bought about four or five cans of the stuff."

In late afternoon, detectives arrested the 31-year-old customer. He at first refused to make any statements but changed his mind when detectives said they planned to charge him with murder.

"I didn't kill no cop," he allegedly replied. "I ain't going to the gas chamber for something I didn't do." He then said that two friends, Thomas Martinez and Eugene Gonzales, had paid him to paint the car and then dispose of it. "They said they wanted to get rid of it because it was hot," he admitted.

Authorities across the nation knew all about the two desperados now fingered for the killing of the CHP officer. Thirty-three-year-old Eugene Gonzales had served hard time in several prisons and went by a number of aliases, including Eugene Dale Vaccaro, Dale Azard, and James Gallegos. The 5-foot-6-inch, 160-pound ex-con had the monicker of "Gato," Spanish for cat. Convicted of armed robbery, he was listed as being violent and dangerous.

Equally dangerous was 35-year-old Thomas Martinez, a convicted armed robber and drug abuser who went by the nickname of "Piojo," the Spanish word for louse.

The two were being sought on a federal warrant charging them with bank robbery in La Jara, Colorado, on May 15, 1981. Two men wearing Halloween pighead masks took $60,000 from the First National Bank. FBI agents had placed the men in La Jara at the time of the robbery along with alleged evidence and information that they had committed it.

With information gained from Rose, detectives obtained an arrest and search warrant naming Gonzales and Martinez as suspects for the murder of Officer Martinez and the attempted murder of Officer Szabo. It was learned the men and a woman were living in a two bedroom, $310 a month apartment in Lincoln Avenue in Anaheim.

When the detectives served the warrant, they found Martinez, his common law wife and their five month old child.

The manager of the complex said the couple had been living with their baby in the apartment for about five months. She said Martinez had identified himself as a fabric salesman.

"They were real low key people," the manager said. "We never had any complaints."

At a news conference that afternoon, Sheriff Pitchess handed out a press release with the photos of Gonzales and Martinez. It stated that Gonzales was believed to be driving a 26-foot, 1976 Itasca motorhome, painted white over orange, with either Colorado or Arizona license plates. It stated Gonzales was believed to be armed with a .357-Magnum revolver and to have two other firearms in his vehicle. "He should be considered extremely dangerous," the sheriff said.

Gonzales was still a fugitive two months later when Officer James Szabo stepped before a press conference on December 12th to announce his return to duty.

"It feels good to be back," he said, flashing a boyish grin. The joy of his official welcome back to the force was dampened by the absence of his slain partner.

"He was close with everybody," Szabo said. "The biggest factor in my mind from this whole thing is how fast life and death goes. You are talking to your partner and the next minute he's gone."

Szabo had been back on the job a month when the second suspect Eugene Gonzales, was slain on January 18, 1982 in a Salt Lake City, Utah shootout that left one lawman dead and another seriously injured.

Eight days later Martinez was charged with 18 felony counts, including first degree murder. Deputy District Attorney John Watson said the murder charge against Martinez alleged special circumstances — shooting a police officer and murder committed during another felony — that could lead to the death penalty.

"And I intend to ask for the death penalty if Martinez is convicted," Watson said.

The prosecutor said he had planned to seek grand jury indictments against Martinez and his alleged accomplice Gonzales, before Gonzales was gunned down.

"This won't change the case," Watson said. "The death of Gonzales will actually simplify my case against Martinez. I guess I'm paraphrasing Nathan Hale when I said I regret that Gonzales had only one life to give for his crimes. I wanted to bring him back to California for trial."

In addition to the murder charge, Martinez was charged with eight counts of robbery and six counts of assault with a deadly weapon in connection with a series of robberies in Bellflower, Torrance, Burbank and San Gabriel.

Martinez had no comment about the charges. When arrested, he allegedly told police, "I got nothing to say. You get me a lawyer before you ask me anything. I've been down this road before."

But she had plenty to say. The attractive, dark haired teenager testified on February 8, 1983 before a Los Angeles Superior Court jury that she met Martinez and started living with him at age 17. They first lived in Denver, then Arizona and finally in Southern California. A cousin of Martinez lived with them for about a month before the shootings and Gonzales was there nearly every day, she testified. None of the four worked and they all used narcotics.

She said that Martinez had left their apartment on the morning of October 1, 1981 with Gonzales, who was carrying a suitcase containing "things for a robbery," including guns. They left in a green and black Riviera, she said.

She then apparently suffered a momentary memory lapse and said she couldn't remember what happened next. After being shown court documents and other statements she made to police following her arrest, her memory returned.

She said her boyfriend left the apartment that morning wearing a mustache and returned that evening clean shaven. He acted "scared, nervous, irritable," she testified.

When she asked what was wrong he replied that "you ask too many questions" and told her to shut up.

"When I asked him where Gonzales was he said he wouldn't be seeing him again, because they couldn't be seen together."

She knew about the CHP officers being shot because she had been watching a report of the shooting on TV news.

"They said on the news that the officers had been shot for no reasons," she testified. "I asked Tommy why he did it and he said they pulled us over and it was either do it or go to jail."

Jurors began deliberation on April 19th. It took a record 36 days before they returned a verdict that John Martinez was guilty of second-degree murder.

The verdict was something of a disappointment to

Prosecutor Watson, because the death sentence cannot be imposed for murder in the second degree.

Martinez was also convicted for a string of robberies and assaults. Prosecutor Watson estimates Martinez faces a sentence of 75 years in prison.

"TROOPER'S RENDEZVOUS
WITH DEATH"

by Bill G. Cox

If humans are pawns for unknown powers, destiny's
chessboard was set for cold-blooded murder on that
dark early morning of Monday, September 17, 1990,
in the lonely pine woods north of Houston, Texas. Call
it merely fate or coincidence if you will. But events
were moving three people to a deadly checkmate.
Shortly, the end-game would come in a burst of explosive violence on a rural stretch of Farm-to-Market
Road 1774, about two and a half miles south of the
little town of Magnolia in Montgomery County.

On that night, a man and a woman in separate cars
were engaged in a speeding, careening race along the
narrow road that wound through the forest of pine
trees. The terrified woman had no doubt that she was
running a race for her very life. The man in the pursuing vehicle was in a frenzy and armed with a loaded
revolver.

As the two cars hurtled along the wooded road, with
the one behind trying to bump the other into a ditch,
Texas State Trooper Mark Jeffrey Phebus was on his
way home. The rookie officer was off duty, dressed in
his civvies and driving his personal car. He was

traveling the same road in the same direction as the two vehicles that were engaged in the suspenseful race.

At first, Trooper Phebus was far enough behind to be unaware of the drama unfolding on the road ahead. In fact, his own thoughts were as far away from violence and death as they could be. After dropping off his girlfriend at College Station, Texas, he was on the last leg of a weekend trip to Oklahoma to visit old college friends and then return home for his next duty shift on Monday.

It had been an especially eventful trip for Phebus and his lovely young companion, for they had decided to get married in the near future. Everything seemed to be going smoothly for the 23-year-old trooper. He had completed training and was graduated from the Texas Department of Public Safety Academy on February 16, 1990, just seven months before. From his boyhood, Mark Phebus had wanted to be a police officer. Now, the reality of his professional achievement was even better than he had imagined.

As his car rounded a curve on the road, Phebus was jerked back into the present by a scene suddenly illuminated by his headlights.

Directly ahead were two cars, both with body damage, that appeared to have been involved in a wreck. One vehicle was off the road in the ditch. Two people, a man and a woman, stood beside the cars. It appeared to be a minor traffic accident, but the trooper braked his car to offer assistance.

When he got out of his car and walked over to the couple, Phebus had his gun stuck in his holster and his trooper badge pinned to his belt. Officers normally carry their weapons even when not officially on duty. It is also standard procedure in such an incident that he would have identified himself as a lawman. Exactly how much Phebus learned about the true nature of the episode he accidentally encountered is open to some conjecture.

Another motorist, a woman, also stopped at the scene to see if help was needed. After a brief conversation with the two car owners, the trooper gave a quarter to the woman who had stopped after he arrived. Phebus instructed her to call 911 from a pay phone outside the roadside store in front of which the cars had ended up. Since he was off duty and had no radio in his car, Phebus asked the other witness to request a patrol unit to investigate the accident.

After police were contacted, Phebus talked briefly on the phone himself, giving the location. He then hung up and walked back to his car to get a flashlight from the trunk to direct any traffic around the vehicles.

As the trooper turned and started toward the cars, the man whipped a revolver from his back pocket and fired point blank into Trooper Phebus' face. The lawman was only about two feet away. The bullet struck him below the left eye. He reeled backward and fell as a woman's terrified scream pierced the night.

In the seconds following, the two horrified women fled in the car of the woman who had stopped at the "accident" scene. They sped to another telephone and frantically called the 911 emergency number again to report the shooting.

Within a short time, deputies from the Montgomery County Sheriff's Department, state troopers, and Texas Rangers converged on the location. Trooper Phebus was found mortally wounded but apparently still barely alive. He was rushed to a nearby hospital, where he was pronounced dead about 30 minutes later.

Back at the scene, which now was ablaze with floodlights and patrol car headlights, officers quizzed the two women, who had returned after summoning help.

One of the women identified the gunman as Richard Leland Jordan, 43. She detailed the cold-blooded gunning down of the young trooper and the events that led to it.

The woman said that she and Jordan had become involved in a heated argument while talking in a bar in the little community of Pinehurst.

She recalled that Jordan was drunk and angry as they argued, and he had vowed he would kill someone before the night was over. As she left the tavern in her car, Jordan followed. She was staying with some friends in Magnolia, she said, and she tried to elude Jordan so he would not know where she was living.

She told of speeding along the Farm-to-Market Road through the tall pines with Jordan giving chase and ramming her car when he gained on her. She decided to turn into the darkened food store lot in hopes that Jordan would go on by, but she turned too sharply and swerved into the ditch.

Jordan then pulled up and jumped from his car, and the couple were arguing heatedly when Trooper Phebus arrived. The woman said the trooper showed his badge and identified himself. As she was telling Phebus about the argument and chase, the other woman had stopped to see if she could help.

Phebus had sent this woman to call for another police unit on the phone outside the store, then had walked over and talked briefly on the phone himself. It was then that the witness caught a glimpse of a gun in Jordan's back pocket. When Phebus got a flashlight from his car and started back, the witness said, she tried to signal Phebus that Jordan was armed. But as she finally screamed "Look out," Jordan pulled out the handgun and fired into the officer's face. When she and the other woman fled to escape and call for help, Jordan apparently sped away from the shooting scene in his car.

The witness, badly shaken and tearful after what had happened, gave the officers a description of Richard Jordan and the car he was driving. The Department of Public Safety (DPS) dispatcher in the district put out an urgent allpoints bulletin to all law enforcement agencies in the area, as well as statewide on the teletype network. The shooting suspect, wanted on an arrest warrant charging capital murder, was described as 6 feet tall and weighing 190 pounds, with black hair, blue eyes, and a mustache. When last seen, he was wearing a baseball cap, a white T-shirt with green horizontal stripes, and blue jeans. He was driving a black 1976 Chevrolet Caprice classic four-door sedan bearing Texas license number 323XNA.

The message warned that Jordan was believed to be armed with a large-caliber handgun and was "extremely dangerous."

As county and state police units set up roadblocks on surrounding highways, preparations were made to bring in search dogs from the Texas Department of Corrections. The woman who identified the suspect and the other witness to the shooting were instructed to go into hiding temporarily in case Jordan tried to harm them.

Meanwhile, officers talked to a man who operated the food store and lived in the quarters behind it. He told officers he had just locked up and retired to his trailer at the rear when he heard the sound of cars about 1:15 A.M.

"Then I heard people talking—a man and a woman—but mostly the woman. She seemed to be shouting at the man."

The store operator said he looked outside and saw two cars, and two people, apparently the drivers, arguing. A third car pulled up behind them before he closed the door to his trailer, the witness said.

"I was really scared. There are no homes or anything around here, just me all alone." To make things worse, he had no phone in his trailer and was too frightened to try to use the phone at the store. After a few minutes, the store employee continued, "I heard a shot. Just one shot. Then I heard a car going away very fast. I was afraid to even look outside until in a little while the police came and told me an officer had been killed."

By the time daylight came to the area, a full-scale manhunt went into operation in the woods and on the roads in a several-mile radius. The searchers believed that the fugitive gunman might have abandoned his car, concealed it in a remote area, and taken off on foot to lessen the chances of his being found. Aircraft with spotters on board swept low over the heavily wooded area, maintaining radio contact with the ground searchers who were in cars and on horses.

Directing the overall hunt and investigation was Texas Ranger Captain Bob Prince of the Harris County office in Houston.

Working closely with the Texas Rangers and state troopers were officers of the Montgomery County Sheriff's Department from the county seat of Conroe, where they were headquartered. Crime scene technicians and photographers from the sheriff's department carefully chronicled the crime scene with still and video cameras.

Talking to news reporters at the scene, Sheriff's Detective Tracy Peterson told them, "It was senseless and cold-blooded — absolutely cold-blooded. The trooper clearly identified himself as a peace officer. He had a badge on and a gun in his belt, and they knew he was a peace officer. He was off duty and being a good Samaritan."

The search for the murder suspect at first centered in the area of Sealy. Jordan was thought to be employed by an ironwork company there, but officers learned that he did not work at the plant. Officers also put out a bulletin on a 1976 black pickup after receiving a report that Jordan had been seen with two men in the vehicle. The pickup was later located, and its occupants — Jordan wasn't among them — were cleared of any link to the trooper's slaying.

As the hours dragged on with no new leads on Richard Jordan's whereabouts, investigators zeroed in on the suspect's background. They learned that he had been a production design engineer with a Harris County company for 17 years. He had no prior criminal convictions, but the fatal shooting of Trooper Phebus wasn't the first time Jordan had killed someone with a gun.

Investigators learned that in 1987, a former boyfriend of a woman Jordan had dated for a short time came to Jordan's home looking for trouble. Files showed that the man threatened to kill Jordan, but Jordan shot and killed the man with a .38-caliber revolver. The bullet struck the victim in the face. The shooting happened in the driveway of Jordan's residence, according to the reports.

Later, a Harris County grand jury refused to indict Jordan in the fatal shooting, having decided from the evidence presented that he had fired in self-defense. Jordan reportedly had been investigated for other incidents of violence, but there were no convictions on record.

Sleuths learned that Richard Leland Jordan was a paradox to his neighbors. Descriptions of his personality and the life he led depended on who you talked to, reporters from the Houston newspapers and TV stations learned. One story in the *Houston Post*, illuminated the strange enigma that was Richard Jordan. The staff writers came up with conflicting views of the industrial engineer who lived in a quiet neighborhood in Spring.

Jordan worked for one company for nearly two decades. He lived happily during that time with the high school sweetheart he married. The Jordans and their two children lived in a middle-class home on two acres of land. One neighbor recalled Jordan as "a family man who adored his kids. Just a heck of a nice guy. If you needed help, he was there."

But in 1987, Jordan and his wife were divorced; no one knew exactly why. Afterward, some noticed a big change in Jordan's lifestyle. He dressed sloppily and let his mustache and beard grow. He hung out at the local taverns. It was in one of these bars that he met the woman he would several months later pursue in the speed duel that preceded the tragic death of the young trooper.

It wasn't long after meeting the woman that Jordan shot down the jealous suitor who came threatening him. Acquaintances said that the divorce from his first wife and the self-defense slaying apparently turned Jordan's life around. For one thing, Jordan began receiving threats after the shooting. He started carrying a gun and showed a bitterness toward the judicial system, which he felt was not protecting him. There were reports, too, that Jordan was drinking heavily.

A story in the *Houston Chronicle* reported still other views of Jordan's character. One neighbor said, "I know he had a hell of a temper . . . Man, when he got mad, he went crazy. He'd go outside and beat up his car, or knock out a window or something. Nobody was surprised when he and his estranged wife broke up, except we were surprised he hadn't killed her."

Another neighbor wondered when an individual

crosses the line between sanity and insanity. "I don't know what made him cross that line," he said. "But I can't imagine him walking out with his hands up now."

As the search for the murder suspect continued, flags flew at half-mast over the DPS station on Grant Road, where Trooper Phebus had been assigned. His co-workers praised their fallen comrade as "generous and conscientious." Though still in his probationary period after graduation from the DPS academy, Phebus had been doing an outstanding job.

He was remembered as a "fine man and a fine officer." He grew up in Hopewell Junction, New York, and he had been a Boy Scout and later a reservist in the U.S. Army. But Phebus' primary aim in life had been to become a law officer. In school, he had been a top student, having combined his junior and senior years in high school to graduate a year early.

One family member recalled to reporters, "He never wanted anything but to be a trooper." He had decided that law enforcement was his career as early as high school, when he would ride with the local police.

The young man's ultimate goal was to become a Texas Ranger, the elite corps of criminal investigators in the DPS whose history as crime fighters is legendary. At the same time, Phebus was looking for what most young men seek: a wife, family, and home. On his weekend trip with his girlfriend, that dream had begun to materialize.

Phebus' tearful 19-year-old girlfriend, the Texas A&M student he had dropped off in College Station before heading for his unexpected rendezvous with death, said, "He wanted a house with lace curtains, two kids, horses for us to ride, that whole white-picket fence kind of thing. He hated being single." And he had popped the question and received an affirmative answer just hours before his untimely death.

It was so terribly ironic that the elated husband-to-be, dreaming of his happiness in the years ahead, had driven into a violent domestic argument between another couple that ended so tragically for the officer. But as the victim's girlfriend said, "There was no way that he could have not stopped to help. He wasn't that way."

Phebus' last act — paying with his own life in the line of duty — had without a doubt saved the life of the woman Jordan had been arguing with, she herself told officers. She felt for sure that Jordan would have killed her had Phebus not shown up when he did.

Fellow officers agreed with the woman's belief that the trooper's timely intervention had probably saved her.

"I definitely believe that," said DPS Officer Bill Nabors. "When you've got an individual who is willing to use his vehicle as a tool of assault, and he's also got a handgun inside that vehicle that's loaded, I think it's a great possibility that was in his mind."

The intensive manhunt for a lawman's killer continued through Monday and into Tuesday, with no trace of Jordan being found. Officers were puzzled by the fact that neither the suspect nor his car had been sighted in spite of the scores of lawmen making the search and the wide publicity that the slaying had received.

The first break in the case came about 7:00 P.M. Tuesday, in a heavily wooded area eight miles north of where Phebus had been slain on Farm-to-Market Road 1774. Two people who were riding three-wheelers in a remote area behind a tavern came upon the abandoned vehicle and notified the authorities. County and state officers converged on the site. Examining the car, they saw that the keys were still in the ignition. But no other evidence was discovered inside the Chevrolet, nor was any weapon found. It appeared that Jordan had parked it and taken off on foot.

The car was recovered at a spot not far from a railroad track. There was speculation that the suspected killer might have hopped a passing freight train and now was long out of the area. Or, probers theorized, he could have made his way back to the highway after leaving the car and been given a ride by a passing motorist. If that had happened, it was possible another homicide victim might turn up, investigators worried.

Another of the lawmen's fears was that the fugitive had forced his way inside one of the residences and been holed up there with the occupants held hostage. As reinforcements poured into the area to search with bloodhounds and on horseback through the thick woods, other teams of officers started checking the isolated houses within a several-miles radius to ascertain the welfare of the residents.

The house-to-house check turned up no leads indicating that Richard Jordan had been in the vicinity. There were no reports of burglaries or forced-entry attempts among the rural residents questioned by the lawmen.

By Thursday, with no signs of the elusive Jordan, the scope of the search was cut back. It was looking as if Jordan had somehow managed to get past the roadblocks and the dozens of searchers in cars, on horses, and in aircraft. Without any sighting of him reported, it was feared that he was still on the run many miles from the homicide scene, possibly even out of state by now.

The description of the gunman continued to fill the airways and a DPS circular carrying two photographs of Richard Jordan—one of the neatly shaven man he was in 1983 and another of the mustached and bearded individual he was in 1989—was distributed to

430

law enforcement agencies throughout Texas and adjoining states.

Officials also conducted routine checks of bus stations, passenger train depots, and airline ticket counters on the possibility that Jordan had escaped by one of these means. Lawmen issued warnings to homeowners and to motorists to take precautions.

On Thursday, Trooper Phebus' colleagues paused in their efforts to track his killer to pay their last respects at funeral rites conducted at a Nazarene church in the small town of Webster. An estimated 300 law enforcement officers and 500 civilians packed the little church and spilled outside. Some officers came from as far away as Dallas and Louisiana to attend the service.

The pastor of the church told the gathered mourners that the trooper's death was beyond understanding, but that Phebus had accepted the dangers of his chosen profession.

"He chose to live a life of service to others," the minister said. "Mark was killed by a killer with a gun, but he died for what he believed in. Mark may have saved a woman's life that night. He died a man of honor and valor."

The slain officer's casket was draped with a Texas flag and flanked by an honor guard of state troopers. Mourners walked through a path bordered by troopers to reach the church. As the long line of vehicles left the service with headlights turned on, motorists along the road stopped, and some stood by their cars with their hats removed.

At the cemetery, a 21-gun salute was followed by the playing of taps at the graveside service. The Texas flag that covered the casket was presented to the trooper's family, as was a memorial cross. One tearful family member told reporters at the cemetery, after Phebus' body was laid to rest, "I don't know what to say right now, except I'm just overwhelmed. I didn't know there were so many police officers in the whole state. And the respect they've shown to us and to Mark, words can't express how much I love them all. He was so proud to be part of that. I can't explain the pride he took in that uniform. He told us one time, honest to God, he said, 'Can you believe they pay me to do this?' That's how much he loved the work."

As the hunt for Richard Jordan moved into Friday with no new leads as to where he might be, residents and businessmen of the Houston area launched a reward fund for information leading to the arrest and conviction of the killer. The reward totaled $8,000 by Friday afternoon. A DPS spokesman said, "We were kind of surprised at the many, many phone calls we got from the public — people wanting to give money for Mark's family or for whatever was needed."

Teams of investigators contacted relatives and acquaintances of Jordan's, seeking information to suggest where the suspect might have gone, but the search seemed to be at a dead end.

With the arrival of the weekend, the lawmen began to wonder how long it would be before some report surfaced on the fugitive's whereabouts, or at least that he had contacted someone or had been seen someplace.

It was early Sunday morning, when searchers were scouring the wooded area where Jordan's car had been found on a remote dead-end road, that they got an answer.

State Troopers Kevin Kennedy and Maurice Neubauer were walking through the woods, which were beginning to be illuminated by the sun's first rays, when they noticed a swarm of vultures in the sky. Walking to the area where the large birds were cir-

432

cling, the officers spotted a man's body about 12 feet from the railroad track that ran parallel to the road where Richard Jordan's car was discovered several days earlier.

The man was lying on his back, obviously dead. A .44-caliber special lay on the ground near the body. The officers retrieved a wallet from the dead man's clothing. A driver's license and other cards inside identified the man as Richard Leland Jordan. The dead man's clothing also matched the clothing Jordan had been wearing at the time of Mark Phebus' slaying.

Richard Leland Jordan had apparently killed a third time with a shot to the face — this time himself, it appeared to the officers who conducted an investigation at the scene. Later, ballistics tests showed that two spent cartridges in the gun's chamber were identical. Texas Ranger Captain Bob Prince reported later that the tests confirmed the gun had fired the shot that killed Trooper Mark Phebus and ended the life of Richard Jordan.

Jordan had stuck the gun in his mouth and fired the fatal slug through the roof of his mouth and into his brain. The decomposed state of his body indicated to the investigators that the killer had apparently taken his own life shortly after shooting down Phebus. He had walked to the spot after leaving his car abandoned on the dead-end road.

One longtime friend of the slain state trooper commented after discovery of the killer's body, "That's one less scumbag on this earth, but it really doesn't change anything for me. This cut real deep, and Jordan's death won't bring my buddy back to life."

APPENDIX

"The Blood of Four Cops!"
Official Detective, October, 1988
"Man Down! And It's a Cop!"
Official Detective, February, 1988
"Requiem for a Blue Knight"
Front Page Detective, March, 1991
"Swat Team Mission — Find the Cop Killer!"
True Detective, September, 1986
"The Executioners of Two Cops!"
Official Detective, September, 1986
"Night of Hell for the NYPD!"
True Detective, April, 1989
"Officer Down!"
True Detective, December, 1985
"Did a Shoplifter Ambush the Beloved Cop?"
Front Page Detective, January, 1987
"All Units. Officer Down. Needs Assistance!"
Front Page Detective, March, 1987
"Flush Out the Cop Killers!"
Front Page Detective, June, 1986
"Oregon Trackdown of a Lady Cop Killer!"
Front Page Detective, July, 1983
"Trooper Was Gunned Down by Mad Terrorists!"
Inside Detective, September, 1984
"Mayday! Mayday! Two CHiPS Down!"
Master Detective, February, 1984
"Trooper's Rendezvous with Death"
True Detective, May, 1991